Building
Family
Competence

Building Family Competence

Primary and Secondary Prevention Strategies

Luciano L'Abate

SAGE PUBLICATIONS
The International Professional Publishers
Newbury Park London New Delhi

10-31-95

For information address:

SAGE Publications, Inc.
2111 West Hillcrest Drive
Newbury Park, California 91320

SAGE Publications Ltd.
28 Banner Street
London EC1Y 8QE
England

SAGE Publications India Pvt. Ltd.
M-32 Market
Greater Kailash I
New Delhi 110 048 India

Printed in the United States of America

Library of Congress Cataloging-in-Publication Data

L'Abate, Luciano, 1928–
    Building family competence : primary and secondary prevention strategies / by Luciano L'Abate.
        p.   cm.
    Includes bibliographical references and index.
    ISBN 0-8039-3488-2
    1. Family—Mental health.   2. Mental illness—Prevention.
I. Title.
RC455.4.F3L33   1990
362.82'86—dc20   90-38948
                                                                        CIP

FIRST PRINTING, 1990

Sage Production Editor: Astrid Virding

Contents

Preface

The purpose of this book is to present a theoretical viewpoint, a practical method, and an integration of over 30 years of work with functional, semifunctional, and dysfunctional families. The field of primary and secondary prevention with families has been neglected thus far. Fortunately, as with prevention, recent advances in the prevention of a variety of physical diseases have demonstrated the validity of the truism: "An ounce of prevention is worth a pound of cure." Furthermore, even greater advances in research show how crucial the family is as the primary support group, which has convinced us that to think about, let alone work with, individuals without their families would be tantamount to working in a vacuum. No matter how much good we do in helping people change, this good will be lost if their immediate families are not part of the process.

Prevention consists of any approach, procedure, or method designed to improve interpersonal competence and functioning for people as individuals, as partners in intimate (close and prolonged) relationships, and as parents. As we discuss in Chapter 1, prevention comprises a continuum of interventions that are challenged by cultural and societal norms that inhibit change.

Myth 1: To be chronologically or biologically an adult means being a fully effective and functioning human being. We assume that qualities of functionality, effectiveness, and competence will automatically be bestowed on us *on the basis of age*. This larger myth, like all myths, is supported by little myths or "submyths." Many of these sub-myths are based on truisms and gender stereotypes often used to make up for incomplete and inadequate self-definitions and personal identities.

Submyth a: Our academic education automatically improves our ability to relate to intimate others in an effective and enhancing fashion.

Submyth b: If we are smart and graduate from high school, college, or even graduate or professional school, we will be able to solve our life's problems. At the same time, we know that emotional, social and interpersonal development are independent of intelligence or at least that they require a different kind of intelligence from just "book knowledge."

Submyth c: Being an adult chronologically means that we are responsible, aware, effective, and competent human beings. Unfortunately, chronological age is related neither to intelligence nor to emotional and interpersonal maturity.

Submyth d: If we do well in our jobs—are adequate or even excellent in them—we will be able to do as well in intimate relationships. However, again, the two sides of this equation are unrelated to each other.

Submyth e: Being a man means keeping all feelings inside and not showing any kind of vulnerability, fallability, or need. Unfortunately, this stereotype of how men "should" behave is reinforced by TV, with powerful effects.

Submyth f: Being a woman means expressing all feelings and showing vulnerability, fallability, and need. Again, how do we distinguish between a stereotype, a truism, and a prejudice?

Submyth g: Our occupational identities are more important than any other identities, even that of being a human being. We often rely on our occupational identities when our primary identity as a human being is incomplete.

Submyth h: To perform sexually means we are adults, with all the attendant rights and privileges. But animals perform sexually too. Does that make them human beings?

Submyth i: To ask for help with your personal problems means being crazy or disturbed. Because I have a good-paying job, I am OK and I do not need any help. Professional mental health help did originate in the context of those who were severely deranged or disturbed; although the context has changed the perception still hunts us.

Submyth j: To admit to needing professional mental health help means being crazy or deranged. I've never been in trouble with the law and I pay taxes; therefore, I do not need any help. As we shall see, performing and producing have little if nothing to do with what kind of people we are, especially in relation to those we love and who love us.

Chronological age, intelligence, and education cannot be equated with competence in intimate relationships. But these submyths are widespread amd general education has not dispelled them. What about a school curriculum directed toward family living, and especially toward loving? The field of family life education, as discussed in Chapter 5, did attempt to address these shortcomings, but unfortunately, it has not succeeded. Furthermore, even if we had such a curriculum, who would teach it? For instance, most high school sex education classes are taught by PE or biology teachers who have little or no academic experience with the emotional and interpersonal aspects of sex and sexuality.

We need mass-produced, inexpensive ways to access as many individuals as possible to increase their levels of personal and interpersonal competence. How can this goal be achieved? We must try many different ways. Most psychoeducational, skills training programs for personal and interpersonal competence are oriented toward individuals. Unfortunately, we lack access to individuals outside of elementary and high school. The technology to develop personal and interpersonal competence in individuals already exists, even though it may still need refinement. It must be refined through application to much larger populations than before. Furthermore, applying this technology to individuals without including their families may be futile. How can we think that one or two hours of intervention a week will change behavior that is being influenced by the family day in and day out? Unless the family is involved in the process of change, it is very difficult for individuals to sustain the change.

Myth 2: To marry or to live with someone in an emotionally, legally, or sexually based relationship means becoming automatically an effective and functioning partner. For most of us, marriage is the most important relationship in our lives. Yet, it is surrounded by many submyths that distort its structure and function. The sheer number of divorces, not to mention suicides and murders between partners, illustrates that most of us do not become effective partners just because we live with someone or are married. The most important, if not the only, marriage we have seen and known intimately was our parents'. An increasing percentage of us have experienced the breakup of our parents' marriage. How can we learn how marriage should work if our experience comes from a questionable or even distorted experience? How can we hope to do better than our parents if no one teaches us? Our often distorted thinking about marriage can be seen in the many submyths that surround it. Ten of these will be described below because they are, in effect, the bases of the larger myth cited above.

Submyth a: Love will see us through. What is love and what does it have to do with solving problems? Love is not a solution; it takes more than love—whatever it may be—to successfully stay in a lasting, close, and committed relationship.

Submyth b: Loneliness or personal inadequacies will be cured by marriage. Unfortunately, marriage is no cure-all or panacea for anybody's inadequacies, especially those of our partners! We tend to think that the burden of perfection lies on our partners, because we are already perfect human beings. Of course, if our partners think the same way, we are in trouble.

Submyth c: Children will improve marriage. This is an awful burden to put on children. Under these conditions, children become surrogates for blame for their parents' failure to take responsibility for improving themselves and their marriages.

Submyth d: Gender differences will cause trouble. Differences in and by themselves in any relationship do not cause trouble. How these differences are used and misused can lead to trouble. Differences can be used to break up a marriage or to make it more exciting.

Submyth e: Anger has no place in marriage. If anger cannot be expressed, how can other, deeper, and different feelings be expressed?

Submyth f: Marital conflict is unhealthy. If by *conflict* we mean "confrontation," no marriage can survive without it. If by conflict we mean "vicious attacks," "unexpected ambushes," and "sudden put-downs," no marriage can survive with it.

Submyth g: Marriage will give us happiness. This expectation is too much to put on any relationship. Happiness—whatever it actually is—is a serious personal responsibility. We cannot make our partners responsible for our individual happiness.

Submyth h: Married couples should spend all their time together. This is not only practically impossible but personally debilitating. How can one remain oneself if all one's self is shared, perhaps taken, by the other?

Submyth i: Sex is the same as love. Sex is a physical act that is only part of our entire sexuality.

Submyth j: The opposite of love is hate. The opposite of love is indifference. Hate means that we are still emotionally involved with our partners and cannot see them any more objectively than we see ourselves.

How can we deal with these widespread myths? How can we reach people *before* they become committed and marry, producing children who will suffer most of the consequences of these distortions? How can couples find a place where these myths will be dispelled and replaced with more effective thinking and behavior patterns? Churches have traditionally been the place where young people planning to get married were expected to find this kind of instruction. Unfortunately, this is an unrealistic expectation. How prepared are the clergy to deal with issues of marriage preparation and the prevention of marital and family problems? What was taught in the seminary and what personal experience does the clergy have? Furthermore, aren't we asking clergy to be all things to all people? Aren't we requiring them to be all-knowing super-people who can deal with and solve all sorts of human relations problems, including those of marriage? If the church cannot do it all, who is going to do it and where? Most mental health clinics are oriented toward crisis intervention and treatment after crises. Their staffs are neither trained nor prepared to prevent marital and family problems. Hence where are we going to find settings where prevention can take place? How can we help people, especially married people, avoid the critical breakup point?

Myth 3: To have children means that we become effective and fully functioning parents. One does not need to mention the abuse, neglect, and punishment that incompetent parents bestow on their offspring. We see it everyday. This big myth may not need elaboration. However, it is supported by many submyths that need consideration.

Submyth a: If you love children, that is all they need. It takes more than love to raise children. It takes sensitivity, awareness, and knowledge of how children need to be raised. Who gave us that knowledge?

Submyth b: I will be better as a parent than my parents were with me. How can we do better if no one has taught us? Good intentions do not make our childhood experience better. At best, we may try to do the opposite of our parents. But in trying to do the opposite of our parents, we are still using them as our standard. Under these conditions, we are not yet free and independent of our parents. Consequently, how can we do better than they did?

Submyth c: Children should be seen and not heard. Rigid discipline and control will shape children into responsible adults, just like we are. This approach would produce conforming, unthinking automatons, who have no awareness of other options.

Submyth d: Spare the rod and spoil the child. Going from the extreme of authoritarian discipline to the extreme of permissiveness is no solution. Where is the middle of the road? The permissive approach precludes the learning of personal, interpersonal, and cultural limits and boundaries. Without these limits, indulgence and self-gratification may be the outcome.

Submyth e: Be like me. If you follow my example and obey my precepts you will be OK, just like I am. This is an arrogant position to take and it does not work. Blind conformity is no solution.

Submyth f: Do as I say, not as I do. This obvious contradiction is one of the many perpetuated on children. Some inconsistency is human, provided we become aware of it and correct it. To require a child to understand this contradiction of this adage is unacceptable.

Submyth g: I, as a parent, cannot make any errors. To admit to errors would belittle and diminish me in front of my child, who must not see that part of me. Is the child supposed to see an unerring, perfect human being? If our standards are too high, don't we destine children to fail?

Submyth h: I will love you if you obey me, perform well, and produce. My love for you is conditioned on your doing well in school and obeying authority without questioned. Where is unconditional love here?

Submyth i: If you are not perfect in everything you do, you are bad. This error is based on equating perfection with "goodness." If we are imperfect, as are all human beings, does it mean we are "bad"?

Submyth j: I may be unhappy, but I want you to be happy, no matter what. This is just a variation on the theme of "do as I say and not as I do." How can a child learn to be happy—whatever that is—if the parents do not know how?

In our society, we are victims of a vicious cycle. Parenting without real partnership is incomplete, and a partnership without personhood is inadequate. How can we become effective and fully functioning, that is, competent persons, partners, and parents? We are not going to learn *how to* be and become persons, partners, and parents from either parents, schools, peers, friends, or lovers. Most of us are going to learn these basic life tasks from our families of origin, mostly through nonverbal modeling rather than through words. However, no matter how functional and competent our families of origin might have been, we are going to have to meet new and different challenges, demands, and role requirements. Even when a degree of competence has been transferred from them, it may not be sufficient to address the cultural and societal changes that take place over time. Thus some of the roles and functions that may have been sufficient and satisfactory for our families of origin may no longer be sufficient for our needs.

We must obtain a driver's license to drive a car, and we spend more time learning how to drive a car than we spend learning to become fully functioning persons, partners, and parents. There are no stated requirements for assuming these three roles, the most difficult in our lives. We study and attend schools to upgrade our academic skills. However, as there is no school or setting to help us learn how to fulfill the basic life roles, how can we learn to become competent human beings, partners, and parents? Most of us learn through trial and error (or horror). Our children pay the price for whatever shortcomings and deficiencies we may have transferred to them, as human beings, as partners, or as parents.

We assume that the skills necessary to fulfill these three roles are given to us automatically, as we watch our parents, peers, and those close to us. How can we do better than our parents? Most of us mean to do just that, but the evidence shows that, at best, if we do just as well as our parents, we are doing pretty well. The fact that this learning is automatic, that is, without our conscious awareness and concern, makes it very difficult to improve. There is no way to improve ourselves in those three roles and life tasks unless we learn new ways of behaving. There is *as yet* no place in our society where this learning can take place, unless things become so critical that we seek therapy. Outside of therapy, we still do not have an institutionalized place to learn basic competencies for intimate relationships.

Prevention is a rather presumptuous term (L'Abate, 1986a). We really do not know whether we have "prevented" anything until a few years after the original intervention, though we hope that what we do now will eventually help. Yet, if we do not follow up the subjects of our initial intervention, we will never know whether they benefited from it. As a result, unless we relentlessly evaluate whether and what changes may have taken place in the long term, we will never know which preventive approach produces effective changes and which does not.

Without evaluation, no progress will be forthcoming. Prevention will become another of the many institutionalized professions in the mental health field without the accountability and verifiability that we expect from our veterinarians, let alone our physicians. As long as the mental health and psychotherapy fields function without the criteria of professional competence and efficacy, there will be little progress at a slow rate. Years ago, I suggested (L'Abate, 1983) that "preventers, " in order to be credentialed, should demonstrate their skills by presenting evidence that whatever they have done as interventions actually worked. They would need to show pre-post and follow-up evaluations done as a *standard operating procedure*. I doubt whether this suggestion will ever be followed or implemented, unless, of course, it is mandated by third parties.

In Europe, for some time now, there have been proponents of what has been called "permanent education," that is, the concept that education should be a lifelong process for all of us to assist in coping with the continual technological and cultural changes that we face in our society. Most proponents of this concept (deSantis, 1979; Guidelin, 1981; Lengrad, 1973; Mencarelli, 1976; Richmond, 1978), however, believe that this education should take place *outside the family context*, mainly in work roles rather than in family roles. Only a few proponents of this concept (Ciotta, 1984; Cusinato, 1985) have considered the vital importance of the family in the life-long formation of more competent life roles, especially those of partner and parent. In Europe, this movement has remained at the programmatic level, as a good theoretical idea but not for implementation; in North America, its pragmatic counterpart has developed in the last two decades under the general title of "social skills training" (L'Abate & Milan, 1985). Most of this movement, however, is still oriented toward teaching individuals in groups, mostly outside the family context. Only a few representatives of this movement, as we shall see in Chapter 5, have devoted themselves to the development of specific programs for couples and families.

Another development that has taken place during this time is the phenomenal rise of family therapy as an important addition to the large repertoire of traditional psychotherapeutic techniques (for individuals and groups.) Unfortunately, family therapy, as an example of tertiary prevention, by definition and in its methods of intervention, deals mainly with families in crisis. What happens to families not yet in crisis who are either at risk or in dire need of some kind of help that would forestall and even avoid future breakdowns and crises? As things are now, most of these families have to wait until things get bad enough to require therapy. For each family in therapy there are at least five to ten families that could profit from some kind of help, although not necessarily therapy. Where is this help to come from? Where are the institutions from which this help could be given? There is none as yet. I hope that in the future there will be family centers that can deliver all types of interventions at primary, secondary, and tertiary levels of prevention.

As a solution to the problem of the need for varying levels of prevention, I will present a proposal for a model national marriage center. This center would be devoted to the study and promotion of preparation for marriage and prevention of marital problems. It would not accept couples in crisis for therapy. They would be referred elsewhere.

Although there are many programs and institutions dedicated to the promotion and promulgation of parenting skills, marriage and marital skills have not received the crucial attention they deserve in the form of an institution specifically dedicated to that purpose. I hope this proposed center can redress this past imbalance.

The audience for this book can be fairly wide and difficult to specify because the family, as well as prevention, should be of interest to everyone. This book is addressed to middle- and upper-level mental health workers, community leaders, researchers, and members of various professions who are interested in and convinced that *prevention is the key factor in the field of individual health promotion, marital fitness, and family wellness.* I hope prevention will be a challenge to many family therapists, who, in the haste to cure and to deal with crises, have forgotten that, for every family in crisis and in need of "tertiary prevention," many others need help, even if they are not yet in crisis.

The public health model advocated here may be, in some ways, incompatible with a private practice model. Instead of seeing either model as exclusive and even antagonistic to the other, I attempt to show that it is possible to integrate them. Although it is possible to help more families per unit of the professional's time than before, this will take place only if professionals give up simply being direct service providers. Instead, professionals would need to learn to allocate and delegate some interventional, pre-, and paratherapeutic functions to others with less training and experience but with good personal, human, and emotional qualities independent of degrees or of expertise; qualities such as warmth and empathy. Issues of cost-effectiveness and personnel utilization are considered throughout this book including the training of a future professional group of *preventers.*

1

The Importance of Primary and Secondary Prevention

Primary and secondary prevention did not arise in a vacuum. They are the result of historical evolutionary processes that have convinced us of the usefulness of intervening *before* human breakdown occurs. This conviction needs to be supported by workable plans and programs relevant to the goal, that is, *to increase personal, partnership, and parenthood competence in all of us.* Most of us, no matter how functional, could use some learning in any of these three basic areas of competence. We only have room here for a very brief account of the historical antecedents of preventive efforts.

Historical Perspective: The Evolution of Human Interventions

Let us review the milestones in the evolution of mental health service delivery. Pinel is credited with breaking down the system that allowed patients in so-called psychiatric hospitals to be treated as criminals or worse. After Pinel, the next advance was Freud's introduction of "talk" as a therapeutic medium and the beginning of the psychotherapeutic movement, at least in the Western hemisphere. A parallel advance was Adler's, who was in some ways a follower and in some ways an opponent of Freud, who requested to see the whole family with the referred index, or identified, patient. This request lead to the child guidance clinics movement and, more recently, to the community mental health clinics movement. A third advance, that has been hailed in some quarters as being even more important, has been the paraprofessional revolution (Sobey, 1970)—the use of individuals selected or self-selected on the basis of personal, rather than solely professional qualities to work with people in trouble. This third advance allowed us to realize that we should help not only people in crisis but also people at risk and in need. Thus the idea of prevention in mental health came about, because prevention cannot take place without the availability of a large pool of interested and specialized personnel.

Prevention in the mental health field is a relatively recent phenomenon, with a great many advocates and proponents (Albee, 1984, 1986; Buckner, Trickett, & Corse, 1985; Edelstein & Michelson, 1986; Felner, Jason, Moritsugu, & Farber, 1983; Goldston, 1986; Hefferman & Albee, 1985; Joffe, Albee, & Kelly, 1984; Kessler & Albee, 1975; Klein & Goldston, 1977; Lieberman, 1976; Murphy & Frank, 1979; Wandersman & Hess, 1985). However, it has not yet reached the level of widespread institutionalization already reached by the many kinds of psychotherapy. Furthermore, most of these advocates do not seem to stress the importance of the family as the first and foremost support system (Mace, 1983). Especially in the mental health field, prevention still has a long way to go. In regard to the family, the mental health field has been even more behind the times. It has been very slow in recognizing the importance of both prevention *and* the family. Prevention with families has an even longer way to go than prevention in general. We might first establish a curriculum for a Ph.D. in prevention (L'Abate, 1987).

Why "Should" Mental Health
Professionals Be Involved in Prevention?

Granted that prevention, like the family, is not of exclusive interest to any single profession, why should mental health professionals, and even psychotherapists, become concerned with and involved in preventive activities with families more than they have already been? There are at least three reasons. First, professions interested in interpersonal competence, involving the whole range of behavior from functional to dysfunctional, need to be involved theoretically, evaluatively, and interventionally with functional, semifunctional, and dysfunctional people (individuals, couples, and families). A great deal of what we know in mental health came from the treatment of very disturbed or disturbing people. The mental health professions have been concerned with crisis and pathology, almost completely ignoring the remainder of the population that does not ask for help because it is not in crisis—an unfortunate point of view. What we know or we think we know about "normal" or "functional" behavior derives from pathology rather than the other way around.

Second, being involved with the whole gamut of behavior, from functional to dysfunctional, would allow mental health workers to learn more about behavior in general and, specifically, more about functional behavior than we would learn from dealing only or mainly with dysfunctionality. In fact, one of the definitions of *normality* has been in terms of the absence of pathology, a definition that can hardly help us understand what normal or functional behavior is, especially when we have trouble defining either the norm or the extreme.

Third, the mental health disciplines do not incorporate the scientific aspects of mental health, such as designing research, statistics, and evaluation. Instead, they concentrate on more immediate, important human aspects, applications and clinical practice, but not on evaluating (e.g., psychotherapy). As a result, even though many mental health workers, especially psychologists, are trained in research methods, very few of us use them once we start practicing professionally and clinically with people, unless we are asked solely to perform psychodiagnostic functions. Otherwise, few of us follow up our clients with pre-post treatment evaluations. Despite this inadequacy in evaluation, our research tools should allow us to sharpen theories and methodologies in the area of prevention. If we do not evaluate our methods of intervention routinely, prevention will repeat the errors of previous theoretical movements, such as psychoanalysis, humanism, and systems theory, with the exception, perhaps, of behaviorism, as will be discussed in the forthcoming chapters.

The importance of research, that is, evaluating the effectiveness of a prevention program, is underscored by Price, Cowen, Lorion, and Ramos-McKay (1989) in their review of effective prevention programs. They found that the most effective programs shared a number of common features: (a) a focus on understanding risks and problems of behavior to be prevented in the target group; (b) a design to change the "life trajectory" of the target group, by making available to them options and opportunities for the long term that were not available before; (c) an opportunity to learn new life skills to allow participants to cope more effectively with stress through social support; (d) a focus on strengthening natural support from family, community, or school settings (p. 51); and (e) the collection of rigorous research evidence to document effectiveness (p. 51). In fact, these authors lament that "rigorous evaluations of preventive programs are scarce" (pp. 51–55). The major ingredients of this rigor are shown in (a) clearly defined instructions as could be found in a manual, (b) pre- and postintervention evaluation, and (c) long-term follow-up to evaluate the "enduring achievement of preventive goals" (p. 55). In conclusion, Price, Cowen, Lorion, and Ramos-McKay (1989, p. 56) commented: "Although preventive programs are time consuming and costly to develop and evaluate, their cost is trivial compared to the social costs of drug abuse, school dropout, depression, or delinquency."

Definitions and Confusion

The term *prevention* in the mental health field describes a variety of individual, group, family, and societal forces and approaches that attempt to reduce emotional dysfunction and disorder by improving interpersonal competence. As already discussed in the Preface, we will define *prevention* here as any approach, procedure, or method intended and designed to improve one's interpersonal competence as an individual, as a partner, and as a parent. But we need to compare this definition with other commonly accepted ones. In this comparison, some confusion will arise between different definitions from different sources. For instance, how does *therapy* fit into our definition? Many therapists would contend that therapy is a way of improving interpersonal competence just like any other preventive approach. Therefore, therapy should be considered a form of prevention. Preventers, on the other hand, would argue that dealing with crisis and breakdown is not prevention, because prevention is intended to avoid that very breakdown by dealing with populations that may or may not be at risk for it. How can we reconcile two equally valid viewpoints with completely different approaches and different populations? It is apparent that therapy deals with critical and clinical populations, but prevention is intended to deal with the population at large: the norm but not the exception as in therapy. One way to reconcile these two viewpoints is to postulate a continuum of preventive approaches, each with its own characteristics and differences.

As noted in the Preface, prevention is commonly divided into three different levels or types: primary, secondary, and tertiary. This division, however, is not free of controversy and confusion. Consequently, this chapter attempts to classify these three types and, hopefully, clarify the confusion and decrease the controversy. We will discuss these three types as different approaches with their own specific characteristics as well as their interrelationships with each other.

Primary Prevention: Intervention for Everyone?

Primary prevention has been defined by some sources (Joffe, Albee, & Kelly, 1984) as the proactive decreasing of incidence of emotional disorders *before* debilitating deficits and/or stresses appear, through reduction of stresses and incidences of dysfunctionalities. Not that the entire definition deals with counteracting negative extremes ("disorders," "deficits," "stresses," and "dysfunctionalities") rather than with norms and positive goals. Furthermore, as I will argue later, this definition confounds primary with secondary prevention. If we are unclear on how to differentiate primary from secondary prevention, how can we be clear about either one of them or even about tertiary prevention? For instance, Albee (1984) proposed an equation that encompasses most, if not all, the *negative* factors related to such an incidence of dysfunctionality:

$$\text{Incidence} = \frac{\text{Organic Factors} + \text{Stress} + \text{Exploitation}}{\text{Coping Skills} + \text{Self–Esteem} + \text{Supporting Groups}}$$

Organic factors, stress, and exploitation or abuse are the constants that we all meet in the course of our lives. These constants, however, are mitigated and modified by our coping skills—by how well we are able to deal with these constants. The negatives on the top of the equation are supposed to be corrected and changed by the positives on the bottom of the equation. However, even the so-called positives have negative aspects. If a person has insufficient coping skills, it is very likely that that person will also show poor or low self-esteem and may lack or have insufficient social support. Furthermore, Albee defined the ability to cope in terms of support groups and self-esteem, the latter an intrapsychic concept that will be considered critically in greater detail in the next chapter. However, he failed to specify that the most important of all support groups can be the family. Preventive efforts should be directed toward helping families cope with their individual members as well as helping individuals cope with their families.

As the foregoing equation indicates, the family is not even mentioned as a major support group by one of the most prominent advocates of primary prevention. In fact, thus far, the family has received short shrift from the prevention literature, and the importance of the family in primary and secondary prevention has not been acknowledged as it should have been. The family is a major, and sometimes the only, natural support group for most individuals (Galdston, 1961; Kahn & Kamerman, 1982; Keniston, 1977; Mace, 1983; Moss, Hess, & Swift, 1982; *Congressional Record*, 1973). For instance, in a recent annotated bibliography on prevention (Buckner, Trickett, & Corse, 1985), consisting of 1, 008 entries, only 19 entries were primarily concerned with families and 24 more entries only secondarily concerned the family. Thus fewer than 5% of all references in the prevention literature focus on marriage and the family. But how can we ever conceive of working to help individuals outside of the natural context and main support group, the family? It is very likely that, after treatment or training, many of these individuals will go back to the same family contexts, which may undo any positive changes that may have taken place. Even though most (95%) of primary and secondary prevention approaches have, thus far, dealt with groups of individuals, most of these individuals live in families. We cannot ask individuals, even in groups, to change if their families do not also change. Consequently, most primary prevention approaches will need to include families. It remains to be seen whether secondary prevention approaches will include families *with* individuals.

A more positive way of looking at primary prevention would be as an approach promoting conditions to increase competence and coping skills. Ideally, this could consist of building new family centers or using empty Sunday school classrooms as family centers. These centers would be used for social and interpersonal skills training through existing psychoeducational programs (Levant, 1986). Again, we return to the basic point that training individuals apart from their family contexts, no matter how dysfunctional these contexts may be, can be practically useless. What good will these newly acquired skills be, if we cannot use and apply them with the very people who care for us and for whom we care? Many individuals give up on their families and separate themselves from perceived pathology and felt pain, thinking that physical separation will be sufficient to avoid becoming engulfed by, and regressing to, family patterns of behaving. Avoidance of issues of closeness and family problems will not teach us how to solve problems in intimate relationships.

We do not learn through avoidance. We learn through confrontation, conflict, pain, and clarity of vision. Eventually an individual trained or treated outside of the family context will become involved with someone with whom he or she will eventually relate in the same ways learned from the family of origin. Thus solution by avoidance is no solution at all. These individuals must learn to practice new and positive skills for the rest of their lives, with the same family members who brought about whatever painful condition may have existed. To learn new psychosocial or psychoeducational skills in a vacuum or with other individuals who do not have blood or emotional history can be artificial and, eventually, wasteful. The same fallacy is present in the field of individual psychotherapy in which individuals learn newer and more positive ways of relating. The new behaviors break down when applied to intimate relationships where the partner who has not been in therapy should have been as well. Instead, why not start with therapy from the beginning of problems in the relationship?

Thus, primary prevention stresses programs of education and social engineering with the population at large and with special populations at high risk for potential breakdown. Unfortunately, here we must deal with the difficult issue of discriminating between primary and secondary prevention. As soon as we use the concept of risk to identify potential populations, we have to distinguish between low, medium, and high risk. Should risk be assessed by special categories (children of alcoholics, children of jailed parents, and so on) or should the approach deal with the entire population (all children, all engaged couples, all newlyweds, and so on) given that all children could potentially be abused, all engaged and newly married couples could potentially divorce, and so on. In any population, how can we identify those couples, families, and children who are at high risk? How can we distinguish between low, medium, and high risk?

Furthermore, we can discriminate between at least two types of primary prevention. One type consists of community-based changes that help alleviate stress. For instance, the creation of nursery schools and kindergartens in or close to the caretaking parent's workplace would reduce the parent's worry about the well-being of the child and allow the parent to be immediately available to the child in case of emergency or sickness. This physical closeness would go a long way toward reducing the stress of working parents with below-school-age children.

Another type of primary prevention refers to any approach designed to help people learn how to cope with stress. Given the inevitability of stress throughout the life span (i.e., death and taxes) for all of us, we as individuals must learn how to deal with stress and not expect external sources to reduce it for us. No amount of community intervention to reduce stress will ever help people learn *how to control their own reactions* to it. Thus, we should assume that competence training would serve as a way of improving people's reactions to stress; that is, the more competent the individual, the couple, or the family is, the more able they will be to cope with stress. Hence, competence and coping skills are intrinsically intertwined, if we accept the definition of primary prevention presented here.

To differentiate further among different degrees of risk, it is necessary to introduce and expand upon the concept of *need* as being synonymous with what others have called *high risk*. Although primary prevention may deal with general or even selected populations—children, adolescents, the newly married, and so on—can we identify among these populations individuals, couples, and families that need help, and help that is not necessarily psychotherapeutic?

If we are not able to differentiate between these three types of prevention conceptually, perhaps we may be able to on the basis of methods, media, and modalities of intervention. Although this discrimination can still become fuzzy, confusion between primary and secondary prevention becomes even greater when one adds the concept of promotion. What is promotion? Does it consist of primary or secondary prevention or does it consist of activities that do not overlap with either one? We can decide that primary prevention consists of at least three different approaches: (a) the creation of conditions, settings, and physical arrangements and facilities that reduce stress, such as nursery schools close to the parent's workplace; (b) the promotion of healthy attitudes and habits, as could be found in education, such as sex education for adolescents, marriage training for engaged couples, or parental training for expecting couples; and (c) the increase of levels of personal and interpersonal competence through psychoeducational skills training, such as the creation of a more appropriate sex education curriculum for adolescents with additional experiential components designed to apply academic learning to real life situations. The same kind of experiential enrichment could take place with engaged couples as with expectant parents. This latter approach is considered in Chapter 5.

Secondary Prevention: Not for Everybody

Until now, the term *prevention* really meant *primary prevention* and also implied a continuum of preventive efforts, including the prevention of recurrences of a disorder or an irritant or toxic condition that may produce dysfunctionality and pathology (Cowen, 1984, p. 36). Few sources bother to discriminate between primary and secondary prevention and some confusion is still present (Joffe, Albee, & Kelly, 1984). Secondary prevention either is not mentioned or implies the application of preventive approaches to special populations. Secondary prevention, therefore, is defined by early identification, diagnosis, and the treatment of cases in need before they break down.

The major distinction between primary and secondary prevention lies in how *risk* and *need* are defined. Does *need* mean high risk? What does *risk* imply? Are we all at risk for headaches, colds, and pneumonia? Unless a more specific conceptual and methodological differentiation is achieved, confusion about definitions of *primary* and *secondary* prevention will continue. Some authors, for instance, Albee (1984), have attempted to differentiate between primary and secondary prevention, but have not cleared up the confusion. Goldston (1986, p. 33) defined *primary prevention* as taking place with "high risk groups within the community that have not been labeled psychiatrically ill." Like Goldston, Cowen (1983, 1984) called *primary* what others would call *secondary* prevention. He defined *primary prevention* as any approach that (a) reduces new instances of a disorder (after it has been identified?), (b) reduces irritants to dysfunctioning people *before* irritants exact their toll, and (c) builds psychological health, that is, competence. It is not clear, therefore, whether primary prevention deals with functioning populations, with populations at risk, or even with populations at "high risk."

Thus far, primary prevention has received a great deal of attention as has tertiary prevention (i.e., therapy). Where do both emphases leave secondary prevention? In a recent reference work on prevention (Felner, Jason, Moritsugu, & Farber, 1983), 8 out of more than 300 pages were devoted to secondary prevention; the rest were devoted to primary prevention. Other references, most of them already cited above, fared no better in terms of attention to secondary prevention. How can we distinguish between these three types of prevention conceptually, clinically, operationally, and concretely with a minimum of confusion and conflict? To achieve this clarity, we can look at the types of prevention along a continuum of functionality-dysfunctionality.

An example may help us discriminate among the three types. In this country, there are currently approximately 28 million children of alcoholics. Many of them would probably like to believe that they are or will be better off than their parents (Goglia, 1985; Thaxton, 1989), without any emotional disturbance or addictive behavior. Even assuming that they will be better off in general, we can expect at least 10% of them (2, 800, 000) to be in need of some kind of help. What kind of help? If all our help consists of is hospitalization, medication, or psychotherapy, then that is all we can offer them. That is, we may have to wait for a serious problem requiring professional attention to develop. At the very least, 1% of this population will break down and need professional help consisting of hospitalization (or incarceration), medication, and psychotherapy.

Could we have helped beforehand? Can we provide help to add to either primary or tertiary prevention? What would something beforehand consist of? How can we distinguish it from either primary or tertiary prevention?

Tertiary Prevention: Magic or Method?

We can easily define *tertiary prevention* in terms of crisis-oriented, psychotherapeutic activities of professionals clearly identified as therapists, counselors, or professional helpers. This approach applies to or implies face-to-face contact between an individual, couple, or family after breakdown or after having reached levels of personal, marital, or family crisis. Dealing with people in crisis requires a great deal of both personal and professional skill. From all we know about the outcome of psychotherapy as tertiary prevention, successful psychotherapeutic results are due to both, personal and professional skills. Psychotherapy's outcome depends in part on the therapist's *style*. We can account for approximately 50% of the outcome in psychotherapy through non-quantifiable factors such as the therapist's personal ability to make people feel at home and comfortable, dealing positively with their crises, and reassuring them of their worth. These qualities are called "relationship skills," warmth, unconditional regard, empathy, respect, and support. Because of their ephemeral nature, these qualities may oftentimes border on the mystical, the mysterious, and the magical (Kazdin, 1986). The other factor involved in therapy's outcome is *professional* qualities—expertise, knowledge, and experience designed to help produce changes in people above and beyond the therapist's style and personal qualities. This set of skills is called "structuring skills," those that relate to a method or a methodology.

Style and relationship skills are peculiar and specific to each therapist's personality and are nonreplicable or, at best, difficult to replicate. Structuring skills, on the other hand, represent those methodological skills that constitute the "professional" or even "scientific" armamentarium of each therapist. Style consists of individual skills that vary from one professional to another. Hence these skills are not replicable and are difficult to control, except through years of supervision and practice. This style arguably represents the ability of the therapist to be *present and emotionally available* to people in crisis, a quality that will be explained further in the next chapter. Styles can vary along a dimension defined by activity at one end and passivity on the other. Activity may imply being directive, confrontational, conductive, and prescriptive and may thus be closely related to structuring skills. Passivity may imply being reflective, reactive, supportive, and nondirective, thus being closely related to the relationship skills described above.

The distinction between style or method is not an idle or irrelevant one with regard to primary and secondary prevention with families. Most primary and secondary prevention approaches are based on method, that is, they consist of a sequence of repeatable steps that are independent of the trainer's own style. Of course, with increasing functionality, it is possible that the professional style of the trainer or facilitator may not be as relevant in primary and secondary prevention as it is in tertiary prevention.

Thus, in tertiary prevention, we have two different but overlapping and synergistically related sets of skills. One set, structuring skills, is more related to the specific symptom; and the other set, relationships skills, is more nonspecific and more related to the person than to the symptom or problem. The first set consists of prepared, already rehearsed and objectively standardized nomothetic (group-oriented) plans. The second set consists of unrehearsed, spontaneously and subjectively individualized ideographic reactions. The first set is based on the rational aspects of intervention. The second set is based on the emotive, affective aspects of intervention.

How is this distinction between method and style related to primary and secondary prevention with families? Both primary and secondary prevention approaches utilize methods more than style, but tertiary prevention utilizes *both*, style as well as method. Neither aspect alone is sufficient by itself. Both are necessary at all levels of prevention. They may well represent two different orientations to life, a *deterministic* one, stressing normative predictability and standard programming, and an *indeterministic* one, stressing variability, unpredictability, and uniqueness in the human experience. Both views represent different but related contexts. One represents the *context of discovery*, stressing the aesthetically dialectical and nonrepetitive impressions basic to relationship skills. The other represents the *context of justification*, stressing the demonstrably pragmatic and the reductionistically repeatable. The former stresses the plausibly seductive qualities of human nature and the latter stresses the accountably verifiable. This ultimate duality will be elaborated in the next chapter.

Psychotherapeutic schools and approaches, however, vary in how much value they give to either quality which we can look at as both sides of the coin. For instance, humanistic approaches would like to maintain an aura of mystically mysterious and hence nonrepeatable uniqueness that magnifies the importance of the therapist's subjective "self" as well as the client's subjective experience and phenomenological views, that is, feelings. At the other extreme is behaviorism, with its stress on the observable, the measurable, and the objective. This school of therapy maintains the importance of repeatable methodologies that can be replicated from one therapist to another, regardless of the importance of the therapist's self.

As stressed earlier, *both* the personal and the professional aspects are important in psychotherapy (L'Abate, 1986). As psychoanalysis falls somewhere in between these two polarities, so-called systems thinking falls close to the humanistic perspective in its antiempirical stance, stressing complexity and nonreplicability for a unique process that cannot be captured by the simplistic nature of psychological investigation or rigor. We shall come back to these four theoretical schools and therapeutic approaches during the course of this book, evaluating them from the viewpoint of their contribution and fruitfulness to primary and secondary prevention with families.

From the viewpoint of primary and secondary prevention, however, the problem of many psychotherapeutic approaches lies in their lack of flexibility in linking, integrating, and allowing for a synergistic combination of all three levels of prevention for the betterment of all families, and not just those in crisis. There is no question that preventive approaches could not have developed evolutionarily without all the knowledge and experience we have gathered from the various psychotherapeutic modalities (individual, marital, group, and familial). By the same token, can the psychotherapy community profit and learn from primary and secondary prevention? Thus far, these enterprises have taken place independently; one mostly ignoring the other and each, in some ways, taking away from the other.

If we want to understand the effects of a therapeutic approach, we will have to practice it ourselves independent of other approaches. How could we otherwise demonstrate whether or not it is useful? Before we combine synergistically different methods of intervention and prevention, we need to demonstrate that each approach produces positive outcomes in and by itself, separate from other approaches. Rather than an either-or position—either psychoeducational practices or therapy—why not think in ways that would allow us to integrate them and use them together?

One of the most serious issues facing the various types of psychotherapy deals with the intellectual and practical gulf that divides family therapists from family enrichers (facilitators, trainers, preventers, and so on). These enterprises operate in completely different ways and, at the present time, unfortunately, exclusionarily if not antagonistically. This takes away from each profession and ultimately from the very families we all claim to want to help. This gulf between professionals relates to the either-or thinking that characterizes most of the arguments as well as the thinking of many family therapists, who look down on psychoeducational practices as being less important than therapy.

There are at least two ways of reconciling these two fields and seeing them as complementing each other. The first way is conceptual; the second is practical. In the first place, we need to think about a continuum of functionality-dysfunctionality, where instead of either-or thinking, such as normal-abnormal, we have a wide range of families with at least three degrees of functionality: (a) *at risk*, (b) *in need*, and (c) *in crisis*, as shown in Table 1.1. As a result of these three gradations, we can now differentiate among three different fields or types of prevention: primary, secondary, and tertiary, each with its specific characteristics and methods. A public health approach would encompass all three gradations, while a private-practice approach would of necessity need to focus mainly on crisis, because that is the only one of the three approaches that pays in the marketplace at the present time.

Second, integrating all three approaches implies the use of a wide range of semi-, pre-, and paraprofessional personnel working together with full-fledged professionals. The latter would remain responsible for directive and supportive decision-making functions. At the outset of a family crisis, full-fledged professionals might use tertiary crisis intervention approaches. As the family is normalized, intervention can progress to secondary and then primary prevention approaches in the hands of nonprofessional personnel. The less disturbed the family, the more it can learn from other, less credentialed facilitators rather than just professionals.

TABLE 1.1: Criteria to Differentiate and Discriminate Among Preventive Approaches

	Types of Approaches		
	Primary	*Secondary*	*Tertiary*
Criteria	*Proactive Pretherapeutic*	*Para-active Paratherapeutic*	*Reactive Therapeutic*
1. Risk	Low to minimal	High: in need but not critical	Very high: critical
2. Reversibility	High: 100% to 66%	Medium 66% to 33%	Low to very low: 33% to 0%
3. Probability of Breakdown	Low but potential	Medium but probable	High and real (actual)
4. Population	Nonclinical: labeled but not diagnosable	Preclinical and diagnosable	Clinical: critical and diagnosed
5. Ability to Learn	High	Medium	Low
6. Goals	Increase competence and resistance to breakdown	Decrease stress and chance of crisis	Restore to minimum functioning
7. Type of involvement	Voluntary: many choices	Obligatory: decrease in choices	Mandatory: no other choices available
8. Recommendations	"Could benefit by it." "It would be nice."	"You need it before it's too late." "Recommend strongly that you do it."	"It is necessary." "Nothing else will work." "Other choices would be more expensive" (i.e., hospitalization, incarceration).
9. Cost	Low	Medium	High
10. Effectiveness	High(?)	Questionable yet to be found	Relatively Low
11. Personnel	Lay volunteers and pre- and paraprofessionals	Middle-level professionals	Professionals
12. Types of Intervention	General, learning, strengthening, enrichment	More specific to behavior, that is, programmed materials	Specialized therapy
13. Degree of Structure	High	Medium	Low
14. Degree of Specificity	General and topical	Individualized	Specific to the symptom

How can we put all three types of prevention together synergistically and on an equal footing, so that each approach can benefit from the other? One reason for the schism between preventers and therapists has been the inadequacy of a model or models to bridge the gap between these approaches. Can we find an all encompassing model to allow us to integrate all three approaches, demonstrating that they all are working toward the same goal, the betterment of society and its members?

Discriminating Among Types of Prevention

The rest of this chapter will be devoted to more practical ways of discriminating, at least conceptually, between the three types of prevention, according to the 14 criteria summarized in Table 1.1. One way of differentiating among these three levels is based on the *type of activity* demanded by each level. For instance, as primary prevention has been defined as *proactive*, and tertiary *reactive*, secondary prevention, consequently, could be called *paraactive*: taking place alongside activities that are either proactive or reactive, somewhere between the two. Secondary prevention practices may be used while the symptomatic behavior is occurring, even though a crisis requiring more severe interventions may have not taken place.

The distinction among three different types of interventions—*pro-*, *para-*, and *re*active—also applies to a definition of what constitutes *therapeutic practices*, that is, face-to-face interactions between people in crisis and professional helpers. Using the notion of *therapy*, we can have pretherapeutic practices in primary prevention, paratherapeutic practices in secondary prevention, and therapeutic practices proper in tertiary prevention. How can we differentiate further among these three different kinds of interventions? Operationally, this distinction will be made more specific in the rest of this chapter and in the rest of this book.

Differentiating among types of prevention according to types of activity and therapeutic practices, one can work out a tentative list of at least 14 qualitative criteria, thus far admittedly quite subjective and tentative (Table 1.1) according to degree and extent of (1) risk and impairment, (2) reversibility of behavior, (3) probability of breakdown, (4) characteristics of the population, (5) ability to learn,

(6) goals, (7) type of involvement, (8) recommendations, (9) cost, (10) effectiveness, (11) personnel, and (12) types of intervention, varying in (13) structure and in (14) specificity.

(1) A traditional way of differentiating among these three types of prevention is according to *degree* of risk. *At risk* means that practically all families, even functional ones, need improvement, betterment, and enrichment in their coping skills, competence, and enjoyment of life to decrease the chances of future breakdown. Out of this population, there may be many (50% to 66%?) who do not cope as well as the rest of the same population. Thus they would be at greater risk than others, as the assumption of individual differences would predict. Hence risk assessment is necessary to discriminate highly competent from less competent individuals and families. From an *at-risk* population, there will be a certain percentage—depending on criteria yet to be determined, and according to which behavior we are targeting—that will be *in need* of specific help. This help will be necessary to prevent further acting out and incarceration, addictions, depression and suicide, and mental illness. These individuals or their families may not be either able or willing to use tertiary prevention approaches. Tertiary prevention deals rehabilitatively with emotional problems and dysfunctionality *after* breakdown has taken place, that is, with families *in crisis* who have an identified patient and are not able to cope by themselves, such as a family that has discovered incest or an adult child of an alcoholic who has developed an addiction or an emotional disturbance as evidenced by an impending divorce.

An example that might help to sharpen this differentiation is, for instance, the area of prevention of sexual abuse. Primary prevention of sexual abuse would consist of helping *all children* because all of them would be at risk for sexual abuse. In the same way, all adults who were abused as children are also, in turn, at risk for sexually abusing children, because the rate of abusers having been abused themselves as children is very high. Out of these two general populations, the abused and the abusers, secondary prevention would take place with children who have been abused at least once and with perpetrators who may have been caught at least once, before, during, or after they go to jail or receive harsher punishments. Both need help, but this help need not be therapeutic. It could be paratherapeutic. Tertiary prevention would deal with families of individuals who have abused or have been abused and are now in crisis because this behavior has reached the level of coming to the attention of authorities.

One could also argue that primary and secondary prevention follows a public health approach (the most for the most), while most tertiary prevention practices follow a crisis and private practice approach (the most for the least). However, regardless of the merits of this differentiation, even group, marital, or family therapy, which may be more cost-effective than individual therapy, is not sufficient to cope with the sheer quantity of families at risk and in need.

(2) *Reversibility* refers to the probability that a temporarily disturbed or disturbing behavior may return to its original "normal, " that is, not disturbed and nondisturbing, state. What may start as a temporary reaction, if handled improperly, may increase in duration, frequency, and intensity to become more and more resistant to intervention. The more and more resistant to intervention that particular reaction becomes, the greater the difficulty of going back to an original state of functionality. For instance, an adult child of alcoholic parents, just by being so labeled, is at much greater risk of becoming an alcoholic or an addict in some other form. Once this addiction becomes a reality, it might be much more difficult to treat than if that adult had been helped preventively, earlier, during his or her formative years (L'Abate, Farrar, & Serritella, in press). During childhood, however, that individual would not have been able to fully realize the dangers transferred from the family of origin.

How can one find a way of evaluating "degree" or "extent" of reversibility? Reviewing all of the outcome studies of psychotherapy (Garfield, 1986), the major if not the only sure finding that is consistent from one study to another is that, regardless of theoretical approach and method used, practically any population treated therapeutically divides itself into a one-third, one-third, and one-third split. That is, one-third improves a great deal, one-third improves somewhat, and one-third remains the same or gets worse. What does this finding mean? It implies that we have not as yet solved the problem of specificity and match between client's needs and characteristics and the therapeutic approach that would best fit that client for an optimal outcome. Another way of interpreting the same result would be from the viewpoint of variability. People are to variable for us to hope that one method of treatment will fit everybody—the uniformity fallacy (Kiesler, 1966). We shall

find the same uniformity fallacy or bias when dealing with all purpose, "funnel," primary prevention programs in Chapter 5. Sometimes, in these programs, the same approach is deemed useful for
everybody, without regard for socioeconomic status (SES), education, personal needs, and other independent variables.

Thus, taking any population at random, we would expect that,
without intervention, at best 33% of that population will continue to
function relatively well even under stress or will be able to go back
to a satisfactory level of functionality after a crisis without external
intervention. How about the remaining 66%? Given the variability
of human behavior, we could expect that 33% to 66% of any population at random would be at risk for some type of breakdown.
Without intervention of any kind, the disturbing condition might
get worse and produce a crisis, which then may or may not be
reversible. There is no reversibility after murder or suicide. Thus
the degree of reversibility decreases with the extent of pathology
and dysfunctionality.

(3) Many of these criteria, of course, overlap a great deal in
terms of the *probability of breakdown*. For instance, in primary prevention attention is given to populations in which everybody has a
potential for breakdown, for example, children of alcoholic parents
would be at greater risk for future addictions than children of non-
alcoholic parents (Goglia, 1985; Thaxton, 1989). Secondary prevention is for populations *in need*, that is, individuals who, for instance,
as children of alcoholics, have already started to drink or show
indications of incipient addictions. This behavior indicates that
breakdown is now a much greater *possibility* than in primary prevention. In tertiary prevention, breakdown, or *crisis*, is a *reality*; it
has already happened or is about to happen. It is taking place. The
adult child of an alcoholic has now been arrested for driving under
the influence. Consequently, primary prevention deals with much
larger pools of cases than secondary prevention, even up to 100%,
as in the case of education as a prepreventive approach. Out of this
large pool, there are fewer cases that may not profit from primary
prevention and could need secondary prevention approaches, such
as (a) abused and neglected children (i.e., children of abusive parents); (b) children of divorce, children born out of wedlock, or chil-
dren of psychiatrically ill parents; (c) children of single-parent families; (d) families of lower SES and unemployed heads of households; or (e) children and adult children of alcoholics or addicts.

Secondary prevention, therefore, would then deal with dropouts from, and families who do not or cannot profit from, primary prevention approaches, such as (a) acting-out or runaway adolescents (and their families), (b) depressed children and adolescents (and their families), (c) learning disabled or underachieving children and adolescents (and their families), or (d) adult children of alcoholics. Tertiary prevention would deal with populations that cannot or are unable to use either primary or secondary prevention approaches at the outset. But, after appropriate tertiary help, many critical and clinical families may eventually be able to learn from secondary and even from primary prevention approaches.

(4) As far as populations are concerned, by now we should be able to start discriminating among different groups to find families who are more at risk than others. Degree of risk can be predicted fairly easily if and when certain predictors are in place. For instance (a) SES may be a predictor of greater chances either of acting out and/or of psychopathology; (b) gender differences may be predictors of greater risk for acting-out disorders in males and depression in females (L'Abate & Bryson, in press); and (c) children from single-parent families may be at greater risk for delinquency or addictions than children from intact families.

Once we start to compound predictors—that is, low SES plus a single-parent family with an alcoholic parent—we may no longer talk of being *at risk*. We may need to start talking about *need*. Thus we may have a population that is nonclinical in the sense of not having, as yet, an identified patient and not being in immediate need of professional help. For instance, in the case of children of alcoholics, they may have a label (COAs) but are not yet diagnosable as "alcoholic" or "addicted." On the other hand, an adolescent child of an alcoholic parent from a low-SES, single-parent family may be in need, especially if he or she is performing poorly academically and his or her character and conduct in school are poor. By then, the adolescent child of an alcoholic may be diagnosable as a status offender or prejuvenile. It may only be a question of time before this adolescent acts out to the point of requiring the attention of authorities.

Once this occurs, a label becomes a diagnosis. Children from single-parent families are at greater risk for delinquency or addictions than children from intact families. Thus we may have a population that is nonclinical in the sense of not having, as yet, an identified patient, not being in a crisis, or requiring professional help, as in the case of children of alcoholics.

(5) The ability to learn from experience and from training and education is another important way of distinguishing between these three types of prevention. The greater the degree of psychological health, the greater will be the ability to learn. In the same way, the greater the degree of pathology and dysfunctionality, the greater the inability to learn. Hence populations at risk, in general, can learn from almost any experience and training. However, being at risk is a very wide criterion that includes practically everyone. Out of this population, we will find a certain percentage of individuals, couples, and families who cannot profit from primary prevention approaches because they are too troubled, too conflictual, too disturbed, or too stressed. They may need either secondary prevention approaches or even tertiary prevention. Once these families have been helped to decrease stress, disturbance, and conflict, after crisis intervention, they may then profit by either secondary or primary prevention approaches.

(6) What are the various goals for the three types of prevention? Obviously, they are different. The main goal of primary prevention is to increase interpersonal competence and to instill greater resistance to stress and breakdown. The goal of secondary prevention may be to decrease stress and chances of a probable crisis *as well as* to increase competence and resistance to stress and breakdown, all through learning to curb and control problematic behavior. The goal of tertiary prevention is either to restore the family to an original or minimum level of functionality or to help the family achieve a greater level of functionality than the one achieved in the past. All preventive approaches share the goal of families being able to learn new and more positive ways of interacting. These ways should eventually translate into greater competence and resistance to breakdown. This newly acquired level of functionality will help the family for the long term. In other words, if the family has learned new and more positive ways of relating with one another, these new ways should allow the family to withstand future stresses and strains with minimum breakdown.

(7) What type of involvement can be asked of the family? In primary prevention this involvement can only be voluntary and

certainly not forced by external pressures. Families could be informed of the possible choices they have. For instance, there may be different parenting classes in the community. If a couple does not like one class, it may switch to another class of a different persuasion. The degree of voluntary choice starts to disappear once the behavior from one member of the family starts to disturb either the family itself or the community (school, neighborhood, and so on). The behavior may not yet be critical, but it could be unpleasant and worrisome. It may even be denied by the family ("boys will be boys") or, especially, by the member who is exhibiting the disturbing behavior. This denial could only exacerbate the situation to the point of producing a crisis. At this point, the family may deny any awareness of precursors that should have alerted them to the need for help, as in the case of many suicides.

(8) Although involvement is not obligatory in primary prevention, the degree of forced choice increases with need and with crisis. Although a functional family may even choose not to participate in a primary prevention program, a semifunctional or dysfunctional family may find itself without a choice. For example, the school principal may recommend that both parents participate in a parent-training group or that their acting-out youngster may receive individualized tutoring. If the disturbing behavior continues in spite of the parents receiving parenting training, the whole family may be referred to a mental health clinic for crisis intervention.

Ministers, teachers, physicians, and lawyers are among the other professionals who need to make recommendations for the welfare of the family. They, of course, need to be educated about prevention and preventive efforts in the community that could help a particular family. Without this knowledge no informed recommendation could take place. Although recommendations are made, many families may refuse to follow them, because of many fears about and resistance to change and because of the need to protect each other and themselves. The greater the degree of resistance to recommendations found in a family, the greater the likelihood of eventual serious disturbance and need for crisis intervention. How a family uses feedback from informed or caring professionals tells a great deal about the level of functionality of that family. Inability to follow recommendations and resistance to change are two of the many criteria to be used in reaching conclusions about the level of dysfunction in a family.

(9) Costs are usually lower for primary prevention because most approaches are based on groups of individuals, couples, or families. To be effective, these approaches are group oriented and relatively inexpensive per unit of professional time. Exercise, diet, and control of food intake are much cheaper than a heart bypass operation, which might have been prevented if these precautions had been taken long before the need for surgery. In the same way, secondary prevention may be a bit more expensive than primary prevention. However, secondary prevention has not been practiced long enough as yet for us to judge its efficiency. Tertiary prevention costs more because (a) professionals' time is more expensive and (b) it takes longer and is much more difficult to treat symptomatic behavior that oftentimes took years (or even generations) to develop. At best, however, we know that tertiary prevention may help up to two-thirds of the families in crisis who ask for help. What happens to the other third that cannot or does not want to be helped? Here is where secondary prevention approaches may become helpful, although we must recognize that certain types of families may not want to change and may refuse help of any kind. Under the latter conditions, hospitalization, incarceration, and lifelong medication may become inevitable.

(10) Effectiveness and the cost/effectiveness ratio are issues that need serious consideration. Psychotherapy and crisis intervention are expensive enterprises because of the degree of professional expertise and time required; primary and secondary prevention approaches need not be expensive. They would be even less expensive if we were to rely on middle-level, paraprofessional, preprofessional, and nonprofessional personnel. Effectiveness would be even greater if therapists were to rely on adding primary and secondary prevention approaches to their therapeutic tools to boost the level of competence of their patients' families. Hopefully, in the not too distant future, we will be able to integrate all three approaches, combining them synergistically for a much greater impact on families than a single approach alone could have.

(11) A professional-paraprofessional hierarchy, alluded to earlier in this chapter and discussed in greater detail in the rest of this book, alerts us to the need to rely on different levels of professionalization. The sheer number of families at risk, in need, and in crisis makes it impossible for existing professional therapists to help them. The sheer number of families in crisis is sufficient to keep

these professionals busy for some time to come. Consequently, we will need to rely on new and different types of personnel, not necessarily credentialed, but with special qualifications to allow them to learn how to administer specific programs of a pretherapeutic and paratherapeutic nature.

(12) As noted in item 5, above the degree of functionality is directly related to the ability to learn and to retain learning for some time. The more functional the family, the greater will be its ability to learn. Dysfunctional families in crisis are not able to learn as much. Consequently, methods of prevention need to be sensitive to differences in ability to learn according to levels of functionality. Methods that may work with one family may not work with another. Why? It is likely that there are individual differences, based on SES, motivation, and other factors, that make it possible for some families to learn and impossible for others. Hence different methods need to be used. Operationally, we should be able to distinguish between what could be called an enrichment approach for primary prevention and a more specific approach for secondary prevention, that is, workbooks and programmed materials.

The relevant issue here among the various modalities of learning is *interchangeability*. For instance, although structured enrichment programs were originally designed to be administered by a trainer or facilitator orally to functional and semifunctional families, they could be administered in writing as well, as if they were programmed materials. The latter materials, instead of being administered by a trainer, are designed to be self-administered and self-instructional, for families to complete on their own at home. Consequently, they can be used in addition or as an alternative either to primary or to tertiary—crisis-oriented, face-to-face therapy—prevention approaches. Furthermore, either structured enrichment or programmed materials can be administered orally in the therapist's office if the therapist were willing to use a script, allowing a definite plan to be followed in face-to-face therapy sessions.

This interchangeability suggests that we can distinguish between the three types of prevention on, among other criteria, the basis of the medium of communication. In writing, both structured enrichment and programmed materials can be administered as self-instructional approaches in addition to any other face-to-face approach, either primary or tertiary. Although primary and secondary prevention programs rely mostly on already written, prearranged "blueprints," tertiary prevention relies usually on the immediate, spoken word, with little if any structure to program the delivery. As some therapists would like to believe, if and when such a nonstructure is present, it is difficult if not impossible to record and study it. However, both media of exchange, oral and writing, can be used interchangeably, both of them affecting the third medium of therapeutic exchange, the nonverbal.

(13) Differences among methods should help us clarify the three types of prevention. For instance, the degree of structure is quite high in primary prevention programs. Its intended audience knows the general topic, such as parenting, in advance as well the number of sessions it will take to complete the course, and the cost. These characteristics may be difficult or impossible to state in tertiary prevention, where there is no topic stated beforehand, except what is defined by the family; the number of sessions is hard to predict; and the cost (if not to the family, to the agency providing the help) is high, because of the professional time required.

(14) Using degree of specificity, the topic to be addressed in primary prevention programs is very specific, for instance; "parenting." All parents taking this course are subjected to the same topic, parenting, in all of its practical principles and applications, considered in terms of generalities, as they are related to parenting in general and not related to the specific needs of a particular couple. This generality could be called a "funnel approach," that is, everybody who attends this course gets the same treatment. In secondary and tertiary prevention, the approach is much more individualized to the specific needs of each family. For instance, instead of a group of parents, each couple may be treated according to its needs, which are different from the needs of another couple.

Conclusion

The purpose of this chapter has been to clarify and differentiate among three types of prevention: primary, secondary, and tertiary. Although this differentiation has taken place at the conceptual level, along a continuum of preventive types, in the following chapters it will be possible to make this differentiation operationally. We will differentiate them according to various methods of intervention, which differ in degree of structure, specificity, level of learning required by trainers and preventers; the degree of functionality of the family; and the family's particular needs. The need for an encompassing theory to integrate all three types of prevention seems necessary, however, before proceeding further.

2

A Developmental Theory of Interpersonal Competence

One of the main shortcomings of prevention practices has been the lack of an adequate theory relevant to and encompassing all three types of prevention and their goals. One could conservatively argue that many preventive practices have muddled along without a clear theoretical background (Gesten & Jason, 1987; Murphy & Frank, 1979). And we could ask whether primary and secondary preventions even need a theory. The purpose of this chapter is to attempt to answer this question affirmatively and to present a theoretical framework consistent with and relevant to all three types of prevention discussed in the previous chapter. Before presenting the framework, I will address the question: Do primary and secondary prevention practices need a theoretical framework and, if so, why?

The Importance of Theory in Prevention

Prevention approaches would be helped by a unified and unifying theoretical framework for at least five reasons. First, theory helps make sense of reality and direct applications. Without some theoretical background, we would be practicing in the dark, without directions and with inadequate goals or criteria. We would, therefore, have to question the validity of our practices, because there would be no criteria to evaluate their validity. How can we begin to enrich and help families change unless we have some idea about how families function or fail to function? A theory would also allow comparison of the validity of one theory with that of another. This latter point will be pursued further when we compare some existing theories.

Second, theory can link and relate disparate factors. If we are going to spend a great deal of energy and time in prevention, how are we going to know whether we have done any good? Not only does theory help us make sense of reality, it can also help us link and tie together a variety of seemingly disparate findings and results. Without theory, we would be wanderers without the protection of an umbrella or map to find where we should be going (getting wet and lost in the process). Therefore, these two metaphors are useful in understanding theory: (a) Theory is an umbrella to unify and protect us and (b) theory is a map to give us some direction in where we should be going and how we should get there.

Third, theory would allow us to test and verify derivations from that theory and to compare results from derivations of other competing theories. Out of this inevitable and necessarily competitive evaluation, we can select the theory that seems to fit results and data in a more parsimonious fashion than other theories. How is a theory to be selected? It can be selected on the basis of seductive plausibility or it can be selected on the basis of results of comparisons with other theories. Up to now most theories in the mental health field, especially in the field of family therapy, have been selected on the basis of the former criterion. Such a criterion can be bolstered and improved by adding those of accountability and verifiability. The first criterion, accountability, deals with the outcome of clinical applications of a theory. The second, verifiability, deals with how the components of a theory are testable.

Fourth, currently theories of interpersonal competence in the family either are lacking in or are unable to fit into prevention strategies. When we use the criterion of fruitfulness and generativity in producing preventive programs to evaluate various theories, we can rely on a robust and concrete criterion to render a relevant judgment. For instance, in regard to psychoanalysis (with the sole exception of Adlerian theory, which has produced a variety of primary prevention parenting programs), it is very difficult, if not impossible, to apply psychoanalytic theory to a verifiable understanding of functional or semifunctional families. The theory is either untestable or very difficult to test and to validate empirically.

It has failed to generate programs for primary or secondary prevention. The humanistic-existential school may be antiempirical and seem just as untestable, in some respects, as psychoanalysis. However, it has provided many useful models of primary and secondary prevention, such as the marital encounter and enrichment movements, Relationship Enhancement, Couples Communication, and many other programs that will be presented and discussed in greater detail in Chapter 5. Behaviorism, on the other hand, is eminently testable though limited because of its acontextual emphasis, that is, its emphasis on observable behaviors, excluding surrounding events, limits our understanding of complex family transactions. In spite of this shortcoming, behaviorism has produced many prevention-oriented programs, both for marriage and parenting. So-called systems theory, which has achieved a virtually unchallenged hegemony in the family therapy field, has produced one small parenting program without supporting evidence as to its usefulness, public acceptance, or consumers satisfaction (Efron & Rowe, 1987).

Finally, we need a developmental theory of interpersonal competence in the family that is relevant to all three types of prevention and that will fulfill other necessary requirements, such as (a) being *concrete* enough to allow for (b) *accountability* of results and (c) *verifiability* of component parts. In addition, such a theory should be (d) *reducible* as much as possible to psychological constructs that are either valid, validated, or relatively easy to validate, (e) using concepts that are *valid and relevant* to most individual, dyadic, and *multipersonal* family levels. If at all possible, a theory should also be able to (f) *supersede and even integrate* existing theories.

Reconciling Family Functioning with Psychological Constructs

How can one reconcile family functioning with psychological constructs? This task requires keeping the importance of the family context primary, relating individual determinants to family functioning, and using a relational rather than a systems language. If the family is a unit(y) of interacting personalities (Burgess, 1926, 1927), then we need to define *personality* within its context or, as we shall see, within various contexts or settings.

The field of personality development and psychological theory has been strongly influenced by what has been called "interactionism" (Ekehammer, 1974; Endler & Magnusson, 1976). Personality and competence development in the family, however, is a topic completely neglected both by interactionism in psychology and by systems thinking in the field of family therapy. Both movements need to be considered critically for reconciliation of individual and family constructs and a view of the family as being *in part* the outcome of individual antecedents and determinants, just as individuals are the outcome of the same family factors.

Interactionism in Personality Theory

In the early to middle 1970s, a great discovery was made in personality psychology: Personality and behavior are the outcome of interactions with situations (Bem & Allen, 1974; Bem & Funder, 1978; Ekehammer, 1974; Endler & Magnusson, 1976; L'Abate, 1976). Finally, personality theory (but not yet psychology) discovered that individuals do not develop or live in a vacuum. They are the products and the producers of relationships. This discovery created expectations of breakthroughs in personality theory, to the point that any self-respecting personality textbook had to include a section, or even a whole chapter, on the topic of personality × situation interactions.

Unfortunately, since this great discovery, which may have been new for psychologists but was really old hat for family theorists and practitioners, none of the anticipated advances and breakthroughs in personality theory took place. Why? Because of the difficulties and vagaries inherent in the definitions of both terms, *personality* and *situation* (Bem & Allen, 1974; Bem & Funder, 1978; L'Abate & Bryson, in press). If we cannot define either term precisely, how can we understand their interaction? Consequently, if we cannot specify what is meant by either term, we may need to go beyond both of them to find new and more specific ways to understand, describe, predict, and, when needed, control this interaction. One way to avoid such confusion is to speak about *competence* (instead of *personality*) and *settings* instead of *situations* or, for that matter, *contexts*. People do not live in general contexts; we live in specific and specifiable settings. As L'Abate and Dunne (1977) have found, most psychology and personality theory textbooks either do not mention or devote less than 1 page out of 100 to family-related topics or links. According to most textbooks, personality and behavior develop in a vacuum. Consequently, interactionism was a great step forward in theory development. However, it failed to specify and to stress that the situation in which most of us grow and develop is the family. The family remains the primary setting basic to the development of other competencies.

Systems Thinking

At the same time that interactionism became prominent in the field of personality theory, although seemingly independent from it, systems thinking made powerful inroads in the family therapy field. This "new, " seductive, provocative, and challenging way of looking at families (and reality) captured the intellectual zeitgeist of the time, to the point that systems thinking was heralded as the wave of the future. It was to supersede, improve upon, and encompass old, shopworn traditional theories like psychoanalysis, humanism, and behaviorism. It became the hobbyhorse of the family therapy profession. The expectation that systems thinking, stressing emergent constructivism at the expense of reductionism ("the whole is greater than its parts") and interdependence of parts in a unit ("no one part of a system is independent from other parts"), would produce new and brilliant methodological advances to improve on past methods finally dissolved with the test of time. No new breakthrough occurred and no evidence was ever produced to indicate that this metaphor was indeed as verifiable as a theory needs to be. In fact, this theoretical viewpoint took an eminently antireductionistic and antiempirical stance. However, it did contribute to the same emphasis found in interactionism, that is, that most of us look at and study *relationships* among us as well as between us and the environment. Terms such as *personality* or *situation* do not mean anything if they are void of relationships. Even so-called inferred intrapsychic concepts, such as "self-esteem, " are still the outcome of a relationship between the respondent and the questions on paper. We must still ask: What environment? Interactionism attempted to break down this very large term into the concept of human and physical situations, leaving, however, this basic term *environment* undefined, vague, and too general to have any descriptive or predictive validity.

The Concept of Competence

Both movements, interactionism and systems thinking, therefore, underscore the concept of competence not as an intrapsychic internal state or trait but as an interpersonal characteristic. Our interpersonal competence is observed and studied through our behavior in social situations and especially *in close and prolonged social situations like marriage and the family.* Short-lived and superficial relationships are not an adequate test. We can treat salesclerks or our office coworkers well because we do not live with them. How nice can we be to those we love and who love and are committed to us? Since White (1959) presented the concept of competence, it has captured considerable attention in motivational and personality theories (Brody, 1980; Ford, 1985; Marlowe & Weinberg, 1985; L. Phillips, 1968; Wine & Smye, 1981). It seems more relevant, specific, and concrete than the concepts of personality and environment. The concept of competence implies an interaction of one thing with another. We cannot talk about competence without specifying the context in which such competence is manifested.

Ford (1985), for instance, in reviewing past and present definitions of *competence,* referred to it as (a) capabilities to formulate and produce effortful, persistent goal-directed activity, (b) one's behavioral repertoire of specified and specifiable skills and abilities, and (c) effectiveness in relevant contexts. Consequently, we need to specify the nature of the contexts where these sets of capabilities, effectiveness, and skills are manifested and used. Competence can be specified and even assessed in a specific setting much more easily than personality can. Although personality seems to encompass a wide range of traits and states, most of them are internal and difficult to measure. Competence, however, is limited to a finite and specific number of settings. It may be a more restricted term than *personality,* but it may also be easier to define and measure because it pertains to a more specific interaction than that of a person and a situation. Instead of a generic person × situation interaction, a competence × setting interaction is proposed as more specific and testable.

Consequently, because of the inadequacies of existing theories, especially their failure to stress the importance of the family in the development of interpersonal competence, it became necessary to stop looking at personality as a global unit in continuous interaction with selected others in unspecifiable situations. Instead, although the term *personality* was useful in communicating about a general topic, in competence theory, *personality* could be defined and broken down in terms of *specific competencies in interaction with specific settings*. We have expanded this specificity of terms over time into a full-fledged developmental theory of interpersonal competence (L'Abate, 1976, 1983, 1987; L'Abate & Bryson, in press; L'Abate & Colondier, 1987; L'Abate & Harel, in press).

Components of a Developmental Theory of Interpersonal Competence

The purpose of this theory is to link individual, so-called monadic views of interpersonal competence to family functioning and dysfunctioning. This theory is based on a reductionistic perspective of family functioning. It attempts to derive family functioning from individual characteristics as well as the other way around, a perspective that would make family functioning continuous with monadic psychology. We cannot deal with the family as a whole, because, it is assumed, the whole is different from the sum of its parts. Nor can we understand and describe individual behaviors solely as the result of transactions among family members. We cannot deal with family transactions as separate and independent from the individual contributions to those transactions from family members. This view would put us in the position of trying to understand behavior as discontinuous from the knowledge derived from psychology as a science and as a profession. A developmental theory of interpersonal competence needs to rely on psychological concepts that will link individual with family functioning as a two-way process. Individuals affect families as much as families affect individuals. The issue here: How, how much, when, and where does one effect the other—an issue of reductionism. Two individuals start a family by conceiving a child and living under the same roof. Both individuals are the products of the contexts of their families of origin, which they carry with them into their new family of procreation. These individual characteristics must be adapted to new demands from different settings, which, in turn, influence functioning in the family of procreation.

The acquisition of personal and interpersonal competence is a developmental process that includes the specificities particular to a given setting. Behavioral outcomes are due to the interaction between specific task characteristics and demands of settings that interact with specific skills and abilities in individuals. A family makes different demands than an employer. A shopping mall demands different skills than a fitness center. A theory of developmental competence in the family needs to meet at least three requirements: (a) to define personality according to relational and contextual concepts, (b) to reduce such relational and contextually relevant concepts to known and accepted psychological constructs, and (c) to verify these concepts empirically as well as applicatively (i.e., preventively). This theory, as summarized in Figure 2.1, is made up of two assumptions, two postulates, three modalities, six resource classes, three sets of skills, five settings, and a variety of models. On the dimension of abstraction, the theory progresses from the general and the abstract to the particular, the specific, and the concrete. Before dealing with the basic assumptions of the theory, we need to consider three extratheoretical assumptions that precede the rest of the theory.

Extratheoretical Assumptions

Extratheoretical assumptions pertain to statements that could apply to any theory. They are considered important for the construction of any theory. They must be enunciated before elaboration of the theory proper. The present theory makes at least three separate assumptions of this type in regard to (a) levels of interpretation, (b) development, and (c) the experience-expression distinction in behavior (L'Abate & Bryson, in press). Levels of interpretation pertain to how behavior is seen along varied strata of public-private, explicit-implicit, and inferred-attributed views. Some theories, like behaviorism, for instance, see behavior as a ranch house without an attic or a basement—just one floor will do. Psychoanalysis, on the other hand, sees behavior as a two-story house, with an attic and basement, for a total of at least four floors, as described by the unconscious, preconscious, verbalized, and unverbalized expectations (Sager, 1976).

The current theory views behavior as taking place at two different levels, *description* and *explanation*, each with its own internal

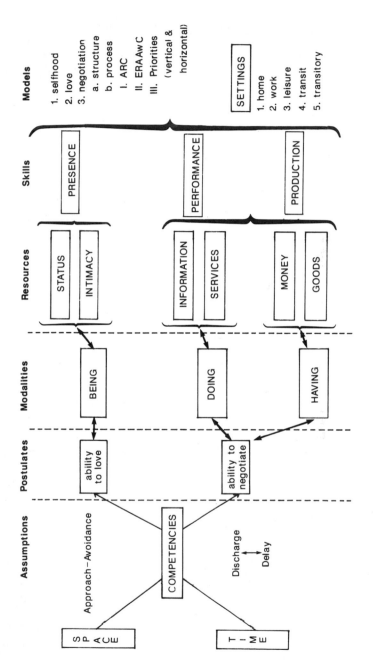

Figure 2.1 A Developmental Theory of Interpersonal Competence

division. Behavior can be described at an obviously visible level. However, description is not sufficient; we need also to *explain* how behavior takes place at the descriptive level. Description consists of two sublevels. At the most public, observable sublevel, we develop a *self-presentational* facade or mask, that is, how we manage to make a superficial impression on others in general, either positively or negatively—our *public* facade. The second, more private sublevel, the *phenotypical*, describes how we behave inside the home, without our public or social mask or facade. This phenotypical level includes the way we behave under the stress of intimate (prolonged and close) relationships, such as those of marriage and family. One, for instance, may present oneself as nice outside the home but behave very nastily within the home. How do we explain possible discrepancies between self-presentational and phenotypical sublevels? We usually explain consistencies and inconsistencies between presentational and phenotypical behavior through two sublevels that are either structurally internal to the individual or are historical. The first sublevel, the *genotypical*, usually consists of inferred, intrapsychic, or attributional concepts, such as self-esteem. This sublevel, in addition to the other two descriptive sublevels, is explained ultimately by the individual's *developmental history*. The first explanatory sublevel refers to how the individual sees him- or herself in the present (competent-incompetent, effective-ineffective, good-bad), and an individual's past history helps us explain how that individual learned or was trained to see her- or himself. The developmental history, if fully available to us (although it usually is not), would help us understand (i.e., explain) how one sees oneself (genotype) and how this genotype may help us understand relationships or discrepancies, consistencies or inconsistencies, between levels of description as well as between levels of description and the genotype.

The historical explanation includes, of course, a contextual explanation. The current context, both internal and external to the individual, can serve as an explanation only *after the fact*. To explain behavior in context, we need to have knowledge of all or most of the various antecedent events that preceded the behavior being explained. Hence the present context can be explained by how and how much past events impinge upon and influence it. Perhaps one way of differentiating between historical and contextual explanation would be in terms of past versus present. For instance, psychoanalysis has stressed the past as being the major determinant of the present, and behaviorism and systems thinking have stressed the importance of the present context in understanding and explaining behavior. Humanism has stressed also the importance of the future as a determinant of the present. Both perspectives, the past and the future, are, of course, important. We need to understand fully what happens now, both as the outcome from the past and as determined by expectations about the future. Contextual factors are too important to be excluded. Their importance postulates five settings that are an intrinsic part of the theory. We will reconsider context formally, in greater detail, later on with the ERAAwC Model. Suffice it to say here that the most important context with which to understand behavior in the past and in the present is the family.

How is this assumption related to families and their functioning and dysfunctioning? Most families, both functional and dysfunctional, need to cling to and rely on a presentational facade, make a good impression, and, most of all, appear normal: "If it weren't for so and so's behavior [the index patient] we would be OK." Thus many families do not have a contextual awareness of how behavior, both functional and symptomatic, came about. However, the more dysfunctional the family, the greater the need to rely on a facade that proclaims social acceptability and normality. By the same token, the greater the stress on appearance and external acceptability, the lower the sense of internal self-importance felt by family members. Perhaps, for some people, the more one feels important and competent at the genotypical level, the less the need to *appear* important and competent at the external level (L'Abate, 1976).

In addition to levels of interpretation, we need to make a second, similarly extratheoretical assumption about the process of development. Development over the life cycle goes through at least four distinct stages: (a) dependency in childhood; (b) denial of dependency, most likely in adolescence; (c) autonomous interdependence in adulthood; and (d) a return to dependency in old age. Development, however, takes place throughout the life cycle through a process of automatic modeling that follows a continuum of likeness in a bell-shaped frequency distribution. This continuum of likeness is the foundation of genotype, the sublevel that refers to one's identity or identification. We develop a sense of identity—that is, a sense of self—by a continuous, unrelenting, and oftentimes automatic comparison with others, especially with those who are close or important to us. This distribution ranges from two dialectically related, extreme sides of symbiosis-autism to two inside ranges of sameness-oppositeness and two central ranges of similarity-difference. The sequence in the frequency distribution of these ranges is as follows: symbiosis-sameness-similarity-difference-oppositeness-autism (L'Abate, 1976). From these six ranges, we derive three styles determining the functionality-dysfunctionality of the individual, couple, and family. The combination of symbiosis-autism in likeness results in abusive-apathetic intimate relationships (AA). The combination of sameness-oppositeness results in reactive-repetitive patterns in family relationships (RR). The combination of similarity-difference leads to conductive-creative family relationships (CC). These styles form the bases for the ARC model, one of the four models for successful negotiation that will be explained below (L'Abate, 1986b).

A third extratheoretical assumption pertains to the experience-expression continuum. Existing theories differ on which part of this continuum they stress. For instance, humanism stresses subjective experiencing on the receptive, input side; behaviorism stresses the expressive output side of the same continuum; psychoanalysis and the rational approaches stress a middle, rational range between the two polarities. Families vary along the whole continuum of experiencing-expressing. There are families who stress the subjective at the expense of the objective—all feelings and no activity. Other families stress expression at the expense of the experience, acting without much time for reflecting. Some families fall somewhere in the middle of this continuum, which has been described by linguists according to the competence-performance distinction. This continuum is encompassed by and elaborated in the ERAAwC model to be discussed later.

In addition to the requirement that a theory should be applicable to all three types of prevention, a developmental theory of interpersonal competence needs to acknowledge and insist on the importance of the family as a unit of interacting personalities (Burgess, 1926, 1927). Within the family both continua of likeness and experiencing-expressing are developed, differentiated, and refined. A sense of self and how feelings are experienced and expressed are all multidirectional processes. Children are affected by adult caretakers and siblings, but, in the same way, they affect the very adults and siblings who take care of them, through bi- and multidirectional effects.

Bond and Wagner (1988, pp. 344–346) listed 19 characteristics of effective prevention and promotion programs, which will be used throughout this book, including four characteristics that are relevant to the theory presented here: (a) a multisystem, multilevel perspective; (b) an emphasis upon the promotion of competence; (c) empowerment of individuals and groups; and (d) sensitivity to the developmental process. As will be shown, the theory presented here attempts to fulfill all four characteristics by (a) being relevant at intra- and interindividual levels; (b) defining and elaborating the meaning of *competence* not as an abstract concept but as a set of specific and specifiable abilities and skills; (c) denoting and implying empowerment through the concept of status, or the attribution of importance to self; and (d) utilizing a life cycle view of developmental competence primarily for the family, because the family is the primary setting for the development of a sense of *self-importance*, or *status*, which here is seen as synonymous with terms such as *self-definition* and *selfhood*.

As noted above, a developmental theory of interpersonal competence in the family needs to be concrete and explicit and to relate to the rest of psychology as a science and as a profession. It also needs to be testable, and tested, through the evaluation of process and outcome (accountability) in its clinical, primary, secondary, and tertiary prevention applications or interventions.

Theoretical Assumptions

Space and *time* are the two basic assumptions of the theory. Development of personal and interpersonal competence is a function of both spatial and temporal processes. Space subsumes a dimension of distance defined by extremes in the approach-avoidance continuum. Extremes in approach, dependency or attachment, produce symbiotic conditions that result in apathy. Extremes in avoidance produce rejection, neglect, abandonment, and aggression that result in abuse. Somewhere in the middle of this dimension is the proper balance of distance, which ultimately culminates in closeness and intimacy. Space determines various degrees of competence in interpersonal distance: as seen in the nature of attachments, closeness, and intimacy, on one hand, and in alienation and autism, on the other. Ultimately, this spatial competence leads to the ability to *Be* and to *Being*, that is, the ability to love oneself and selected others (partner, parents, children, friends, and so on) unconditionally, without demands for performance, production, perfection, or problem solving. Closeness and intimacy mean being emotionally available to oneself and to selected others in a reciprocal fashion, because self and other (partner, parents, children, friends) are considered as important to our emotional survival.

Time subsumes a dimension of control defined by extremes in the discharge-delay continuum that determine competence to negotiate in interpersonal relationships. Eventually too much control (delay) or too little control (discharge) leads to failures in negotiation. Extremes in discharge tend to produce hyperactivity, impulsivity, and acting out, and extremes in delay tend to produce obsessive-compulsive thinking and behavior as well as withdrawal. They are derived from the temporal assumption of control, defined by extremes in discharge-delay. Effective problem solving is the outcome of a balance in discharge-delay functions. Too much delay relates to overrationality and obsessiveness. Too much discharge relates to underrationality, immediacy, and impulsivity. Functional problem solving involves a process in between these extremes, that is, the ability to think through various options and to choose the option with the highest rewards and the least cost. Thus competence and coping abilities are the outcome of both the ability to love and the ability to negotiate between individuals, within couples, and within families.

Normality, then, as seen through both assumptions of space and time, means an appropriate (in age and space) balance of approach-avoidance and of discharge-delay tendencies. For instance, possible combinations of extremes in avoidance and discharge may eventually lead to denial in action and to hyperactivity; which, combined with drivenness or impulsivity, plus hostility and aggression, may lead to the formation of character disorders and delinquency. Possible combinations of extremes in approach and delay may lead to overattachments, dependencies, and depressions. Possible combinations of extremes in avoidance and delay could lead to extreme psychopathology, such as schizophrenia, while possible combinations of extremes in approach and discharge could lead to narcissistic personality development.

Both assumptions underlie *competencies*, which become developmentally transformed into two postulates dealing with two more specific *abilities*: to *love* (distance) and to *negotiate* (control). The notion that these two abilities, the ability to love and the ability to negotiate, are indicative of the competence level and coping strategies of families is supported by a great many theorists of different persuasions, disciplines, and interests (L'Abate & Colondier, 1987). Regardless of the terminology used, there seems to be a consensus among these theorists that most interpersonal behavior, especially in the family, can be reduced to these two abilities. They are considered to be the two fundamental abilities necessary for personal and interpersonal competence. This concept should be distinguished from abilities and skills on the basis of the same differentiation made by linguists, that is, competence lies on the subjective, experiencing side (input) and skills lie on the expressive side (output), with abilities in the middle (throughput) of this continuum (Figure 2.1). Competencies underlie assumptions; abilities underlie postulates; and skills underlie models. Assumptions then subsume a notion of competence in regulating distance, which transforms itself developmentally into the ability to love.

Postulates

Individual, dyadic, and family functioning, as determined by the ability to love and the ability to negotiate, derives from competencies in distance and control regulation. The ability to love and to negotiate are basic to individual, dyadic, and family functioning. The modality to love is based on two resources to be shared and not to be negotiated. These two resources (Foá and Foá, 1974), are (a) status and (b) intimacy. We cannot offer for sale or bargain for either of these two resources. If they become commodities traded in the market of the family, they lose their inherent qualities of being freely given and freely shared, as is required for unconditional love. Both resources constitute the developmental bases for family relations. Distance and its extremes in approach-avoidance form the bases for subsequent parent-child and lover-lover attachments (Shaver, Hazan, & Bradshaw, 1988). The observation, moderation, and modification of approach-avoidance tendencies lead to amplifications, variations, and failures in attachments that last for the rest of our lives. The most important and vital of all family attachments, one that defuses and decreases stress, is *intimacy*, defined as the ability to share past and present hurts and fears of being hurt, the essence of being emotionally available (L'Abate, 1986b; Sloan & L'Abate, 1985). Intimacy means acknowledging our fallability, vulnerability, and neediness. The disclosure of these feelings can mainly take place within a context of equality and reciprocity: "I need to be close to you when you are hurting, because I want you to be available to me when I am hurting."

It takes a strong person to admit weaknesses. People who perceive themselves as weak cannot allow themselves to admit weaknesses, because they are afraid that their admission may be seized upon and used against them. Hence intimacy can mainly take place in functional (approximately 25% to 30% of the total population, at the most) and not in dysfunctional families (L'Abate, 1986b). We need unconditional love and an attribution of importance (i.e., status) to become intimate with someone. Consequently, in families that cannot share love or attribute status to one another, it is extremely difficult to experience intimacy as defined above.

Physical and interpersonal distance between and among family members is the outcome of the process of the expression of intimacy and status in the family. Both are based on emotions. Functionally and ideally, both love and status should be independent and not controlled by rationally constituted schemes. Love and status are the bases of emotional attachments that lead to intimacy. Rationally constituted schemes are the bases for the negotiation of and problem solving with issues concerning *Doing*, or the combination of services and information, and *Having*, the combination of goods and money, in the Foás' theory (1974). Both sets of abilities are relevant at individual, dyadic, and multipersonal levels. Both sets are relational. Both are relevant to levels of functioning in individuals, couples, and families: that is, functional families *at risk* know how to love and negotiate more successfully than families *in need*, and families in need are able to love and negotiate relatively better than families *in crisis*. Chaotic families who are in continual crisis cannot show and share their love for each other and cannot negotiate their differences through effective decision making and problem solving.

Modalities, Resources, and Skills

Both postulates are related to three different modalities partially derived from resource exchange theory in social psychology (Foá &

Foá, 1974). Six classes of resources are continuously exchanged interpersonally and in the family: love, status, services, information, money, and possessions or goods. These six classes of resources are reducible to three different modalities of living (L'Abate, 1986b): Being, as shown by the skill of *presence;* Doing, as shown by the skill of *performance;* and Having, as shown by the skill of *production.* The ability to love and to be intimate is demonstrated and expressed through the two modalities of Doing and Having. Both performance and production are the bases of power, which can or should be negotiated but may or may not be negotiated depending on the level of competence of the family. The greater the level of competence in a family, the greater the possibility for successful negotiation. The negotiability or nonnegotiability of power is the basis for family struggles when power is not negotiated, but it is a solution to problems when it is based on feelings and attributions that are impossible to negotiate. One does not negotiate how much one loves or how important other family members are. Presence, in the sense of emotional availability to oneself and to significant others, can only be shared. *Personal* and *interpersonal competence,* therefore, is defined by what an individual *is, does, and has in different settings.*

In functional families, presence remains separate from performance and production. In dysfunctional families, of course, power and presence become confused, diffused, and fused to the point that issues of power (performance and production) are confused and mixed up with issues of presence (L'Abate & Hewitt, 1988)— that is, love and status are no longer expressed unconditionally; they become conditional based on performance and/or production. Consequently, Doing, Having, or both oftentimes become substitute expressions of Being ("If you loved me you would do . . ."; "If you loved me you would buy me . . ."). Therefore, Being deals with the ability to love, attributing importance to self (status) and to other intimates (family members and/or friends).

More often than not, conflicts over Doing and Having suggest an inability to Be together, that is, to share and divide stress according to an emotional modality of Being and presence rather than modalities of performance or production. In our society, it is easier to learn how to Do and how to Have than it is to learn how to Be. We are trained to Do in order to Have. Very few families are able to share and teach their offspring how to Be together unconditionally, without demands for perfection, performance, production, or problem solving. Yet, the modality of Being is much more important for sharing stressful events than the two modalities of Doing and Having. Being is crucial to dealing with most stresses *as soon as* they happen, but Doing and Having are important in dealing with stresses *after* they happen, to deal realistically with practical issues in the aftermath of a stressful event. If a family cannot share Being together, it will have even more difficulty negotiating and problem-solving together. Most if not all stressors, whatever their nature, have an immediate, direct or indirect, emotional impact (L'Abate, 1985b). Unless a family is ready and able to use (experience, express, and share) their presence by being available emotionally to each other, it is unlikely the family will be able to negotiate issues of power (i.e., performance or production). This is how this theory differs from a monadic model of stress (Lazarus & Folkman, 1984). The monadic model emphasizes cognitive appraisal as primary to emotions, and this theory emphasizes the primacy of emotions as the basis of love and of family living as well as of competence (L'Abate, 1985b). The skills required in love are more receptive in that they require the ability to experience feelings and, consequently, to be present and available emotionally to oneself and to significant others, to show and share joys and sorrows, victories, and defeats. Skills required for negotiation, on the other hand, are more on the expressive side, consisting of more active problem-solving and decision-making initiatives.

Functionality, either individual, marital, or familial, means a balance of Being, Doing, and Having. Dysfunctionality is the outcome of the inability to clearly separate what is mainly sharable (Being) from what is mainly negotiable, that is, power, as shown through victories and defeats over Having (goods and money) and Doing (information and services). For instance, money, food, sex, or services are provided out of love for loved ones. The same resources, however, may provide grounds for power struggles in which any one of these resources may become grounds for conflicts, used to manipulate and defeat rather than to win. More specifically, sex may be one avenue for the expression of love between partners, especially at the beginning of the relationship. Eventually sex may become a power struggle, if the partners are unable to use sex and sexuality to enhance self and other (L'Abate & Hewitt, 1989). The content of the power struggle, that is, the conflictual resource, which has acquired an emotional amplification, may vary from one family to another. Therefore, there are many ways in which issues of love are confused with issues of power. Thus one of the major sources of dysfunctionality in families stems from the inability to be available emotionally to each other, substituting or stressing Doing and Having at the expense of Being together.

Settings

The way different sets of skills are expressed pertains to the concept of *setting*. The importance of interactions within various settings is understood when one uses the concept of *priorities* among settings, interacting with individual's priorities among the modalities of Being, Doing, and Having. Competencies, abilities, and skills vary as a function of the task requirements of a setting. Instead of the abstract, vague, and nonspecific term *situation*, it is preferable to use the more specific and concrete concept of *setting* (Barker, 1968; Moos, 1976). There is a finite number of settings—five—in the order of functional importance to the development of interpersonal competence: home, work, leisure, transit (going from one to other settings), and transitory ones (church, shopping stores and malls, bars, barbershops, beauty salons).

Home. The home setting has task requirements related to the maintenance of a family as an emotional unit and of the home as a physical entity. At home, we need to fulfill at least four different and sometimes nonoverlapping roles: (a) caretaker, (b) provider, (c) partner, and (d) parent. The first two roles depend on what kind of people we are. Personhood, in turn, will affect what kind of partners we will be. The partnership will determine what kind of parenting will take place. Each of these roles demands specific skills. For instance, responsibilities in the *caretaking* role are of two kinds. One kind encompasses to nurturing qualities that deal with love and being present and available emotionally. The other kind encompasses to instrumental qualities relating to the physical and material well-being of the home, such as cooking, cleaning, purchasing, and repairing. The role of *provider* deals with the economic aspects of family living. Salary, income, credit, mortgages, and the like are aspects of this role. How much money comes into the home and how is it spent? Both the caretaker and the provider roles depend a great deal on what kind of people we are. How well we function as *partners* depends on a variety of personality competencies that can be summarized in the selfhood model that will be presented later. In this role, both abilities to love and to negotiate are necessary. The fourth role, *parent,* is probably one of the most difficult and demanding in our lives. Often this is the role for which we have received little if any training except through what we learned automatically as children by watching our parents. Most of us perpetuate their errors and may forget their assets because the task requirements today are different from those of a previous generation. Being able to love and to negotiate becomes crucial at this stage. Consequently, a proper and appropriate developmental sequence would first require the development of personhood, as basic to partnership. Being a partner is basic to being a parent. Unfortunately, few of us are lucky enough to follow such an orderly sequence. Even if we are, this sequence does not guarantee us a positive outcome.

Work. At work, one needs to distinguish between two sets of separate but intertwined skills: those necessary for the specific job and those extrajob, interpersonal skills necessary to get along with authorities, peers, and subordinates. The first set consists of specific occupational skills that are necessary to perform a job, such as filing, typing, drawing, writing, ditch-digging. The second set of interpersonal skills requires interpersonal sensitivity, political gamesmanship, and contextual awareness. They may have little to do with the substantive job skills necessary for success; yet, these very skills may make the difference between promotion or stagnation on the job.

   In Western culture, many people, especially men, identify themselves according to their occupational roles (Crandall, 1984) just as some women identify themselves through a nurturing, housekeeping function. In fact, this nurturing role often provides the major source of gratification for some women and, therefore, may require a great energy investment that takes away from other possible roles. We identify ourselves by what we *do* or what we *have* (possessions) instead of who we *are* as human beings. What happens to us when we lose our jobs or retire? Do we have any self left? How does this role (unemployed or retired) interfere with other roles?

Other Settings

In this category we find the leftover settings that are neither home or work related. There are fewer demands and requirements here. The skills used may be considered more discretionary than obligatory.

Leisure settings. Leisure activity sometimes takes place at home, sometimes in other settings. It can take place in the company of others or it can be solitary. It can be active or sedentary, indoor or outdoor, oriented toward people or toward things. Working in one's basement on a hobby, participating in the Elks Club once a week, watching TV, going to church, or running a marathon are all examples of activities important to the enjoyment of life and competence development (Franken & van Raaij, 1982; Hirschman, 1984; Stamps & Stamps, 1985). They are an integral part of how we function as individuals. These activities specifically define how much value we put on friends and relationships in our lives. Leisure settings require skills that are specific to the activity being performed in a particular setting as well as skills to develop and maintain relationships formed within each setting.

Transit. These settings may not have been as important in the past as they are today, with our capacity to travel long distances in short periods of time. This capacity has the effect of increasing the number and variety of transit settings within which we interact each day (roads, highways, airports, cars, buses). With changing perceptions about distance and time spent in transit settings, time and activities in these settings may take on their own identity. Increased time spent in commuting to and from various settings requires the acquisition of skills to learn to commute and to make the best of it. But the ease of commuting within various settings may also increase the chance of overlap among settings. For instance, having an office in the home may be a more comfortable way of reducing commuting time. However, it may produce conflicts in fulfilling responsibilities we might not be required to fulfill if we had an office away from home. Lee and Kanungo (1984, p. 6) noted: "It is clear that there are new problems and opportunities in coordinating work and personal life and achieving personal well-being. There is clearly a need for theory and research that might offer insights and guidelines that would be helpful to those most affected by these (social and economic) changes." This insight can be achieved through the concept of priorities in the present theory (L'Abate, 1986b; L'Abate & Bryson, in press).

Transitory. These settings are temporary and vary in importance from one person to another. Purchasing goods and services, shopping in a mall, going to a beauty salon, attending church, or frequenting a bar may require different time and energy requirements depending on how important we think that activity is. Getting the oil changed at the corner garage, waiting in an unemployment line, completing the requirements for automobile registration, buying a bottle of aspirin—all of these bring us to different settings. Each of these settings has its peculiar role demands and codes that need to be observed. They may seem less important than other settings; yet, our ability to transact in these settings allows us to survive in the most important setting to many people, the home.

Of course, these five settings may overlap with each other. For instance, leisure time activities may take place in the home or, sometimes, in work settings. Competence in one setting does not necessarily predict competence in another setting. One could be a terrific parent at home but a mediocre employer at work. By the same token, one could be a strong athlete during leisure hours but not function as well either at work or at home. Further study is needed to determine whether there may be a general "g" factor that predicts cross-setting transfer of certain, yet to be specified, competencies (Bem & Allen, 1974). To understand how we allocate time and energy from one setting to another, we need to invoke the concept of priorities, which is motivational in nature (L'Abate, 1976, 1986b). These priorities stem from definite choices we make about what is important in our lives.

Models

Models have been an integral part of this theory from its inception (L'Abate, 1976) to its more recent elaboration (L'Abate, 1986b; L'Abate & Bryson, in press). Models are inventions that serve a variety of functions, such as (a) being concrete and testable expressions of the theory; (b) being visual summaries of more abstract notions; (c) integrating different and various viewpoints into all-encompassing wholes; and (d) covering all degrees of the whole range of functionality through dysfunctionality. This theory, thus far, has produced various models to describe (a) status or self-hood, (b) love or intimacy, and (c) negotiation. The complexity of negotiation requires that we break it down into structure and process, each described in turn by other models.

A Model for Status

From the ability to love and its modality of Being, we can derive two models. The resource class of "status" produces a model of selfhood and self-definition based on the attribution of importance to self and to selected significant others (spouse, child, parent, friend)—a process crucial to the development of a stable, integrated sense of self. Dysfunctionality arises from our inability to experience an appropriately positive sense of self-importance and to express it constructively. Status may be considered the other side of love. We learn how important or unimportant we are from our families of origin. Direct and indirect, verbal and nonverbal, consistent and inconsistent messages are continuously given by all family members concerning their esteem for themselves and for others in the family. This attribution of importance is basic and crucial to the development of interpersonal competence within and outside the family. A whole typology of self-definition that we can derive from this fundamental attribution has implications for an understanding of the genesis of functional and dysfunctional patterns in personal and interpersonal competence, as shown in Figure 2.2.

Theoretically and practically, the attribution of *importance,* as the most fundamental resource exchanged among human beings, is viewed as being a much more useful concept than that of self-esteem. At best, esteem can be inferred about oneself but not about another. Unless we ask people about how they feel about themselves, we have to infer their self-esteem from their behavior. Self-esteem, an intrapsychic process, remains an inference without interpersonal implications. Once we infer, directly or indirectly, someone's level of self-esteem, what interpersonal implications can we find? We do not transact business, and especially family business, on the basis of self-esteem.

Importance, on the other hand, is an attributional process with crucial interpersonal implications. We transact and share whatever

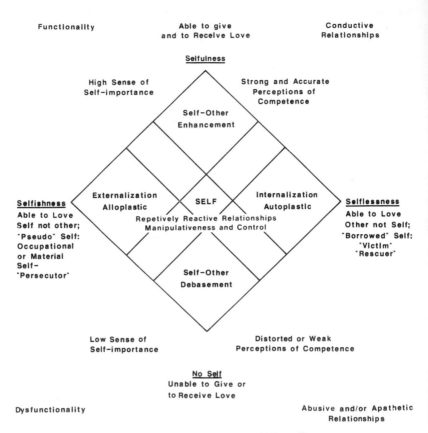

Figure 2.2 The Domain of Self-Definitions and Their Excesses

is relevant to family members because *love means the attribution of importance to self and to selected, significant others.* We do not grieve people's loss on the basis of self-esteem, either ours or theirs. We grieve on the basis of a person's importance to us. Hence the concept of self-esteem, as one way of defining status, has outlived its usefulness because of its limited, if nonexistent, interpersonal significance. The sense and attribution of personal importance, instead, has a much more definite theoretical and practical significance from a relational viewpoint than the concept of self-esteem.

Once we accept status as an attributional process, not based on just the objective reality but on subjective feelings and perceptions, we are essentially asserting our importance and the importance of significant others. In extreme cases, such attribution may reach symbiotic proportions ("I cannot live without you") as in love addictions. And there is a destructive extreme, such as in murder and suicide. If we even provisionally accept the fundamental relevance of this process of attribution of importance, then we can develop a model with which we can derive four possibilities from this attribution with different interpersonal outcomes: (a) *self-fulness* ("I win, you win, we both win"), (b) *selfishness* ("I win, you lose"), (c) *selflessness* ("You win, I lose"), and (d) *no-self* ("I lose, you lose."). These qualities form personal and interpersonal competence as well as marital and familial functionality.

(1) *Self-fulness* refers to the process of attribution of importance to self and other, which interpersonally would lead to more victories than to defeats. Victories are based on equality of importance, reciprocity of positive behaviors, intimacy, and a generally conductive stance (L'Abate, 1986b). We are able to take care and to be in charge of oneselves and to manifest the same care toward loved ones.

(2) *Selfishness* results from the attribution of importance to self and denial of the importance of the other. This stance leads to Pyrrhic victories and interpersonal defeat, to negative reciprocity, or reactivity and repetitiveness in intimate relationships. Most men (approximately 40%) have been and still are being socialized for selfishness. Extremes of selfishness are visible in addictions, character disorders, various criminality, and murder.

(3) *Selflessness* refers to the attribution of importance to the other, with a parallel denial of self-importance, also leading to interpersonal defeats and to the formation of self-defeating personalities, expressed in such ways as depression, affective disorders, manic-depression, and suicide. Most women (approximately 40%) have been and still are being socialized for selflessness. Both selfishness and selflessness produce reactivity and polarization in intimate relationships, especially when, as often happens, a selfish man marries a selfless woman.

(4) *No-self* results from denial of the importance of both the self and the other, leading to severe defeat, apathy, and abuse, as found in borderline, schizophrenic, and psychotic reactions and conditions.

The range of functionality through psychopathology can be described according to this model. Self-fulness is equated with constructive and creative styles in intimate relationships. Equality of importance between partners leads to reciprocity of exchange and, ultimately, to intimacy. These qualities form personal and interpersonal competence as well as marital and familial functionality. Intimacy with selfishness and selflessness is salutary and occasionally experienced, but it does not last for long. It is practically impossible to be intimate with anyone at almost any time in the no-self position.

If we assume that Self-fulness represents the highest functional level of competence in personality development, with selfishness and selflessness representing an intermediate level, and no-self the lowest level, we can postulate a complex interaction among exchanges—giving and taking—according to (a) the three skills of presence, performance, and production with (b) the three levels of status or self-definition (self-ful, selfish-selfless, and no-self) in (c) five settings (home, work, leisure, transit, and transitory). This interaction allows us to make even finer distinctions among levels of functionality. Within this matrix, for instance, we can now distinguish at least three different levels of self-ful competence (Figure 2.2): (a) a *creative* level, highly skilled in modalities and settings; (b) a *competent* level, with one or two skills in presence or performance and in one of the five settings; and (c) an *adequate* level, barely competent in one or two skills and settings (L'Abate & Bryson, in press). The greater the degree of self-fulness, the better the ability to cope with stress and trauma. Creative individuals are able to cope with stress better than competent individuals, who, in turn, should be able to cope better than adequate ones. The notion of "better" is explicated by the use of winning or losing strategies in intimate relationships. According to an old German proverb: "When we share joys they multiply. When we share sorrows they divide."

This model of status and self-definition predicts that each of the four diamonds in Figure 2.2 includes approximately 25% of the population. Among the American population, today, one-quarter of the population has attained a modicum of self-fulness and functionality, as shown in the ability to form lasting and creative intimate relationships. Functional families cope best with stress, with a minimum of disruption and a brief period of aftereffects. The left-middle diamond indicates that 25% of the population is characterized by selfishness: 80% of the population in this quadrant consists of males who have been socialized for selfishness—shown by criminality, addictions, and character disorders being most prevalent among males. Selfishness, of course, is another way of defining narcissism, and, as Emmons (1989, p. 33) concluded: "Few personality traits have captured the attention of as diverse a group of scholars as has narcissism." The other 20% of the population in this quadrant is made up of women. When one looks at ratios of incarcerated criminals, for instance, one finds five to seven times as many men in jail as women. When we look at diagnoses of acting out and character disorders in psychiatric hospitals, we find a four to one ratio in favor of men. In the same way, in the other middle-right diamond, sex ratios are reversed. Many more women (four to one) are diagnosed with depression than are men. Selflessness is the developmental basis for depression. More women are socialized for selflessness than men (Lemkau, 1984).

Individuals high in self-fulness tend to attract and marry others who are similar and can achieve the same level of intimacy, according to an integration of similarity and differentiation, producing positive and constructive relationships with family members (L'Abate, 1976). Because of their inherent equality as individuals, they follow the norm of reciprocity. They respect themselves and each other to the point of allowing individuality, differentiation, growth, and creativity in their partners and family members (Stinnett & DeFrain, 1985). Intimacy is mainly possible within the context of equality and reciprocity. It is not possible in the other three quadrants of the model. If present at all in the two middle quadrants, it is occasional and short-lived, as at funerals. It is almost nonexistent in the bottom quadrant.

The next two levels of status are related to each other because selfish and selfless individuals tend to attract and marry each other, according to the norm of complementarity rather than the norm of similarity and differentiation. They operate in the relationship from unequal positions, either up or down but rarely as equals. Consequently, there is little room for reciprocity and intimacy here. Stereotypically, in terms of gender differences, four women to one man in the selfless position have been socialized to define themselves through a "borrowed" or vicarious identity, by taking on the status of their mates (as in codependency) or the identity of a diety or of a patron saint or martyr. These women tend to attract and be attracted by men who have been socialized to behave selfishly in intimate relationships. Four out of five men in the middle-left quadrant are socialized (by selfless mothers and selfish fathers) to become self-centered and self-indulgent, as shown by an emphasis on a "pseudo"self based mainly on occupational identity, material success, or work (e.g., Doing and Having). This extreme is fertile ground for addictions, such as smoking, overwork, and driven Type-A personalities, that are socially sanctioned and condoned. Relationships between individuals socialized in either selfish or selfless fashion are characteristically reactive and repetitive with little or no change for either the worse or for the better. Complementary and polarized unions of this type, with manipulation and control, yield the normative context (at least 50% of the population) of most family relationships. They serve as the basis for most offspring either gravitating toward extremes at the same level of reactivity or, in fewer cases, gravitating positively upward or negatively downward (Figure 2.2).

At the bottom of Figure 2.2, in the lower-middle diamond, at least 25% of the population is socialized for the defeat of themselves and others, producing the most intense levels of psychopathology, with no-self. When individuals in this diamond marry, they usually tend to seek others who will match them on the same level of abusiveness and apathy ("misery loves company"), that is, an apathetic person marrying an abuser, as seen, for instance, in incestuous and battered families. Stress in these families is so prolonged and intense that people either seem impervious to it or tend to break down continuously, through crisis and upheaval, at least once a week.

A Model for Love and Intimacy

Love has finally reached a long overdue level of legitimacy in psychology; look at how many publications there are on the subject from a variety of prominent psychologists and researchers (Gaylin & Person, 1988; Sternberg & Barnes, 1988; Swensen, 1985). As one reviewer (Murstein, 1988) concluded, there seem to be as many definitions of *love* as there are people and professionals who think and talk about it. In addition to defining *love* as the attribution of importance to self and other, there are at least four ways of showing and expressing it. These ways allow us to assess the extent and consistency of attributed importance of self and other.

The *ability to love* and to be intimate consists of a set of discriminable skills characterized by the same qualities as any other behavior, which are: duration, intensity, and frequency. These processes are part of: (a) seeing the good in self and other; (b) caring for self and other physically, practically, and financially; (c) forgiving errors in self and loved ones; and (d) maintaining intimacy, defined as the sharing of hurts and fears of being hurt. Thus the ability to love— Being that is present without demands for perfection, performance, production, or problem solving—is made up of skills in the attribution of importance and the development of intimate (close and prolonged) relationships.

Seeing the good is a cognitive process, a choice that allows us to value ourselves and our loved ones in positive terms (Stinnett & DeFrain, 1985). As long as the perceived good overshadows the perceived bad, love is everlasting and unconditional, that is, we stress the good and minimize the bad, considering it to be imperfection that is part of being human. The idealization of the beloved one represents one extreme example of this process. Once the balance tips in favor of bad over good, love may become either conditional or withdrawn, as in the case of divorce.

Caring includes all of the various physical acts and chores we perform to show commitment and to ensure the well-being of the self and of loved ones. It ranges from making a living to cooking, cleaning, and taking care of family members when they are sick. It shows in delicate lovemaking, in surprises for birthdays or for special occasions, and in performing routine, mundane, and trivial but necessary tasks that are, in the long run, important for smooth family living. Caring is the physical representation and expression of seeing the good.

Forgiving, in spite of its obviously theological connotation, represents a process of acceptance and tolerance of self and loved ones that acknowledges the essentially imperfect nature of human beings. It is necessary for unconditional love. It allows us to avoid trying to be perfect or expecting loved ones to be perfect. It is a necessary (albeit insufficient) ingredient of family relations that, when absent under stress, leads to blaming, hurt collecting, tensions, and conflicts. Without forgiveness, all previous errors and traumas are catalogued and preserved to be used against each another, producing a reactive self-other defeat pattern that makes family members distant but at the same time dependent on each other (L'Abate, 1985b), because the locus of responsibility is externalized from the self. This pattern of manipulative reactivity is especially evident among selfish-selfless polarizations in couples (Figure 2.2). Seeing the good and forgiving, as cognitive processes, underlies the *duration* of intimate acts and relationships; caring underlies their *frequency*; and intimacy underlies their *intensity*.

Without presence, or Being, as defined here, and the effects of these three processes of seeing the good, caring, and forgiving, it is unlikely that the family can get close and become intimate in sharing individual and family hurts and fears of being hurt. In families that cannot be intimate, there is temporal overreliance on the past or on the future rather than on the present. Spatially, these families may be physically close but emotionally distant. Families that can cry together to share their hurts, when appropriate, represent the ultimate level of intimacy and closeness and the most functional ability to withstand and cope with stress.

Because of the socialization practices mentioned above, however, some men cannot cry and cannot relate to the pain and grief of their wives ("strong men don't cry"). Their wives, by the same token, may externalize blame to their husbands for whatever trauma may have taken place. A great many families go to great lengths to avoid being close and intimate with each other on a prolonged basis. When intimacy is present and prolonged, it becomes the basic ingredient for immunization from stress and breakdown (L'Abate, 1986b). Unfortunately, for those who have not experienced intimacy, it is to be avoided because it is seen as threatening and, therefore, dangerous. Families who cannot be intimate emotionally make contact with each other through sporadic and sudden ambushes, uproars, upsets, and conflicts over Doing and Having. They cannot share Being with each other because their major orientation to life is one of performance (or lack of it) or production (or lack of it). Being, therefore, means being emotionally available to ourselves and our loved ones, sharing victories as well as defeats.

Ability to Negotiate Resources

The ability to negotiate resources yields different models. Both Doing and Having are negotiable commodities and together represent *power*, which is negotiable in democratic families where all the members count as equally important, even though each member may have different functions. In dysfunctional families, power is misused, abused, or unused; family members cannot show and share their love in ways that are enhancing to self and other. The ability to negotiate, which involves decision-making and problem-solving skills, is basic to competence development inside and outside the family (L'Abate, Ganahl, & Hansen, 1986). To negotiate we need a sense of successful self-mastery and control, which is usually visible in conductive stances (self-fulness); relatively absent—or sporadically and accidentally present—in reactive stances (self-ishness-selflessness); and almost completely absent in abusive-apathetic stances (no-self). Negotiation needs to be divided into two separate entities: (a) structure and (b) process.

Structure of Negotiation

Before considering the *process* of negotiation, it is important to evaluate the structure under which negotiation succeeds or fails to take place. To understand this structure the following distinctions are necessary: (a) decision making, (b) the nature of decisions made, and (c) the content of decisions. Decision making can be broken down into authority and responsibility. How we reach decisions represents authority, and who carries out those decisions and how they are carried out represents responsibility. An equitable distribution of authority (who makes the decisions) and responsibility (who carries out those responsibilities), is functional. An inequitable distribution is dysfunctional.

The nature of decisions can be divided into *orchestration* versus *instrumentation* representing big versus small decisions. Is the decision a crucial one for the family, such as moving to another city or taking another job (orchestration)? Or is the decision concerned with routine, trivial everyday matters, such as what to cook for supper (instrumentation)? Who makes these decisions and who carries them out? If the husband decides to take a job in another city without consulting the wife, how will she feel after she is left to take care of the move: selling the house, packing, and taking care of the children?

The content of decisions is tasks relating to services (chores and responsibilities) and information ("Which TV channel should we watch?"), in the modality of Doing, and to money and goods in the modality of Having. How much money is available and which goods should be purchased (or sold)? For instance, in one clinical family, the father assumed complete and absolute authority for decisions about every task that had to be carried out by his wife and two children—ranging from what to buy at the supermarket to what TV programs the children should watch—requiring them to fulfill their quotas of chores. The wife (a daughter of missionaries) followed her husband's orders submissively, unquestioningly, and uncritically, requiring from and enforcing on the children the same kind of blind conformity. Eventually, in adolescence, both children started to rebel by acting out in various ways.

In spite of this acting out, the father remained rigid in retaining his authority (and no responsibilities), continuing to demand complete assumption of responsibilities (without any authority) from the rest of the family. No negotiation on any issue was possible under this regime.

How clear, definite, and understood is this structure? What roles are assumed by the family and how are such roles assigned or rejected within the family? Without such clarity, it would be impossible for the family to carry out and complete any type of negotiation and problem solving. Levels of personality functioning and dysfunctioning relate to bargaining, problem solving, decision making, and negotiation.

A review of the literature on this topic (L'Abate, Ganahl, & Hansen, 1986) showed that, although the terms may be different, the processes are very much the same, following invariant sequences of steps. For example, creative negotiation and problem solving cannot take place in families unless certain feelings are expressed at the beginning of the process. When these feelings are not expressed and shared (nonjudgmentally), the whole process of negotiation is derailed or destroyed. We already know that functional families can negotiate more efficiently than dysfunctional ones (Winter & Ferreira, 1969). The former can reach an "I win, you win" consensus that respects the rights of each individual in the family. The latter are unable to reach such consensus. Whatever conclusion may be reached, it is usually based on manipulation and coercion rather than on genuine problem solving. Thus the outcome is that someone wins at someone else's expense—a Pyrrhic victory. To understand negotiation and teach families how to negotiate, the following series of models has been found helpful and verifiable.

Thus far, the *structure* of family negotiation can be described concretely and concisely. It will be somewhat more complex to describe the process of negotiation.

The Process of Negotiation

To understand, describe, and teach the process of negotiation to families, I have found it useful (L'Abate, 1986b) to divide it into three different subprocesses requiring a description of (a) degree of functionality or coping style at the time of negotiation (Ill), (b) level of competence or mastery available to the family at that time (Skill), and (c) desire or willingness to negotiate that would motivate the family to want to come together to solve problems (Will). Thus the ability to negotiate in a family (negotiation potential) is a multiplicative function of these three processes (Ill × Skill × Will).

Styles of coping: The ARC Model. This model was derived from a continuum of personality factors along six ranges of likeness from symbiotic to sameness, similarity, differentness, oppositeness, and alienation (L'Abate, 1976). From these six ranges, three distinct and distinguishable styles, two dysfunctional and the third functional, in intimate relationships were derived (L'Abate, 1986b). Combining symbiotic and alienated ranges produces an *abusive-apathetic* (AA) style, where physical, chemical, substance, and verbal abuse derive from a context of helplessness and hopelessness, as in the downward spiral of poverty and homelessness. This style leads to deterioration, breakup, and breakdown, without victories and mostly with defeats. There is neither intimacy nor problem solving in the relationship, except in sporadically rare, accidental, and short-lived situations. Most no-self definitions are found in this style (Figure 2.2).

Combining the sameness (demand for blind conformity) and oppositeness (rebellion) ranges produces a *reactive-repetitive* (RR) style based on vengeful rebuttals and manipulatively coercive patterns of response, as found in perhaps 50% to 60% of the interactions in most families. For instance, with few exceptions in the selful position, most parent-child and husband-wife interactions are of a reactive nature. This style furnishes the normative context for repetitive sameness and stagnation in most cases, with differentiation upward toward self-fulness and creativity or, in a smaller number of cases, downward toward abuse or apathy. The ability to withstand stress and to use intimacy as a buffer and defense against stress is somewhat more pronounced in the RR than in the AA style. However, the outcome with or without stress is still unsatisfactory, because the RR style, like the AA style, increases rather than reduces stress—it may do it to a somewhat lesser degree than in the AA, but still enough to decrease the level of functioning and coping resources. This style is usually found in marital polarization based on selfish-selfless definitions of the two mates (L'Abate & Hewitt, 1989).

Combining the similarity and difference ranges of a likeness continuum yields a conductive-creative (CC) style that indicates commitment to change and to improvement through a variety of positive plans ("reactors explode, conductors keep cool"). Individuals characterized by this style usually follow a plan or a score (hence a second meaning for *conductors*) that allows them to think ahead and ask for and gather relevant information before reaching a decision or going into action. This style is found in individuals, couples, and families whose coping strategies are characterized by democratic decision making and winning interactions as well as conductively creative, change-oriented family relations. These conductive relationships, characterized by equality of importance but by difference in functions, tend to produce reciprocity and intimacy, with positively prolonged outcomes for the family in spite of stresses and traumas. These families are more resistant to stress effects than families characterized by reactive-repetitive or abusive-apathetic coping styles.

Although immediacy and impulsivity are the characteristics of the first two styles (A and R), delay and control are the major characteristics of the conductive style. Here the individual is in charge of the self and respects loved ones enough to allow them to give relevant information before responding. Intimacy is much more likely to be found in this style. Consequently, stress is handled better—more successfully—because it is shared equally among various family members.

Competencies for negotiation: The ERAAwC Model. To negotiate and to deal successfully with stress, families need to rely on at least five different sets of competencies: (a) emotionality, (b) rationality, (c) activity, (d) awareness, and (e) context. They need to experience, express, and share feelings and emotions (E) before they can even begin the process of negotiation. After this sharing has taken place, if problem solving is required in the situation, they then can rely on cognitive brainstorming and give-and-take strategies based on realistic rewards and costs (R). From this brainstorming about choices and options, one course of action may appear to be better than the others considered. This course of action may then be put into effect (A). As this course of action is taking place, feedback about its relative rewards and costs (Aw) may produce eventual revisions in maintaining or changing the course of action. This corrective, change-oriented feedback is based on an awareness of the internal context (how family members feel about the issue) and external realities defining the issue (C).

The ERAAwC Model has been found useful in various ways: (a) as a classification of past theoretical schools and therapeutic movements (humanism stresses E, psychodynamics stresses R, behaviorism stresses A, Gestalt stresses Aw, and family therapy stresses C) and (b) as a diagnostic system to characterize how individuals and families use each of these components primarily, secondarily, and tertiarily. For instance, an individual who short-circuits feelings (< E) may rely on either overrational obsessions (>R) or on impulsive behavior (>A). A couple may be polarized around the way the man overrelies on rationality while his wife overrelies on emotionality. Thus this model can be used (c) as a way to describe and prescribe necessary negotiation skills, either informally, in the therapist's office; more formally, through systematic written homework assignments to be carried out in the family's home (Chapter 6); or through structured enrichment programs for couples and families (Chapter 5).

Willingness to negotiate: The Priorities Model. To understand how we allocate time and energy from one setting to another, we need to invoke the concept of *priorities*. This concept is motivational in nature (L'Abate, 1976, 1986b). Priorities stem from definite choices we make about what is important in our lives. How important is a person, an object, or an activity to us? How important is oneself in relation to others? How important are Being, Doing, and Having? Motivation to negotiate within the family takes place on the basis of what is important to each family member. Emphasis on one priority may make other priorities secondary or even irrelevant. Priorities can be *vertical* or *horizontal*. Vertical priorities are intrafamilial or extrafamilial. They are developmental in nature, starting with Being and progressing over the life cycle to Doing and Having. Intrafamilial priorities are (a) self; (b) spouse; (c) children; (d) parents, siblings, and in-laws; and (e) work. Extrafamilial priorities are (a) friends and (b) leisure time.

Horizontal priorities are settings, respectively: home, work, leisure, transit, and transitory settings. Vertical priorities are developmental, and horizontal priorities are structural, that is, they exist regardless of anyone's level of development. One may value Doing more than Having or Being, stressing the work setting at the expense of the home and leisure settings. This emphasis, for instance, could define the American workaholic man. To use another stereotype, of course, a woman may be described by her stress on Being present emotionally and practically at home, considering work and leisure secondary to her emotional availability. In other words, vertical and horizontal priorities intersect and interact with each other.

Therefore, functionality and competence in negotiation imply (a) reliance on conductive rather than on reactive, abusive, or apathetic styles; (b) a flexible balance in the use of component resources, such as emotionality, rationality, activity, and awareness of internal and external contexts, without relying on one component at the expense of another; and (c) a flexible and life stage-appropriate ordering of priorities, both intra- and extrafamilial, and the even ordering of Being, Doing, and Having modalities over the family life cycles. Under these (ideal) conditions a family can withstand stress and cope with only a minimum of breakdown.

Less than ideal abilities and skills to cope produce conflicts, symptoms, and somatizations among family members. Dysfunctionality and a relative inability to deal with stress imply (a) overreliance on repetitive, defeatingly reactive, or abusively apathetic styles; (b) exclusive or extreme reliance on one skill at the exclusion of other skills, such as overrelying on emotionality to the exclusion of rationality or overrelying on activity at the expense of awareness and reflection; and (c) confusion about priorities, such as putting work ahead of the family, children ahead of the marriage, or our family of origin ahead of our family of procreation.

These priorities can be measured easily by time analysis: How much time does one spend in each of the settings and what modality of expression among Being, Doing, or Having is used primarily, secondarily, and tertiarily (Juster & Stafford, 1985)? Being, of course, is much more relevant to the home setting than are the modalities of Doing and Having. The latter two modalities, on the other hand, are more relevant and primary at work and in leisure settings.

How successful we are in any of these settings depends a great deal on the priorities of each particular individual. If a person defines himself primarily in occupational terms—"I am an engineer"—rather than domestically—"I am a husband and a father"—it follows that this individual may be more successful at work than at home. In the same way, avocational pursuits sometimes may overshadow both domestic and occupational roles. We all need to balance modalities and settings so that no one modality or setting is stressed at the expense of the others.

The salience of and satisfaction derived from each modality and setting remain an individual prerogative that determines how each modality and setting is ranked with respect to the others. Each one can be reduced in importance by increasing the importance of the others. For example, activities in the leisure area can become direct antidotes for the negative effects of stresses at work or at home. How this juggling and counterbalancing of demands and of difficulties takes place to maintain balance in life is reflective of priorities. Priorities motivate us to negotiate, or to avoid negotiating—with ourselves and significant others—important issues in our lives.

Theoretical Implications

The primary purpose of this theoretical framework is to link individual with family psychology (L'Abate, 1976, 1983, 1987) in both functional and dysfunctional aspects. The models derived from this theory are applicable to individuals as well as to families because they use concepts that derive reductionistically from monadic psychology, namely, the ability to love and the ability to negotiate. For instance, in developmental psychology, the basic concept of development is relevant to the individual as well as to the marital and family life cycles. A secondary, more practical and applied purpose is to bridge inevitable gaps between theory and practice, between theory building and theory testing, and between theory and types of prevention. If this theory is valid, the purpose of any intervention, at any level of prevention, is to increase the ability of individuals, couples, and families to love each other and to negotiate successfully. To fulfill both purposes, this theory attempts also to meet two additional formal requirements, which are reducibility and verifiability.

Reducibility: Links Between Monadic and Family Psychology

Reducibility, of course, does not mean an all-or-nothing process. The issue here is: What portion of the variability in functioning and dysfunctioning is due to individual, dyadic, and superdyadic, multimember, multiperson interactions? Eventually this is a theoretical as well as an empirical measurement issue that will be solved when we have adequate measures of individual, dyadic, and superdyadic determinants. This requirement is met, first, by using psychological terms that are at the same time interactional and relational, by drawing from and linking to various areas of psychology as a science and as a profession. Love and negotiations, for instance, imply the presence of another partner with which to love and to negotiate. Both sets of abilities are vital for individual, dyadic, and familial functioning. In fact, most family dysfunction is the outcome of deficits in either or both abilities. This framework also draws from and is linked to developmental and cognitive psychology and personality, social, and stress theories (Lazarus & Folkman, 1984). We (L'Abate & Hewitt, 1988) have discussed how this theoretical framework applies to a classification of sexuality and sexual dysfunction, and we have applied the same framework to a classification of addictions (L'Abate, Farrar, & Serritella, in press).

The theory of interpersonal competence presented here seems continuous and consistent with monadic psychology through at least six different links. The first link is found in an emphasis on constructs such as *self* or *personality*, which, although derived from individual psychology, have been redefined here according to relational and interrelational concepts, for example, in the definition of love as attribution of the importance of self and other. The concept of self is and will continue to be a psychological construct in personality theory. Even though, in the past, the *self* may have been defined in intrapsychic and inferred terms, such as *self-esteem, self-image,* or *self-worth,* it is defined here strictly in interpersonal terms. Attribution of importance is an absolutely relational process that supersedes the construct of self-esteem or equivalently inferred constructs. These intrapsychic constructs by now have reached a dead end in theory and in research (L'Abate & Bryson, in press). They have outlived their past and pervasive usefulness.

The second link is in *attachment theory*, which is related to the spatial assumption of approach-avoidance and the development of dependencies and interdependencies. Attachment can be generalized from parent-child to man-woman relationships. Love can be derived from a spatial assumption of approach-avoidance, leading to psychological concepts such as dependency and distance (L'Abate, 1985b). Ultimately, distance predicates the degree of closeness and intimacy we allow ourselves to achieve (L'Abate, 1983, 1985a, 1985b, 1985c, 1986b). *Intimacy* and *love* are the two basic concepts that have been given new meanings in the recent upsurge of research interest in both topics (Gaylin & Person, 1988; Shaver, Hazan, & Bradshaw, 1988; Sloan & L'Abate, 1985).

The third link is in the temporal dimension of *discharge-delay* that is basic to the development of personal controls and the ability to negotiate. The transmission of competence or incompetence from parents to children takes place through a *psychophysical continuum of likeness* (L'Abate, 1976; L'Abate & Bryson, in press), leading to the establishment of functional and dysfunctional styles (the ARC Model—Ill). In abuse-apathy (AA), there are inconsistent and contradictory extremes of discharge-delay. In repetitive reactivity (RR), immediacy of discharge and delay may not be as extreme or contradictory as in AA, but this immediacy is substantial nevertheless. Only in the creatively conductive style (CC) is there a balance of discharge-delay, shown in the ability to delay enough to reach an appropriate and constructive response. The fourth link is in reordering and applying resource exchange theory in social psychology (Foá & Foá, 1974) to modalities and skills that are basic to the models developed in this theory. A fifth link is in *sex* and *sexuality*, which are two, among others, of the biological and social bases for the formation and development of the family. L'Abate and Hewitt (1988, 1989) have applied the same theory of power (performance and production) and presence (love, Being, and status) to a classification of sex and sexuality. They have argued that most sexual dysfunction is based on the inability to Be, with cultural emphasis, instead, on sexual performance or production. Functional sex and sexuality imply an ability to be emotionally available to one's partner *before* one can be available sexually. Performance or production, that is, just the physical act of intercourse at the expense of emotional presence, is bound to produce deviations and disturbances that will affect the subsequent development of sexuality in the family. The sixth link, the relevance of individual differences, and especially gender differences, is too important to bypass. It deserves a separate section.

The importance of gender differences. Individual differences, especially gender differences, are the outcome of different socialization practices for males and females. As stated earlier, men (40%) are usually socialized for selfishness, and women (40%) are traditionally socialized for selflessness. For both sexes, 25% are socialized for self-fulness and 25% for no-self, with few gender differences in either category. This model of gender differences is also drawn from and linked to the field stress theory, as formulated by Lazarus and Folkman (1984). Their theory maintains the importance of individual differences in coping skills through the distinction of emotion-focused and problem-focused coping strategies. This distinction, in turn, relates to the importance of gender differences in level and type of competence and coping strategy. Stereotypically, at least, most men tend to follow problem-focused strategies, and most women tend to follow emotion-focused strategies. In addition, these two strategies are relevant to the ERAAwC Model. Women are socialized to be more emotional and aware than men, who, in turn, are socialized, relative to women, toward rationality and activity. Evidence for this polarization is found in the work of Gore (1979), who supported one derivation from the self-definition model presented in this chapter, which is that there would be no sex differences between functional, self-ful (CC) and very dysfunctional, no-self (AA) couples. The highest degree of conflict and polarization between partners would be found in couples defined along the extremes of selfishness and selflessness (RR). The attribution of importance would be strongly and positively reciprocal in functional couples just as it would be reciprocally, apathetically, and abusively negative and denied in very dysfunctional couples. Gore (1979), for instance, supported this prediction from the status model: "Differences between the sexes being much greater for the neurotic disorders than for the psychotic disorders" (p. 47), "in modern western industrial societies more women than men are mentally ill" (p. 54). This conclusion, of course, means that more women tend to be diagnosed as depressed and men classified as criminal and, therefore, not mentally ill. Acting out and externalization are characteristics of criminal and narcissistic character disorders (predominantly found in "selfish" men), and depression and its derivatives are more predominant in "selfless" women. As Weissman and Klerman (1979) concluded in their review of the literature on this very topic: "Most diagnosed depressives are women" (p. 384). "Women predominate in the rates of depression" (p. 392). "Women report more symptoms, especially affective distress. Women go to doctors more often (than men)" (p. 394). "Men use more alcohol (than women)" (p. 395). "Men predominate in the Law Enforcement and Correctional Systems" (p. 397). "The female preponderance (in depression) is 'real'" (p. 398).

Recently, we have been able to pinpoint specific gender differences in response to stress (Barnett, Biener, & Baruch, 1987). The crucial and basic importance of these differences has prompted the need to consider a theory of personality that distinguishes sharply between the two genders (L'Abate & Bryson, in press). At least provisionally, and admittedly stereotypically, we need to consider that many (at least four out of ten) men are socialized in many ways to be different, if not opposite, from women (and, of course, vice versa). What is the nature of these differences and what are their implications for a theory of interpersonal competence?

When the foregoing distinction of problem- versus emotion-focused strategies is applied to gender differences (Barnett, Biener, & Baruch, 1987; Belle, 1987; Miller & Kirsch, 1987), usually most men tend to use problem-focused strategies, whereas most women tend to use emotion-focused strategies. Most men in our culture, at least in the past, were socialized to, and, therefore, tend to, strive to be rational problem-solvers (i.e., power) expressing themselves mainly through actions. Most women, in our culture, were socialized to, and, therefore, tend to, strive to relate emotionally and to experience, acknowledge, and express their feelings verbally (i.e., presence).

This major gender difference in competence and coping strategies has profound implications for functioning and dysfunctioning in intimate relationships. Each of these two strategies, when used in a mutually exclusive fashion, represents a deeply ingrained socialization process that leads many individuals to answer, and cope, automatically with confrontation and conflict without much awareness of how their coping strategies are different from their spouses'. This difference, if and when left unresolved, produces polarization in couples and becomes counterproductive for a joint solution and resolution of hurtful events. Emphasis on one strategy at the expense of the other not only restricts the coping repertoire of either partner but, when this emphasis produces mutually exclusive strategies, it prevents family members from being available to each other in times of stress and hurt. The man tends to fall back and maintain his rational facade of instrumental problem-solving performer, while the woman tends to express her emotionality, sometimes blaming the man or at least making him feel guilty for whatever may have stressed the couple: She cries; he gets angry.

Defeat as well as victory in problem solving and negotiation relate to the model of selfhood, self-definition, and status presented above. None of these terms would have any meaning without another person to defeat, to be defeated by, or with which to share victories. Any form of discounting, criticism, putting down, and name-calling would produce a lowering of the sense of self-importance in both parties, that is, defeat. Any compliment, positive affirmation, and open, nonjudgmental expression of feelings and emotions would enhance the sense of importance in both parties, that is, a victory. Of course, topics such as bargaining, negotiation, and problem solving find their theoretical bases in cognitive psychology.

Verifiability: Evidence to Support a Developmental Theory of Interpersonal Competence

This developmental theory of interpersonal competence can be supported through three different sources of evidence: (a) inferential and independent of, (b) indirectly related to, and (c) derived directly from the theory itself. For a theory, we must develop methods derived from it and isomorphic as much as possible with the theory itself or with the models derived from the theory. Methods, not techniques, are needed to verify this or any other theory. A method is a step-by-step sequence of replicable procedures, while a technique is a personal, stylistic gimmick or a one-time intervention that defies replicability. Once we establish, however, that *both* theory and method are needed to advance prevention approaches, three different possibilities ensue. That is, the present derivation and expansion of resource exchange theory to a theory of interpersonal competence is verifiable in three possible ways: (a) Theory and method can be independent of each other and any link between them would be based on inferences with *no isomorphism* between the two; (b) theory and method may be somewhat related to each other, consequently one can be related to the other indirectly with *some isomorphism;* and (c) theory and method may be so related that one is *derived* directly from the other and the theory is verified directly by methodological applications derived from the theory itself, with *isomorphism* between theory and method. Thus some of the preventive programs presented in the following chapters may be independent of theory, some may be vaguely or indirectly related to the theory, and some programs will be derived directly from the theory. Therefore, these programs can be used to verify the theory directly.

These three relationships will be discussed and illustrated further in the course of this work because they are relevant to the point that a theory, and especially the theory presented briefly here, can be tested not only evaluatively (Chapter 4) but also interventionally through primary (Chapter 5) and secondary (Chapter 6) prevention approaches. For instance, as far as primary prevention is concerned, some structured enrichment programs for couples and families are independent of the theory presented here. Some of them are somewhat related to the theory and others were written specifically to test the theory because they were derived directly from the theory itself.

Inferentially, and independent of the theory, support can be found in work done by other researchers that is related to the ability to love and to the ability to negotiate. In other words, inferential evidence is empirical work that has been done outside the theory itself. For example, a great deal of the construction of this theory was derived from clinical observations (L'Abate, 1976, 1986b). On the other hand, Swensen's (1985) or Steinberg and Grajek's work on love (1984) or work on the process of negotiation (L'Abate, Ganahl, & Hansen, 1986) would be examples of theory-independent evidence that would inferentially affect the relevance and validity of the theory itself.

Indirectly related to this theory is the work of Foá and Foá (1974), from which part of this theory is derived. They developed paper-and-pencil, self-report tests to measure resources exchanged. Results of their work would have some bearing on the validity and viability of the present theory, provided their measures are valid as far as the definition of constructs used in this theory. Even though there is an overlap among constructs between the two theories, some of the same constructs have been defined differently from one theory to the other.

Thus far, the evidence to support this theory more directly has been derived evaluatively from self-report paper-and-pencil or visual tests in a variety of studies reviewed by L'Abate and Wagner (1985). More recently (1988), L'Abate and Wagner published data supporting the validity and reliability of some of these measures. Recently, Schratz (1988) evaluated 72 couples at various stages of the family life cycle (from 19 to 77 years of age) with a battery of paper-and-pencil self-report tests, including a Marital Issues Questionnaire, Loevinger's Revised Sentence Completion Test, the Emotional Intimacy Subscale of the PAIR Inventory, Swensen's Scale of Feelings and Behavior of Love, the Conflict Resolution Scale of Olson's ENRICH program, and Stevens's 28-item Sharing of Hurts Inventory. The latter test was constructed to evaluate the validity of defining intimacy in terms of sharing hurts (Stevens & L'Abate, 1989). Although this test was derived from one statement of the theory, the other tests in Schratz's battery were independent of the theory. Three hierarchic regression analyses of these instruments showed that intimacy and negotiation together accounted for 43% of the variance for marital adjustment in husbands and 50% in wives. Specific ways of testing the theory with other paper-and-pencil tests will be described in Chapter 4.

In addition to self-report measures, the groundwork to test this theory has been laid interventionally through (a) the creation of structured marital and family enrichment programs derived from the same models of primary prevention we will review in Chapter 5 and (b) written, self-administered, and self-instructional systematic homework assignments—programmed materials for couples and families that either are isomorphic with the models presented above or are completely independent from them in secondary prevention (to be reviewed in Chapter 6).

To fulfill both theoretical and practical purposes, this developmental theory of interpersonal competence attempts to meet additional requirements. We will look at how this theory fares in regard to additional criteria, which are (a) concreteness, (b) accountability, (c) validity, (d) relevance, and (e) integration. This theory has several advantages: (a) It is concrete and specific because the six resource classes are finite and easily defined, even though, admittedly, status and love may appear, at first blush, to be less concrete than the other four classes of resources exchanged: information, services, money, and possessions or goods. For accountability, because a great many of its models have been translated into writing, either in structured enrichment programs or in programmed materials, either approach can be applied to both couples and families and we can see what results occur. Relevance is easy to demonstrate in terms of the face-value usefulness of the programs. Validity, however, needs to be established in many more ways and from sources unrelated to the author. For integration, the whole theory, which was originally developed independent from resource exchange theory in social psychology, is found to be wholly consistent with it (Foá & Foá, 1974) as well as with humanistic and behavioral theories. Furthermore, the ERAAwC Model is another way of integrating existing theories.

Implications of the Theory for Primary and Secondary Prevention with Families

Ideally, a theoretical framework needs to be consistent with all three types of primary, secondary, and tertiary prevention. This is an issue of reducibility to concrete, written format from an abstract, theoretical, or oral medium. For instance, although psychoanalysis and systems theory may have been found relevant to tertiary prevention (i.e., therapy), neither of them (with the exception of Adler and his followers in parent education) has produced any programs for primary and secondary preventions. In terms of productivity and fruitfulness, only humanistic and behavioral theories have produced a great many marital and parental programs (Levant, 1986).

We also need to have theoretical models to encompass all three types of prevention. The models presented here seem to do this, provided they are verifiable evaluatively and interventionally. In Bond and Wagner's (1988) list of characteristics of effective prevention and promotion programs, four characteristics were considered relevant to program development and refinement: (a) guidance by scientific theory, (b) ensurance of replicability of the programs, (c) field experience by the researcher and program designer, and (d) longitudinal tracking of program operation and effectiveness. These characteristics are fulfilled as follows: For (a) above, many of the concepts used in our theory, such as dependence, distance, victory, and defeat, are derived from monadic psychology and from theoretically or empirically established principles (L'Abate, 1985b, 1986b). For (b), all of the structured enrichment programs (Chapter 5) and programmed materials (Chapter 6) are completely replicable, because they all are in written form. For (c), these programs and materials have been or are being field-tested (by my students, collaborators and me) to verify their effectiveness (L'Abate & Cox, in press), using (d), follow-up either in consumer satisfaction (L'Abate & Rupp, 1981) or in definite changes in behavior over time (Ganahl, 1981; Wildman, 1977).

Can both humanistic and behavioral approaches be integrated in ways consistent with all three types of prevention? The theory presented above seems to fulfill this requirement also. It integrates both approaches. The ability to love, like that found in *empowerment* and support groups, has been stressed by the humanistic school, and the importance of negotiation and *enablement*, that is, social and interpersonal skills training, has been stressed by the behavioral school (Dunst, Trivette, & Deal, 1988). For instance, in a recent review of social and community intervention, Gesten and Jason (1987) summarized most primary prevention programs and created two major categories, which are also supported by more recent references added here. The categories are (a) mutual help groups that stress social support (Kagan, Powell, Weissbourd, & Zigler, 1987; Stinnett et al., 1982; Wolchik, Sandler, & Braver, 1987) and *empowerment* (Rappaport, Swift, & Hess, 1983), on one hand, and (b) behavioral programs that stress skills training in negotiation (Hermalin & Weirich, 1983), on the other hand. Are these not the two major dimensions assumed by the theory? Does not social support represent a form of caring and loving without conditions or requirements, giving people a sense of importance, that is, empowerment? How about negotiation? Is this not one of the two sets of abilities (after the ability to love) fundamental to the theory? Teaching negotiation skills means enabling families to improve their decision-making and problem-solving skills. Individuals, couples, and families need *both* sets of skills: empowerment and enablement (Dunst, Trivette, & Deal, 1988).

TABLE 2.1: Applications of a Developmental Theory of Interpersonal Competence to Types of Prevention

Abilities	Types of Prevention	
	Primary	Secondary
Love	(Support groups)* (Empowerment) Structured enrichment programs; intimacy program (Chapter 5)	(Self-help groups) Programmed materials: intimacy workbooks (Chapter 6)
Negotiation	(Skills training) (Enablement) Structured enrichment programs: negotiation (Chapter 5)	Programmed materials: negotiation workbook (Chapter 6)

*Parentheses include programs and approaches that are independent of this theory but that in some ways, discussed above, are related to or consistent with the theory.

Do we have isomorphism between theory and practice here? As shown in Table 2.1, this theory encompasses both primary and secondary types of prevention. The relationships between this theory and tertiary prevention will be discussed elsewhere (L'Abate & Cox, in press), because the topic is outside the province of this book. One could argue that any form of therapy and positive attention would tend to increase, either directly or indirectly, the sense of importance of family members. This increased sense of importance may lead to their solving problems more efficiently than they did before receiving therapy. A dysfunctional individual, couple, or family will be unable to love and to negotiate and will, therefore, show signs and symptoms that indicate this inability.

Summary and Conclusion

Competencies and abilities underlie modalities of Being, Doing, and Having that are made up, respectively, of six resource classes—status and intimacy, information and services, money and goods—according to resource exchange theory, developed by Foá and Foá (1974). Thus we are assuming a continuum of competencies containing certain abilities, which, in turn, contain certain skills ranging from the general to the specific. A developmental theory of interpersonal competence derived from assumptions of space and time postulates two sets of abilities necessary and sufficient for functional family living: the ability to love and the ability to negotiate. From postulates, modalities, and resources we have derived various relational models. Love is expressed through (a) the assertion and affirmation of the importance of self and of other loved ones and (b) the ability to be intimate and to be available emotionally to oneself and to others (Being). Negotiation over Doing and Having requires the ability to separate Being from Doing and Having, in five different (home, work, leisure, transit, and transitory) settings, according to one's developmental and structural priorities. We need to distinguish *competencies*, therefore, from *abilities* and *skills*, instead of using them synonymously. *Competencies* lie on the subjective, experiencing side (input), and *skills* lie on the expressive side (output). *Abilities* lie in the middle of this continuum (throughput).

Assumptions then subsume the notion of competence to regulate distance, an internal, developmental process, which eventually transforms itself into the ability to love. This ability to love is shown, manifested, and expressed on the output side by very specific skills. Competence in modulating and modifying control transforms itself developmentally into the ability to negotiate, which is also shown, manifested, and expressed through specific skills. Resources are summarized by testable models that require different sets of skills. Skills related to Being are developed from the ability to love but skills related to Doing and Having are developed from the ability to negotiate. The way the different sets of skills are applied pertains to the concept of setting. The importance of the interactions within these settings is understood when one uses the concept of priorities among settings interacting with the individual's priorities among modalities of Being, Doing, and Having.

This theory seems to fit requirements bridging monadic and family psychology as well as primary and secondary prevention approaches. When types of primary, secondary, and tertiary prevention are coupled with the laboratory method in clinical psychology, reviewed in the next chapter, it will be possible to intervene with more families than has been the case heretofore.

3

The Laboratory Method for Preventive and Crisis Interventions

The purpose of this chapter is to introduce the laboratory method for working with individuals, couples, and families. This method uses standard operating procedures (SOP) in evaluation and in preventive methods, using a lattice and ladder of different personnel with varying levels of professional expertise: from completely unstructured, such as in decision making and therapy with full-fledged professionals, to more structured for middle level-professionals and for paraprofessionals, such as enrichment programs and programmed materials (L'Abate, 1965, 1969, 1973). This method consists of the doctorate-level professional retaining executive responsibilities. These responsibilities would consist of coordinating, directing, supervising, and supporting middle- and lower-level professionals as well as reporting and relating to other professionals involved in the same process of evaluation and treatment. The rationale for this method has multiple components.

First, one needs to consider the high costs of traditional mental health practices, which were already high 20 years ago (Klarman, 1969) and are as expensive, if not more expensive, today (American Psychological Association [APA], 1986). Apparently, this is a consideration that does not seem to matter to many mental health professionals, especially to psychotherapists, because very few if any references are made to it in the professional literature. On the other hand, this expense is a basic and important consideration in service delivery (Sauber, 1983), especially from the viewpoint of offering primary and secondary prevention services *in addition* to offering tertiary prevention for people in crisis. Because the numbers of people that need to be served by primary and secondary prevention services could become absolutely impossible to manage, it would be unrealistic to think that the single-professional/single-client paradigm used thus far in mental health delivery would be sufficient to meet the needs of people at risk and in need. We must think in terms of more cost-effective, mass-oriented, and less expensive ways to deliver mental health services. *We must think in terms of hierarchies of professionals, semiprofessionals, paraprofessionals, and preprofessionals able and ready to administer high-quality services at the lowest possible cost without cutting corners and without reducing the effectiveness of these services.* There will never be enough doctorate-level professionals to take care of the mental health needs of the millions of people who need help.

In a recent survey of mental health providers (APA, 1986), it was estimated that there were approximately 172, 000 psychiatrists, psychologists, social workers, and marriage and family counselors. Even if one were to add to that number pastoral, guidance, and school counselors, one would not go far beyond 300,000 mental health specialists for 250 million people at best, an approximate ratio of 1 professional for every 1,000 people. With this ratio, there would barely be enough professionals to take care of crisis intervention, psychotherapy, or tertiary prevention. Where would the additional personnel come from to deal with primary and tertiary prevention? We need to find new ways to deal with such staggering mental problems facing us today, with AIDS and drug epidemics, sexual and physical abuse, and the ever present danger of murder and suicide.

Psychodiagnostic mental health evaluation and diagnosis, as traditionally and institutionally practiced to date, is a time-consuming procedure, costly in professional time and questionable in its usefulness, especially if it fails to direct and specify particular treatment or preventive strategies and if no postintervention evaluation takes place. A great deal of time and expense is given to evaluating baselines. However, practically no effort is given to evaluating whether any change, for better or worse has taken place *after* treatment. Unfortunately, psychological testing of children and of some adolescents and adults has become so institutionalized that no thought is given to demanding that each child (client, patient) who has been evaluated once be evaluated again to verify that whatever recommendations for treatment formulated initially were indeed followed in treatment. As a result, there is no critical feedback process to allow us to validate, correct, and improve psychodiagnostic conclusions.

Psychiatric hospitalization, as a last resort, is very expensive and can leave a possible stigma, and alternatives to hospitalization, such as community crisis interventions and medication with the families in psychiatric emergencies, have been found to be more effective and cheaper in the long run (Langsley & Kaplan, 1968; Sauber, 1983). Furthermore, unless it is a matter of life or death, hospitalization per se does not seem to reduce psychopathology unless a whole program of rehabilitation, consisting of a combination of various therapeutic modalities, takes place during this period of time.

We need to consider the great cost and relative inefficiency of most mental health practices. For instance, in psychotherapy, there is a great deal of attrition (Edwards, 1988). Only one family in ten who start treatment complete what is professionally considered a full dose of appropriate and adequate treatment. These attrition rates should indicate that psychotherapy by itself may be failing to meet the mental health needs of a large sector of the people who need help.

Interventionally, psychotherapy is by now the most used form of intervention, in spite of the melancholy fact that, when we consider it from the viewpoint of outcome, it is a very chancy process. Attrition rates are extremely high—up to 50% for initial referrals with individuals and probably higher with couples and families (Edwards, 1988; Garfield, 1986; Patterson, 1985; Phillips, 1985a, 1987). At best, only 66% of those who terminate this process receive some relief. At worst, only 33% of all those who terminate psychotherapy receive lasting benefits.

Furthermore, there are very few and very vague standards of what constitutes psychotherapeutic competence and effectiveness, on one hand, and what constitutes successful outcome, on the other. Could it be that—in addition to factors like family characteristics, type of treatment, therapist characteristics, and others—lack of choice (either therapy or nothing) may be at least one factor to explain attrition? Psychotherapy is currently administered as the only available choice with or without hospitalization and/or medication. The consumer has little to say about what type of treatment is available, especially when costs and consequences are not clearly spelled out. We cannot predict how long treatment will last and whether it will bring about any benefit, either immediate or long term. Yet, many of us are willing to take this chance in order to reduce pain and suffering. It may not be very good, but it is the only approach we know. Can we do more and better?

We also need to consider the split between service providers and researchers. Each group has its own sets of values that oftentimes clash with each other. Stereotypically, those interested in offering services are motivated by immediacy, the need to help and to be needed, even if the service rendered may leave something to be desired. Researchers, on the other hand, are a more cautious lot. They would like to see validated and proven methods established before administering them uncritically and sometimes unthinkingly. It is difficult if not impossible to reconcile either value system with the other.

What is even more relevant here is the split between therapists and preventers. Most therapists do perform the service of prevention, but crisis intervention and psychotherapy are tertiary prevention. However, most therapists do not have enough energy, interest, or expertise to perform secondary and primary prevention services. In addition, the number of preventers is quite limited, still in the hundreds rather than in the thousands. They include family life educators, mental health educators, and a great many lay volunteers. The leadership in this field is limited to tens of professionals rather than hundreds. Their interests and commitment are not sufficient to deal with the immensity of the mental health problems confronting us. Hence we need to develop a completely new professional from the ground up if we are going to deal with these problems proactively rather than reactively (Chapter 7).

The laboratory method, with its emphasis on SOPs, a hierarchy of different personnel, and a perspective of preventive interventions on a continuum, may provide the basis for allowing groups *both* of clinicians and researchers and of therapists and preventers to find a mutually acceptable middle ground. The laboratory method is presented here as just *one way* of attempting to resolve some of the dilemmas of expense, quality, and cost-effectiveness (considered here and in Chapter 1) without shortchanging the public.

The Need for a Hierarchic Lattice and
Ladder of Mental Health Providers

To accomplish our goal in primary, secondary, and tertiary prevention, we need a variety of personnel with different interests and skills (Arnhoff, Rubinstein, & Speisman, 1969; Ellsworth, 1968; Grosser, Henry, & Kelly, 1969; Guerney, 1969; Joint Commission on Mental Health of Children, 1969; Joint Commission on Mental Illness and Health, 1961; Sobey, 1970). These skills range all the way from a specialty board diploma at the professional level to a part-time, volunteer student at the preprofessional level. Otherwise, having only doctorate-level professionals as direct service providers would be like trying to build skyscrapers with our bare hands. Engineers and architects design a building. From their blueprints, a hierarchy of workers, each specialized in his or her job *with tools specific to the job*, build what began as a simple design and a blueprint. In mental health, in spite of many blueprints (Joint Commission on Mental Health of Children, 1969; Joint Commission on Mental Illness and Health, 1961; Keniston, 1977), very little change has taken place, whatever the reasons for this complacency, apathy, and stagnation.

It is possible that no change has taken place because, at the time these "blueprints" were published, we lacked the technology for primary and secondary prevention that has been created in the last few years. Hopefully, with the development of new primary and secondary prevention methods, some of which will be reviewed in the next three chapters, we may be able to produce some changes by creating new blueprints. These new blueprints will need new personnel.

Personnel

Just as skyscrapers are not built by architects and engineers alone, so, in the mental health field, we need to start practicing according to different credentials, competencies, and capacities at various levels (lattices or ladders) of human endeavor. At the top of this hierarchy should be professionals with the greatest experience, interpersonal maturity, knowledge, and credentials, as exemplified in our society by the doctorate degree and a board diploma in a psychological or psychiatric specialty or equivalent credential, such as being a fellow of a professional society or another form of professional recognition. These professionals would supervise three or four middle-level professionals with less experience or with lower-level degrees, as with beginning professionals, newly acquired doctorates, or individuals with a master's degree or equivalent, postdoctoral fellows, or predoctoral interns. Each middle-level professional would in turn supervise and support three to four paraprofessional technicians, with a B.A. degree or equivalent and/or volunteers with degrees not necessarily in the mental health field (Lauffer & Gorodezky, 1977; Nash, Lifton, & Smith, 1978). Each paraprofessional would then work directly or indirectly with the help of preprofessional personnel. The latter would include workers at the clerical level with a high school degree or equivalent as well as part-time volunteers, including former patients. The latter may work at whatever level they fit best into in this hierarchy, according to their interests, degrees, and experiences.

The level of experience in this human framework would be based on experiential knowledge and experience in applying methods of evaluation as well as methods of intervention. The more one knows and has experienced, also including research methods, the higher the position in this hierarchy. The higher the level of professionalism, the less structure will be needed in both evaluation and intervention. In the same way, the lower the level, the clearer the need will be for structure in both evaluation and intervention. This point will be considered with more concrete examples throughout this chapter.

Standard Operating Procedures

For instance, to illustrate the point just made, in the evaluation of individuals, couples, and families, technical instruments, such as tests and their scoring, take more time to administer but less time for training and learning than professional skills. The latter skills, such as decision making, interpretating, and reporting, take more time and training than technical skills. Professional skills, once learned and mastered, take less time than technical skills. To wit, it may take one hour to administer an intelligence test, following verbatim instructions in a manual, and maybe 20 or 30 minutes to score it, again following standard instructions from the manual.

However, it would take a full-fledged professional with years of experience just a few minutes to interpret the test results, relating them to other tests or to other historical and situational information. In a few minutes, a seasoned professional can dictate a written report or make a phone call to another professional who may have referred the case. Or, in the case of a child, a professional would discuss the results with the parents including the implications of the results for treatment or other disposition and recommendations. The major difference here lies in the decision-making responsibilities. The professional makes some decisions after gathering all the relevant information. These decisions are then carried out routinely by less experienced personnel, just as in any other fields of human endeavor—business, building, and bureaucracy (except in the mental health field so far).

Evaluation and Prevention

The first application of the laboratory method took place at Washington University Children's Hospital in St. Louis, when in 1963 it was estimated, conservatively, that a complete psychological evaluation, performed directly and solely by a Ph.D. clinical psychologist would cost $120. To provide SOPs, three batteries of tests, according to age, were designed to evaluate intellectual, emotional, organic, and educational functioning in children. These batteries were originally administered in part by "pink ladies," volunteers who received some training in the easiest tests to learn, administer, and score. They were tests of visual motor coordination, like the Draw-a-Person, the Peabody Picture Vocabulary Test, and the Benton's Visual Retention Test. A graduate student administered the more advanced intelligence tests and the Rorschach Inkblot Test. The author was responsible for interpreting test battery results and communicating them both verbally and in written reports to referring professionals (pediatricians, neurologists). During the first year of operation, this laboratory evaluated approximately 50 children where none had been evaluated before. In the second and third years of operation, this number jumped into the hundreds, and after 25 years of operation, this laboratory has evaluated thousands of children. The cost of each evaluation went down then from an estimated $120 to $34.

The issue here is whether test results, blind (without seeing the child directly) interpretations, and recommendations obtained by this method would be as valid or relevant as evaluations based on a direct administration of a test battery by a Ph.D. clinical psychologist. To answer this question, I conducted an experiment with a colleague who raised this issue. After moving to Atlanta to establish a psychodiagnostic laboratory in Child Psychiatry at Emory University School of Medicine, I directly evaluated 15 children, while training an assistant to administer the same test batteries I had used. The assistant completed evaluations of 15 children, but I wrote the reports, however, without having seen the children. The 30 reports were sent to the inquiring colleague, who was supposed to separate them according to whether they had been administered by me or by my assistant. The inquiring colleague's division of reports was no greater than chance. He was unable to recognize any difference between the two types of reports.

The same batteries of tests were also used to evaluate the results of monitored play therapy with children at Georgia State University in Atlanta (L'Abate, 1979). This mode of intervention was the second application of the laboratory method. Instead of a traditional therapeutic playroom, which gives little if no information, a new kind of playroom was constructed. It consisted of two separate rooms, one full of aggressive toys and the other full of constructive ones. The lights in the rooms; the separate electric guns, baseball, or shuffleboard games in the two rooms; and chests of drawers for toys were wired. These connections communicated to control panels in an observation room, behind one-way mirrors, how long a child played with a toy and how long the child stayed in either of the two rooms. The therapy was conducted by graduate students in training under my supervision. The children's test results from these batteries showed some changes after therapy. However, without a control group, it was difficult to judge or reach conclusions about the effectiveness of therapy. The major conclusion that was reached, however, was that play therapy, independent from family interventions, was not very effective or at least not cost-effective enough for the time and effort expended on it. Consequently, the next application of the laboratory method consisted of designing enrichment programs for couples and families (Chapter 5).

The same concept of a test battery for children to be administered by clerical- or technical-level personnel was transferred to the evaluation of couples and families (L'Abate & Wagner, 1985, 1988). These batteries were used to evaluate, on a pre-post basis, the administration of structured enrichment programs (SEPs, Chapter 5). Other batteries of tests are being used in an ongoing research project using programmed materials with college students (Chapters 4 and 6).

The fourth application of the laboratory method was the creation of self-administered, self-instructional, systematically programmed, written homework assignments for individuals, couples, and families. I have used this application in my private practice, using the MMPI as a pre-post measure. Research to evaluate this approach is in progress (Chapter 6).

The major payoff of the laboratory method has been theoretical. For instance, the laboratory method of evaluation with children yielded a theoretical model of intellectual functioning based on receptive-expressive functions (L'Abate, 1971). Monitored play therapy, on the other hand, yielded a developmental model consisting of three sequential stages: (a) exploration, (b) aggression, and (c) construction. The aggressive stage could then be broken down into three different phases: (a) displaced, (b) motoric, and (c) competitive aggression. The constructive stage could also be broken down into (a) competitive, (b) collaborative, (c) productive construction, and (d) creative phases (L'Abate, 1979). The use of SEPs with functional and semifunctional couples and families in part helped the development of the theoretical models (summarized in the previous chapter) that encompass both functional and dysfunctional levels of interpersonal competence. The application of programmed materials helped to specify which individual terminants, for instance, depression and impulsivity, are in part responsible for family dysfunctionality.

The practice of the laboratory method, and the creation of a variety of pretherapeutic (i.e., SEPs) and paratherapeutic (i.e., programmed materials and workbooks) approaches have led to the consideration that, with these riches, we need to plan how to deliver services with some degree of structure. This structure is given by the concept of *successive sieves*.

Successive Sieves in Preventive and
Clinical Interventions with Families

On the basis of the theoretical and pragmatic frameworks presented above, and to elaborate on the discussion thus far, I submit the following model of interventions for all three types of prevention. This model is bidirectional, that is, movement from one type of prevention to another can take place according to the concept of *successive sieves*. For example, there are people (individuals, couples, and families) who, for whatever reason (level of functionality-dysfunctionality, educational and/or socioeconomic limits, family composition, stage of life cycle), cannot profit from primary prevention. They may need either secondary or tertiary prevention programs. The only way we have been able to find out, thus far, has been by seeing whether these people benefit from primary prevention efforts. If they are unable to learn and to profit from a primary prevention program, they will drop out. They may then profit from a secondary prevention approach. If not, it means that they are likely to need a tertiary prevention approach. Thus the movement from one sieve of intervention to another goes from primary, to secondary, and eventually to tertiary prevention efforts.

In the same way, there are people who, after the initial crisis and its reduction through tertiary prevention efforts *for the short term*, may be ready to learn from secondary and/or primary methods of prevention *for the long term*. As indicated in Chapter 1, families in need or in crisis cannot or are unable to learn from primary prevention efforts. They, therefore, need either secondary or tertiary methods. Thus, with families as well as with personnel, it is suggested that the concept of *successive sieves* be used in defining levels of functionality. This definition can be reached on the basis of how and how much a family can learn, retain, apprehend, and actually translate into everyday practice. Functional families learn faster and more efficiently, retaining more than dysfunctional families. The latter, once the initial level of dysfunctionality is reduced, can use and apply the new ways of relating to each other. Although, initially, a full-fledged professional may be necessary to help the family out of the crisis that brought them to seek professional help, less experienced personnel can take over to teach that family new and more positive ways of relating, through secondary and primary prevention approaches, as I (L'Abate, 1987) and coworkers have suggested.

The concept of successive sieves implies that there should be a two-way process in mental health delivery systems, going from primary and secondary to tertiary or from tertiary to secondary and then to primary. Excluding exceptional cases, and in the absence of a clear-cut crisis, with functional people we can start with the simpler, cheaper, and easier sieve, for instance, a primary prevention program. If we fail to help an individual, couple, or family using this approach, we should at least be able to understand how these people are functioning or malfunctioning. We may find that, indeed, they need a more crisis-oriented intervention, such as psychotherapy or an additional assignment of programmed materials to process at home. We can then progress to more complex, expensive, and time-consuming sieves. For instance, with the family of an alcoholic, we could start with mutual support groups, such as Alcoholics Anonymous, which costs practically nothing. If this sieve is not sufficient for either the index patient or the family, we could progress to a more expensive sieve, such as a social skills training program for partners or parents. If that approach is still not enough, we could try group therapy (including marital and family) and psychodrama, which are more expensive, perhaps, than social skills training programs, but less expensive than individual psychotherapy. These approaches are certainly less expensive than environmental modification, including medication, hospitalization, or incarceration.

The concept of successive sieves also applies to different phases of the treatment process in tertiary prevention. Families would go from an initial stage of crisis, followed by secondary stages of symptom reduction, conflict resolution, and finally reeducation. Once a family has reached a level of normalization, after the crisis has been successfully surmounted, most family therapists would consider that family cured and would claim lasting success. There is no question that, by going through these two stages, many family members may learn to consider each other as important and become more loving and more able to discuss and negotiate emotional issues. After the crisis and symptom reduction stages, they may now be able to show and share their love in more constructive ways, learning better ways to negotiate differences. This successful outcome may be reached, perhaps, at best by 33% of the families who receive therapy. What happens to the rest? What skills do they have or have they learned that will allow them to function on their own for the long term? Family therapy may have reduced the crisis. However, what resources and skills are available to the family to allow them to surmount future stresses? Many families who have terminated therapy could use an extra dose of skills training in the form of secondary or primary prevention approaches. Kochalka, Buzas, L'Abate, McHenry, and Gibson (1987) have shown that this process could take place in a mental health clinic. Once therapists felt they had completed their function, they would refer some families for enrichment programs administered by volunteers supervised by two graduate students who, in turn, were supervised by the program's author.

Thus the concept of successive sieves would mean going from tertiary to secondary and then primary prevention approaches for families in crisis. For at-risk families, or families who initially seem to be only at risk but not in need of additional help, the process would be reversed. Families that cannot benefit from primary prevention may receive available secondary and, if necessary, tertiary prevention approaches. They can go back to primary prevention once they have shown they can learn from either tertiary and/or secondary prevention. A summary of this approach is shown in Table 3.1.

TABLE 3.1: Successive Sieves in Preventive Approaches

Types of Prevention	Stages of Treatment	Approach to Be Used	Personnel Credentials
Tertiary	Crisis and/or symptom reduction	Emergency psychotherapy (medication); crisis-oriented programmed materials (Chapter 6)	Doctorate, board diplomate or equivalent degree of knowledge or experience
Secondary	Specific problems (i.e., impulsivity; problems in relationships)	Workbooks (Chapter 6)	Master's degree or equivalent degree of experience
Primary	General issues	Enrichment (Chapter 5)	Bachelor's degree or equivalent

Discussion

This view of successive sieves is not as farfetched as it may at first seem. Of course, if one has not considered different types of prevention with different types of personnel, this view may appear not only farfetched but alien. However, if one conceives of multiple methods of intervention—primary, secondary, and tertiary—working synergistically with each other, then this view appears not only logical and practical but even necessary. Marlatt (1988, p. 479) has suggested a *stages of change* perspective in dealing with addictions, which shows some similarities with the successive sieves view: "The basic idea is that individuals proceed through a series of relatively discrete stages in the change process." He suggested four successive stages: (a) precontemplation, prior to any consideration of change; (b) contemplation, or motivation and commitment to change; (c) an active attempt to change; and (d) a maintenance stage to keep up with whatever changes have taken place thus far. Marlatt (1988, p. 479) viewed the "stages of change model as applicable to addiction treatment *regardless* of the type of interventions employed." In addition to this model, Marlatt suggested how matching strategies should be applied at every stage of the change process. This suggestion, translated into the language and views of this book, means that we need to individualize primary, secondary, and tertiary interventions to the specific and particular needs of individuals, couples, and families using a hierarchy of personnel with specialized skills.

This important issue of matching intervention strategies with clients' needs will be considered in the next chapter. We do not currently have norms and profiles to allow predictions about which family will profit from which type of prevention. With time and effort, through painstaking pre- and postintervention evaluations, we should be able to amass sufficient data to allow this kind of discrimination to take place on the basis of objective judgments. For the time being, however, we have no choice but to let this discrimination take place on the basis of what families can do, do, and want to do. We should make options available to them so that with our help they can discriminate and choose according to their needs and wants, including choosing not to receive any help from any source and paying for the consequences thereafter.

To conclude, we have discussed a two-way process, going from primary, to secondary, and when necessary, to tertiary prevention. And families who are no longer in crisis after tertiary prevention could benefit from secondary and primary prevention. After proposing this model, at least one practical issue arises. Where are these families to receive primary and secondary prevention? Thus far, these approaches have taken place haphazardly, erratically, and on a limited basis. In comparison with the number of therapists, there are very few individuals trained in primary and secondary prevention, especially when we consider that there is a much greater percentage of families at risk and in need than there are in crisis. Where is a family to go? After becoming aware of this crucial issue, it is obvious that a structure is needed for leadership in primary and secondary prevention, especially in dealing with marriage, the most crucial factor in family life (Chapter 8).

Lower costs and increased effectiveness for most mental health practices are possible if we want to build human "skyscrapers" using a variety of human skills and competencies with different tools and instruments rather than with our hands. Thus far, the job has been mainly restricted to professionals who have been trying to deal with limited solutions (i.e., psychotherapy) for large-scale problems (i.e., trying to build a skyscraper with their bare hands). A prevention approach cannot afford to take such a restrictive (and expensive) view of service delivery. To accomplish our goal of prevention, and to deal with large-scale human and social problems (let us not forget the 28 million adult children of alcoholics), we need a variety of personnel at various levels of education, interpersonal skill, and motivation, according to a hierarchy of skills and responsibilities.

Consequently, the relationship between a developmental theory of interpersonal competence in the family and the laboratory method can take place according to three different possibilities, as follows.

(1) There is no relationship between theory and method—one is independent of the other. However, method may facilitate the finding of results and the creation of hypotheses that may, eventually, have a bearing (pro or con) on the theory; that is, empirical results may be related inferentially—positively or negatively—to a theory.

(2) There is some relationship, mostly indirect, between theory and method, primarily through logical inference rather than through empirical results. For instance, the theory could be evaluated through paper-and-pencil tests that are completely independent of it. One could use a test to measure ability to love and to negotiate created either before or independent from the theory. Or one could use the paper-and-pencil tests developed by Foá and Foá (1974) for their theory of resource exchange from which the present theory was partially derived.

(3) There may be a direct relationship between theory and method, in the sense that a method can be used to test (i.e., to verify) a theory or to test parts or derivations (i.e., hypotheses) of the theory. We will see that a theory can be evaluated and tested not only through evaluative instruments but also through specifically designed interventions (Chapters 5 and 6).

Table 3.2 shows how the theory described in the previous chapter is evaluated through various approaches. As this table indicates, the interventional *outcome* of a particular method of prevention can be measured through paper-and-pencil tests, while the *process* of intervention can be evaluated through content analyses of transcripts or videotapes of family interactions. These analyses could use the models of the theory to score the transcripts. Outcome and process, of course, can also be evaluated through theory-independent paper-and-pencil tests and content analyses.

Interventionally, the theory can be tested using a comparison of outcomes between theory-independent and theory-derived enrichment programs in primary prevention or in secondary prevention, using workbooks that were written independent of the theory compared with workbooks derived from the theory itself. The relationship between theory and the laboratory method to evaluate the theory is also explicated in Table 3.2 and will be elaborated in the next three chapters.

Conclusion

This chapter has introduced the laboratory method as a way of linking the practice of prevention with research through SOPs in evaluation and preventive interventions. These procedures can be

TABLE 3.2: Testing a Theory of Developmental Competence Through the Laboratory Method

Abilities	Models of Skills and Resources	Verifications and Applications		
		Evaluatively and/or Processually	Interventionally (prevention)	
			Primary	Secondary
Being or Presence	Love caring, seeing the good, for- giveness, intimacy	Paper-and- pencil tests; Content analyses	Structured enrichment programs (Chapter 5)	Programmed materials; workbooks (Chapter 6)
	Status self-ful- ness, self- ishness, selfless- ness, no self	Chapter 4	Chapter 5	Chapter 6
Doing or Perfor- mance	Information	Questionnaire	Interviews	(L'Abate, 1986b)
	Services	—	—	—
Having or Production	Goods	—	—	—
	Money	—	—	—

delegated to a hierarchy of personnel at various levels of skills, interests, and competencies. This method allows us to reach more families at risk, in need, or in crisis than would be possible through traditional evaluative and therapeutic methods in the hands of pro- fessionals. This method is also cost-effective, allowing the combina- tion of theory and preventive practices, evaluation with prevention, and practice with research. Before we go any further, however, we will need to show how evaluation is crucial in primary and second- ary prevention as well as, of course, in tertiary prevention.

4

The Importance of Evaluation

How are we going to demonstrate that prevention has long-term effects? Thus far, some primary prevention programs have been able to show short-term effects (Bond & Wagner, 1988). However, with the exception of Head Start and the programs reviewed by Price, Cowen, Lorion, and Ramos-McKay (1989), most primary prevention programs have failed to show long-term effects (L'Abate, 1986a). This failure is not due to the programs themselves, because effects may have occurred; however, there was not sufficient evidence to show whether these effects really existed in the long run. Why have these programs failed to show long-term results? Because whoever designed them (including me) was not thinking and planning ahead and evaluating not only to show short-term but also to demonstrate long-term outcomes, using, at the very least, another control group. Furthermore, many primary prevention programs have failed to evaluate their effects even at the very outset of program administration.

Of course, this relative lack of evidence for long-term outcome is not unique to primary and secondary prevention. For those readers who are acquainted with the outcome of psychotherapy (Garfield, 1986), only a third of all the individuals, couples, and families who have undergone some type of psychotherapy can claim long-term results. One-third may show some relatively small, short-term effects. The other third fails to show any effect and, in fact, may show some deterioration. This outcome demonstrates that the medium of psychotherapy cannot boast a great deal of efficiency or cost-effectiveness. Human nature is too variable and too complex to be changed by just one method or medium.

How could this failure in producing widespread positive outcomes be possible? We must consider the inadequate state of assessment and evaluation in the mental health field. We do not lack of measures. In fact, we have an embarrassment of riches in that regard (L'Abate & Bagarozzi, in press). We do, however, lack professional attitudes and practices in regard to SOP evaluation of treatment. Thus far, evaluation has taken place mostly through the subjective experience of professionals or through the consensus of subjective impressions of groups of professionals, as happens in many staff meetings in mental health clinics and hospitals every day. In some cases, this subjectivity is bolstered by fiat, by strong convictions, or by the status of the highest-ranking professional in the meeting. Subjective judgments are important and could be acceptable if and *only if* they are augmented, bolstered, and substantiated by additional, objectively acquired information.

Of course, in the mental health field, *subjectively impressionistic* and *objectively valid*, are relative terms, given that no absolute criterion in either direction or extreme is possible. Evaluation, as a whole, therefore, is either avoided altogether or, at best, given little or no value by most mental health practitioners. This avoidance of or diminished importance given to evaluation is usually rationalized, and often correctly, as being either irrelevant to the treatment process or useless in evaluating change. Professionals argue that changes in behavior are multidimensional and cannot be comprehensively measured by any single test—hence the need for batteries of tests, as indicated in the previous chapter.

Past rationalizations have also focused on the possible dangers of evaluation to the therapeutic relationship, possibly weakening or distorting it. No evidence, of course, is presented to support these biases. Consequently, it might be helpful to briefly consider the status of current evaluative practices in the major theoretical schools as well as in the various mental health professions and therapeutic approaches.

Evaluation in Traditional
Mental Health Disciplines

Theoretical viewpoints have been some of the major stumbling blocks in the practice of evaluation. After all, most theories, once institutionalized, provide the basis for training, which influences the thinking of future practitioners of a particular school. Consequently, one way of tracing the degree of importance or unimportance of evaluation is to review evaluation practices in the four major theoretical ideologies that have influenced the most mental health practices in the last half century.

Major Schools of Thought

The four major theoretical viewpoints that have influenced thinking as well as practices are, in order of historical development, (a) psychoanalysis, (b) humanism; (c) behaviorism, and (d) systems thinking. All these schools have developed their own specific brand of evaluation. For instance, psychoanalysis developed the historical interview, making an individual's past history the major source of information for evaluation. History still remains the most important datum available to us. Unfortunately, historical information is difficult to reduce to quantitative dimensions. In terms of interventions, the past cannot be changed. We can only help people change their perceptions and memories of past hurts and traumas.

Humanism, on the other hand, emphasizes the individual's present perceptions of reality. His or her phenomenological feelings about reality are the most important source of information about that individual. History is not as important as the present and the future, in terms of an individual's aspirations and goals. Again, this kind of information is difficult, although not impossible, to reduce to quantitative dimensions, unless one uses an objective way of measuring clients' affective reactions. However, evaluation is seen by the humanistic school as a mechanistic way of putting down individuals and not relating to them emotionally. In fact, any form of objective evaluation is scorned as irrelevant, useless, and even dangerous to the needs of the patient or client. Human relations are like art, and the aesthetic experience of psychotherapy cannot be ruined by what is tantamount to an engineering approach that would diminish the subtlety and delicacy of the human experience.

Behaviorists sought to develop their own ways of measuring reinforcement values using clear-cut, objectively observable behaviors rather than nonquantifiable historical information or self-report paper-and-pencil questionnaires of questionable relationship to external behavior. Furthermore, tests and questionnaires were based on group norms that were seen as antithetical to a single-subject-as-its-own control methodology. In spite of criticisms leveled at traditional psychometric criteria and standards, eventually behaviorists, working especially with couples, developed their own special blend of self-report, paper-and-pencil tests of the very kind they had originally criticised (L'Abate & Bagarozzi, in press). Eventually, they (or at least some of them) came to realize that information obtained from self-report did not have to correlate with external behavior to be valid or useful.

Finally, systems thinking avoided objective evaluation because traditional assessment practices cannot capture the circular and complex nature of family transactions. They are too linear and do not accurately reflect the recursivity and circular nature of behavior. At best, a videotape of the family's therapy sessions is sufficient to illustrate the way a particular family functions. Nothing else is necessary, because no kind of objective evaluation would be valid, according to the theory. The therapist is ultimately the final authority in arriving at a satisfactory evaluation, a position also shared in both psychoanalysis and humanism.

Apparently, behaviorism is the only mental health school that has emphasized the importance of evaluation and direct observation of behavior in vivo, even though some of its practitioners may have given up this practice in favor of more indirect measures. Thus we must conclude that three out of four mental health ideologies have failed to provide a rationale as well as background training in evaluative practices. How about the mental health professions?

Professions

Psychiatry uses historical information and present status to reach a diagnosis, which, according to traditional medical practices, would dictate the kind of treatment a psychiatrist would administer. This practice may work well in the administration of medication. However, the analogy of medical practices with psychotherapy falls flat. It has been virtually impossible, thus far, to match evaluation with a specific course of psychological treatment. Of course, many psychiatrists and even nonmedical psychotherapists may claim they do just that, that is, individualize treatment to an individual's specific needs. No evidence, however, is available to support this position, as far as I know, because such claims are based on spoken words without a record to back them up.

Clinical psychology developed historically ancillary to psychiatry, in particular, to give to it psychodiagnostic evaluations based on the administration of objective and projective tests (L'Abate, 1964). As clinical psychology progressed to an independent profession, it became more and more involved in the psychotherapeutic enterprise. It adopted the same stance of the psychiatric and psychotherapeutic professions, avoiding the objective evaluation of therapeutic outcomes as an SOP. Although trained in testing, statistics, and research design, most clinical psychologists, when doing evaluation for another referring source, usually do not get the chance to reevaluate the same individual after treatment has taken place. Without reevaluation, we lose important information about the validity and reliability of the original baseline evaluation, altogether avoiding the importance of both criteria as well as whether or not the intervention was effective.

Although clinical psychology is the only mental health profession that prides itself on training its students in statistical and research techniques for the completion of a doctoral dissertation, this training apparently does not seem to be used after the doctorate is obtained. Many clinical psychologists, especially those who become involved in the therapeutic enterprise, give up their scientific training for the more human aspects of their practice, denying and often rejecting the very professional identification they bear. Thus we cannot even rely on clinical psychology to use evaluation as an SOP to apply to lifelong professional practices.

Social work has usually followed, perhaps too uncritically, traditional psychiatric ideologies and practices, making history, with little else added to it, the mainstay of evaluation. Some social workers have suggested home visits as an additional form of evaluation, but no objective data were gathered from this approach. The lack of

statistical knowledge and applications makes this profession one of
the most resistant to evaluative practices, which are seen as an
invasion of privacy for the practitioner as well as for the client.
Counselors and pastoral counselors are not usually trained in evaluation. When they are, they would probably not have the statistical
background to understand basic principles of standardization and
application. Thus we cannot expect this profession to do better
than the larger and more established mental health professions that
have preceded it.

If evaluation is deemed unnecessary or irrelevant by theoretical
ideologies and professions, what about evaluative practices among
the various therapeutic modalities? Can we hope that here we will
find what we are looking for?

Therapeutic Modalities

Unfortunately, there is no need even to consider the various
therapeutic modalities, such as individual, marital, group, and family therapies or even the precursor of primary prevention with families, family life education. None of these approaches uses evaluation as an SOP. Thus we arrive at another melancholic conclusion:
*Evaluative practices in traditional mental health disciplines have been
either inadequate or inadequately followed by most practitioners.* What
should we do to convince ourselves that evaluation is crucial for a
variety of reasons? Should we wait for a legislative mandate? Why
should we evaluate, especially in primary and secondary prevention?

The Purposes of Evaluation

No matter how and how much we may rationalize the need for
evaluation, it is doubtful whether any amount of reasoning, logic,
or even evidence will help change existing evaluative practices. The
main argument in favor of unrelenting and continuous evaluation
as an SOP lies in how and how much we want primary and secondary prevention to progress. It would be an absolute disaster if
these two fields were to follow existing (really nonexisting) evaluation practices of the tertiary prevention field. Without consistent
and routine evaluation, the fields of primary and secondary pre-

vention will be relegated to just another fad in the mental health armamentarium.

Identification and Selection of Families

The first goal and most important reason for evaluation is to identify and select individuals, couples, or families who would benefit from (a) the type of prevention (primary, secondary, or tertiary) appropriate to them and (b) the approach within each type of prevention that would be even more appropriate. This diagnostic goal is a very difficult one to achieve. However, unless we can achieve it, we will be helping people in need of help without a specific direction (the blind leading the blind). As we discussed in Chapter 1, we need to develop objective criteria to distinguish among families at risk, in need, and in crisis. Although families in crisis may be easy to identify, because they present themselves for professional help, this is not a sufficient criterion to evaluate degree of disturbance. There is tremendous variability among families in what behaviors are perceived as troublesome and in need of professional help. A behavior that one family considers troublesome may not be so for another family. In the same way, a large number of families who could be considered in crisis by an external observer, might not, however, agree with that external evaluation. This, for example, may be the case for court-mandated treatment for families who equate being referred for psychological treatment with being "crazy." What makes one family want to receive treatment while another family, probably even more disturbed according to external criteria, refuses it? Why do so many families who are mandated into treatment either refuse it or resist it? We do not know as yet. We need to discriminate *before treatment* which family would profit from which form of treatment by which therapist or preventer and at what price (L'Abate, 1969).

Identification and selection of families for any type of intervention are based on the following information: (a) developmental history (individual, couple, and family) as well as stage of the family life cycle (which can be quantified); (b) present situation and demographic information (quantifiable); and (c) interviewer's subjective impressions (which can be reduced to an objective rating). However, none of this information can serve as a baseline to measure improvement unless one uses clients' and interviewers' objective ratings.

Establishing Baseline Data

The second reason to evaluate is to establish objective baseline measures repeatable from one setting to another and from one family to another. These measures are necessary to assess whether any changes have taken place as a result of treatment. Most evaluation methods used thus far, for instance, the history of the individual, couple, or family, cannot be used as a comparative baseline to evaluate (a) outcome before and after treatment and (b) other families who have or have not received the same or another type of treatment. In other words, to find out which family will benefit from which level of prevention (and which specific approach within each level), we need to evaluate families *before and after* preventive interventions, because the outcome of an intervention provides crucial information about who profits the most and who profits the least from that intervention. Without this kind of knowledge, we would never be able to match specific forms of treatment with the specific needs of each family. Without evaluation as an SOP of treatment, therefore, we will never be able to find out which preventive approach works with which families or determine which approach works better than other approaches.

Ultimately, an objective evaluation, *in addition to* interviews and subjectively impressionistic inferences and conclusions, must consist of standardized, objective tests of established validity and reliability to use to compare and contrast, and as controls for, different individuals, groups, and families on a *before-after intervention basis*. The importance of objective evaluations for families in the field of prevention has been emphasized by many authors (Hermalin & Morell, 1981, 1987; Hermalin & Weirich, 1983; Hess & Hermalin, 1983; Kelly, 1970; Kelly & Hess, 1986; L'Abate, 1985a, 1986a; L'Abate & Bagarozzi, in press; L'Abate & Wagner, 1985, 1988; Lorion, 1983; Powell, 1987; Price & Smith, 1985; Price, Ketterer, Bader, & Monahan, 1980; Seitz, 1987; Zautra, Bachrach, & Hess, 1983; Zigler & Freeman, 1987). However, all of these exhortations remain meaningless unless we can conclude—some would say somewhat harshly—that there should not be primary and secondary prevention *without* pre-post evaluation. Prevention without evaluation would be a complete waste of time and effort because we would never be able to determine whether any changes had taken place.

Specification of Preventive Interventions

Another argument in favor of evaluation is the importance of the comparative evaluation of theories and methods of prevention, that is, which theory and which method are "better" than competing theories and methods. *Better* is a relative term that can be evaluated by assessing the final comparative outcome between approaches as well as their comparative costs. In addition to the preliminary interview, evaluation can occur through paper-and-pencil, self-report tests, which may vary in relationship to a theory.

Up to now we have considered evaluation for accountability, that is: the measurement of change and progress after intervention. However, another purpose of evaluation is to verify a theory through content analyses of family transactions. Again, these analyses could be (a) *theory derived*, such as content analyses of family interactions coded according to the ARC, ERAAwC, and Priorities Models (Chapter 2); (b) *theory related*, such as content analyses conceivably developed either from the Foás' models or from some other related theory; or (c) *theory independent*, as discussed in Chapter 2.

The Need for Prescriptive Instruments

Thus far in the progress of the mental health enterprise, we could argue that most tests developed for assessment and evaluation have been based on *description* rather than on *prescription*. Evaluation has been used to understand and describe dimensions deemed relevant theoretically, empirically, or clinically. However, it seemed impossible to link evaluation with therapy or with other forms of interventions. As Hayes, Nelson, and Jarrett (1987, p. 964) have noted, in the past, traditional evaluation was not directed toward "treatment utility": "An assessment device, distinction, or strategy has its own kind of utility if it can be shown that treatment outcome is positively influenced by this device, distinction, or strategy." Consequently, most psychometric criteria failed to consider this dimension as relevant to the design, validation, and standard-ization of assessment devices.

Evaluation was deemed irrelevant and will continue to be irrele-vant to the treatment process as long as the major if not the only modality of treatment, psychotherapy, relies on the spoken word. Once new pre- and paratherapeutic methods to intervene with individuals, couples, and families based on the written word have been created (Chapters 5 and 6), it becomes possible to construct new instruments with *prescriptive* rather than solely *descriptive* bases. Examples of such instruments are presented here to illustrate the applications and implications of this approach. It is now indeed possible to create *prescriptive* rather than just *descriptive* assessment instruments.

A recent survey has amply demonstrated (L'Abate & Bagarozzi, in press) that most instruments for marriage and family evaluation, including traditional individually oriented instruments, are mainly and strictly descriptive, that is, they stress the importance of under-standing and describing individual, marital, and family dimen-sions, conflict areas, and interaction patterns. However, none of these instruments, no matter how well standardized and validated, leads directly into linking either theory with therapy or evaluation with treatment. Up to now, psychotherapeutic treatment has taken place without any clear or direct links between theory or evalua-tion and interventions:

> To date, the role of treatment utility has been buried by conceptual confu-sion, poorly articulated methods, and inappropriate linkage to structural psychometric criteria. . . . Treatment utility research has been hindered by nonspecific types of therapy, nonspecific types of assessment, unnecessary divisions between the role of assessor and therapist, and an overemphasis on technique over conceptual advancement. (Hayes, Nelson, & Jarrett, 1987, p. 973)

In considering the literature on individually, dyadically, or fam-ily-oriented tests (L'Abate & Bagarozzi, in press), we found that very few instruments are oriented toward the measurement of change per se on idiographic (i.e., individual) bases. Most instru-ments were based on nomothetic (i.e., group norm) bases. One exception to this conclusion is the Goal Attainment Scale (Kiresuk & Sherman, 1968). However, this scale, although useful and oriented toward the measurement of change, is rather complex to learn, not easy to score, and difficult to interpret.

Furthermore, as long as treatment is based on the spoken word, it is difficult to find which factors lead to a successful therapeutic outcome and which do not. We need instruments to use with individuals, couples, or families. These instruments should, at the same time, also be *nomothetic*, that is, yielding normative data, as well as *idiographic*, that is, providing information that is specific to each individual, couple, or family. Of course, they should also be designed to evaluate degree and type of functionality-dysfunctionality as well as the process of change. In addition to being relevant to the assessment of change, they should be easy to administer, score, and interpret.

Consequently, new instruments that attempt to fulfill most if not all of the foregoing requirements have been created. Research on the basic psychometric requirements, such as validity and reliability, is still in progress (see Chapter 6).

In addition to background demographic and baseline information, as exemplified by instruments like the Social Information Form and the Self-Profile Chart, it is now possible to design instruments that would provide more specific links between evaluation and treatment, once we design new ways of intervening with individuals, couples, and families. After these new ways of intervening have been developed, it will be possible to design new evaluation instruments with that purpose in mind, *provided one uses the written rather than the oral medium in therapy* (L'Abate, 1986b, 1987, in press; L'Abate & Cox, in press). When the spoken word is the main or only medium of dialogue and exchange between two or more individuals—client(s) and therapist—it becomes extremely expensive to reduce what is going on between them to meaningful patterns. For instance, it may take up to 28 hours to type and code 1 hour of therapy. Even when some verbal control is achieved by structuring the relationship, there are still myriad intervening variables that cannot be controlled. Even when we can establish control, trying to chart and process the interaction is costly and time-consuming.

On the other hand, when we use the written word as the main and, under certain conditions, the only medium of exchange between clients and therapists, a variety of possibilities emerge. First of all, a variety of subtle interpersonal variables that may interfere with the treatment of certain clients are eliminated. Second, the whole process can be recorded and reported without having to add or remove anything. Third, once the feasibility and usefulness of this process is established, it will be possible to use the written medium synergistically with the spoken word when necessary. Fourth, the written word can be reproduced cheaply and in quantity, becoming, therefore, a cost-effective medium when used appropriately. Examples of such instruments, still undergoing validation, will illustrate what can be done when writing, rather than speaking, becomes the preferred medium of therapeutic structuring.

Theory-Independent Instruments

This section consists of test instruments that are neither derived from nor are related to a developmental theory of interpersonal competence. How is this discrimination possible? Is it possible for an instrument to be theory independent? The answer is affirmative. Most tests are theory-free, just like many other instruments of evaluation. Most traditional diagnostic instruments, like the Rorschach inkblots, for instance, are theory independent. Even the MMPI, based on traditional psychiatric nosology, is not based on a theory of psychopathology. It aims to describe, not to explain or prescribe. Thus an instrument can be defined as theory-free when it aims to describe, in a pragmatic manner, without guidance from or relationship to a theory. It can be considered to be theory derived when it is used to validate the particular theory from which it was derived.

Social Information Form

To measure past history and developmental background, the Social Information Form consists of 85 items about past and present living conditions and perceptions of family relationships, past and present. On the basis of weights for most of the items, the user arrives at one total score that gives a quantitative assessment of the individual's background and past level of adjustment. The higher the score, the higher the level of competence in the individual. This test, of course, cannot prescribe. However, it is useful in measuring the degree of functionality-dysfunctionality. And it cannot be used to assess therapeutic or preventive outcome, as it is based on perceptions of past events. It can be substituted for an interview, quantifying usually subjective impressions for interviewers (L'Abate & Cox, in press).

The Family Profile Form

This instrument is derived from work with structured enrichment programs for functional, at risk, and semifunctional—in need but not critical or clinical—couples and families. These programs, concerning 50 marriage- and family-relevant topics, consist of three to ten lessons per program and three to eight exercises per lesson. Although these exercises have been designed to be administered by trainers relying on reading instructions for each family, they could also conceivably be administered in a written, programmed format as a paratherapeutic addition in secondary prevention. They can be administered by paraprofessional personnel, trainers, or enrichers instructed to read instructions from the manual verbatim but not mechanically. Consequently, a trainer can select programs and/or lessons that are appropriate and specific to the stated and observed needs of a given couple or family. For years this selection was made on the basis of matching the couple's or family's perceived needs and the trainer's perceptions with program titles and the index of lesson topics. Pre-post evaluation batteries were administered as an SOP. However, none of the test batteries used over the years directly links the evaluation and the selection of programs, lessons, or exercises specific to the couple or family's needs (L'Abate & Young, 1987). The process of selecting a program, lessons, or exercises, therefore, was cumbersome, strictly subjective, and based on the whim of the trainer and/or the supervisor. How can one select from hundreds of lessons and among literally thousands of exercises?

The process of selecting programs, lessons, and especially exercises was not sufficiently specific and objective to be satisfactory. It depended a great deal on the clinical experience and knowledge of the supervisor who helped trainers select specific programs, lessons, and/or exercises. Because not objective, it was not readily reproducible and transmittable to others. The problem then became one of finding out whether we could make the process of selection more specific and more objective at the level of the exercises rather than just at the level of the programs and lessons. Therefore, my students and I started to classify and code these exercises. As this attempt at classification progressed, we were able to come up with objective rules for decisions that allowed seemingly reliable discrimination and allocation of exercises into nine functional, different, and nonoverlapping categories: (a) brainstorming, (b) description, (c) evaluation, (d) negotiation, (e) play, (f) reflection, (g) role taking, (h) self-expression, and (i) touching (L'Abate & Weinstein, 1987, pp. 498–499). Although the reliability of these discrimination rules was not computed quantitatively, an informal, separate classification of exercises by two judges (Steven Weinstein and me) yielded a 90% to 100% agreement between us. Because an evident bias is possible here, the reliability of these decision rules still needs to be established quantitatively.

Once these nine categories were used to classify all of the exercises, it became possible to generate items (136 to be exact) to tap into the nine dimensions. Family members can describe their family on each item on a five-point Lickert-type scale and can, by either consensus or disagreement, indicate which of the nine dimensions are more problematic to them than the others. On the basis of the identification of such dimensions, it is now possible to prescribe which among the more than 1, 000 available exercises can be specifically administered to improve the reported area of conflict or perceived deficit (L'Abate & Weinstein, 1987, pp. 471–476). Research to validate this instrument is now in progress (Kochalka, n.d.).

The Adjustment Inventory

This instrument was developed a few years ago with the same goal in mind, that is, to serve as a multipurpose instrument to be used with individuals, couples, families, or groups. It is a versatile instrument that can be used as a structured interview to assess areas of dissatisfaction in individuals, couples, or families, arriving at a quantitative score sensitive to present conditions and to any possible changes that may take place with intervention. It is easy to administer either on a self-report basis or as a structured interview (L'Abate & McHenry, 1983, p. 378). It was preliminarily validated recently by Hall (1987). It consists of filling in three areas of dissatisfaction, the respondent's choice, or those already preselected, for instance, personal, marital, and parental. After these three areas are selected, three specific unsatisfactory behaviors need to be listed for each area, plus one extra behavior unrelated to the nine previous ones. These ten behaviors are then ranked in order of importance for change from 10 to 1 and then given an emotional rating from –5 to +5 (without 0). By multiplying and then adding the rankings with the ratings, one obtains a total number (usually negative) that indicates the present level of dissatisfaction. This instrument, therefore, is nomothetic in relying on established norms. It is also idiographic because it specifies which behaviors need to be changed in a particular individual, couple, or family.

Once we have gathered workbooks reduced from existing self-help books, they will be classified into three different areas of personhood, partnership, and parenting. Respondents will be able to choose which three areas of dissatisfaction to select in the Adjustment Inventory. From their rankings, we can then select whatever programmed materials or workbook(s) seem more appropriate on the basis also of specified troublesome behaviors.

An Empirically Derived Test: The MMPI

In the same way, using programmed materials and workbooks, an old testing standby, the Minnesota Multiphasic Personality Inventory (MMPI), can be used as in the example given above. Thus far, we have administered three appropriate workbooks on the basis of high scores on depression (Scale 2), impulsivity (Scale 4), and anxiety (Scale 8). Consequently, even the MMPI can become a prescriptive test provided we have corresponding written programs for each of the clinical scales. We have also completed 15 different workbooks based on the 15 new factor-pure scales of its revision, the MMPI-2 (L'Abate & Cox, in press).

Theory-Derived Instruments

The following instruments were designed specifically to test a developmental theory of interpersonal competence. They are additions to a previous series of verbal and visual test batteries developed to evaluate past versions of the theory (L'Abate, 1976; L'Abate & Wagner, 1985, 1988).

Self-Profile Chart

To assess self-related views that may reveal some information about the individual's sense of self-importance, the Self-Profile Chart is a quick way to assess how an individual perceives him- or herself past, present, and future: how he or she was, as he or she is, and as he or she would like to be. It takes a few minutes to answer and it is easy to score. Eventually, the Self-Profile Chart may be linked to treatment, if written lessons or programs for the major dimensions resulting from this evaluation will be developed.

The Problems in Relationships Test

In the process of developing a theory-derived workbook for couples, a prescriptive instrument came into being, the Problems in Relationships Test (L'Abate & Fresh, n.d.). The model of status or self-definition in the developmental theory of interpersonal competence (Chapter 2) deals with the attribution of importance to self and to other (mate, parent, child, friend, and so on). This *attribution of self-importance* is the cornerstone of self-definition, or status. From this attribution of importance four different possibilities were derived: (a) *self-fulness,* (b) *selflessness,* (c) *selfishness,* and (d) *no-self.*

Consequently, we summarized most marital problems into 20 conflictful and polarized dimensions (dominant-submissive, weak-strong, and so on) that furnish the bases for the Problems in Relationships Test, (L'Abate & Fresh, n.d.) and the development of a parallel workbook, in which lessons correspond to the 20 dimensions measured by the test (L'Abate & Cox, in press). To validate this model and obtain normative data on the nature and limits (validity and reliability) of this model, a paper-and-pencil, true-false questionnaire was constructed along the 20 dimensions of polarization mentioned above. With at least 3 items for each of the four possibilities (self-fulness, selfishness, selflessness, and no-self) and 20 dimensions, the resulting 240-item test will be validated with various measures of self-esteem, self-concept, narcissism, altruism, and marital conflict.

To achieve this goal, we will evaluate the nomological network of correlations of this test with other paper-and-pencil tests purporting to measure the same or overlapping domains, such as the Rosenberg and the Steffenmeyer Self-Esteem Scales and the Minnesota Multiphasic Personality Inventory (MMPI). We will then evaluate whether the predicted polarization in the 20 dimensions are greater in clinical and conflictual versus nonclinical and nonconflictual couples. With this test, it is now possible to identify which among the 20 dimensions are the most troublesome in a couple, ranking them from the most to the least conflictful. Then the couple can have administered just those lessons that correspond to their most conflictful dimensions. In this fashion, we have a nomothetic method in the test and in the workbook. However, the identification of the most conflictful dimensions for each couple and the administration of the specific matching lessons to each couple is ideographic, that is, these lessons would fit the specific problem areas reported by each couple.

Among the many hypotheses derived from use of this test, which could lead to an evaluation of the validity of the original model, the major one deals with the prediction that most (approximately 40%) men in past and current American society have been socialized for *selfishness*, while more women (approximately 40%) have been socialized for *selflessness*, with important consequences and implications for gender differences, personality development, marital conflict and divorce, and psychopathology. The defective attribution of self-importance, as reflected in selflessness and selfishness, results in many conflicts between the sexes, especially in polarization within couples along a variety of dimensions that may vary from one couple to another. Selfish men tend to attract and to be attracted by selfless women, producing children who follow the same sex role identifications. Boys (approximately four out of ten) tend to follow in the footsteps of selfish fathers, while girls (approximately four out of ten) model their selfless mothers. One out of ten boys and one out of ten girls will show a reversal in this trend and model after the parent of the opposite sex. This model also yields information that might be useful in understanding sex role identification, socialization practices, and the rate of conflict and divorce experienced in the United States today.

From the hypotheses to be tested with this test, three representative examples follow: (a) The more reactive (i.e., clinical) couples would show lower levels of self-esteem (Rosenberg and Steffenmeyer) and more indications of individual dysfunctionality on the MMPI than nonclinical, nonreactive couples; (b) Ss, mostly males, with high scores on Scale 4 (impulsivity) of the MMPI tend to show higher scores on selfishness than on selflessness, while Ss, mostly females, with high scores on Scale 2 (depression), tend to score higher on selflessness than on selfishness; (c) scores on the selfishness dimensions would correlate positively with measures of narcissism (Emmons, 1989) and negatively with measures of depression.

This research is part of a larger project designed to assess the validity of a developmental theory of interpersonal competence (Chapter 2). Findings from research validating earlier versions of this theory have already been published (L'Abate & Wagner, 1985, 1988; Stevens & L'Abate, 1989). Assessing whether this test is valid in its correlations with other established tests that have been designed to measure the same dimension should enable us to validate this and other models of the theory. If the models show a modicum of validity, then the theory on which these models are based might be partially validated.

Problems in Relationships Test Semantic Differential

The Problems in Relationships Test, described above, attempts to measure dimensions of polarization in relationships indirectly; that is, the respondent is not aware of the overt purpose of the questions being asked. A more direct way of finding out how each partner views the relationship along the 20 dimensions of polarization is evaluated according to a semantic differential format, in which two antonyms define each dimension. Each partner rates self and partner on each of the 20 dimensions according to a seven-point scale. In this way, we would be able to assess the relationship between directly and indirectly measuring the same dimensions of polarization.

Interventionally, we would need to find agreement between these two sources of information, the Problems in Relationships Test and the semantic differential before administering the lessons appropriate to the more conflictful dimensions. Here the method— the semantic differential—is independent of the theory. However, the 20 dimensions of polarization are related to as well as derived from the theory, because we expect that the greatest degree of conflict takes place between partners polarized along the selfish-selfless self-definitions.

Conclusion

Without evaluation, primary and secondary prevention will not go forward, because both fields would repeat the same errors made by previous mental health movements. Without evaluation, prevention would remain a fad rather than a credible, respectable approach and, eventually, a respected profession. Prevention would not progress as fast as it can, or should, because it would lack the empirical base for its enterprise as shown in other, more established disciplines. Unfortunately, evaluation might not take place routinely unless it is mandated, either by the profession of prevention (if and when there is one), in its ethical and professional practices as well as in its training curricula, or by consumers, insurance companies, the federal government, or the public in general. In principle and in practice, there is no reason that the same prescriptive approach illustrated above cannot be developed with other existing evaluative instruments, once the domain of treatment is specified, as in the examples of structured enrichment programs or programmed materials and workbooks. Once treatment methods are based on the written rather than the spoken word, it will be possible to create and adopt them as pre- and paratherapeutic interventions to help individuals, couples, and families at risk, in need, and in crisis. Given any evaluative instrument, it is now possible to construct a self-administered, self-instructional program or workbook derived from the same dimension, as we have done with three clinical scales of the old MMPI and with the new factor scales of MMPI-2.

5

Structured Enrichment Programs

Primary prevention deals with families at risk and a few, select families in need. It does not, should not, and cannot deal with families in crisis. *Families at risk* are defined by the theory presented here as being made up of members characterized by a certain degree of self-fulness, where there are more victories than defeats (L'Abate, 1985d). They are able to show and share hurts and are available emotionally to each other in times of stress. They take responsibility for their actions and are free, open, and spontaneous in the expression of feelings. Their styles are mainly conductive, with little repetitive reactivity and no abuse or apathy. They are able to negotiate issues efficiently and with a minimum of stress. How can they be distinguished from families in need, that are, semifunctional?

What Is Functional and
Semifunctional in Families?

It is unfortunate that we generalize to families according to certain negative qualities or, oftentimes, just one characteristic, for example, families of alcoholic individuals may be called alcoholic families, or a person who is blind is called blind, according to the deficit and liability rather than according to strengths. Consequently, we become trapped by our linguistic habits in trying to separate functional from dysfunctional families. Functionality may

126

be the absence of dysfunctionality or the presence of positive qualities that together make a family function "better" than other families. But what does "better" mean? What criteria shall we use to label one family as being "better" than another? Therefore, whatever clarification or classification we make must be considered relative, tentative, and, certainly, in need of improvement. Here is where empirical evidence, as in the Timberlawn research project (Lewis, Beavers, Gossett, & Phillips, 1976), becomes very useful.

One could start with the simplistic generalization that all functional families are at risk. No matter how functional a family is, no one can go through life without some losses, traumas, and accidents. How a family copes with stress is a ready way to assess resilience, functionality, and even creativity. A second, simpleminded way of defining functionality is according to absence of dysfunctionality, that is, the family has no identified patient and is not in need of or asking for professional services. Unfortunately, this definition is defective because there are many families that could be dysfunctional who do, however, meet both requirements. A definition by positive commission is more appropriate than a negative definition by omission. A third way to define functionality, which is derived from a developmental theory of interpersonal competence (L'Abate, 1976, 1983, 1986b; L'Abate & Bryson, in press), is to define functional families as showing, among other qualities, the ability to give and to receive love (self-fulness) and to negotiate emotional issues in Doing and Having. Of course, we need to be clear on what is meant, operationally, by the ability to love and by the ability to negotiate. The ability to love also implies competence in showing and sharing feelings, including crying together and comforting one another in times of stress. A functional family also exhibits a conductive style: They are creative and/or efficient in negotiating and problem solving (as specified in Chapter 2).

In addition, the family's priorities are appropriate to its life cycle stage, to the point that no one in the family wins at the expense of anybody else, producing the aforementioned ability to enjoy life and laugh, in relaxed, rather than rigid or forced, interactions.

Semifunctional families, who are at greater risk, that is, in need, may be adequate but are neither competent nor creative in their interactions among themselves, demonstrating the following: (a) possibilities of more serious problems, as shown by incipient symptoms, either internal or external to individual members or to the family as a whole, such as underachievement, mild acting out, eating disorders, sleeping disorders, discipline problems, sibling rivalry, or temper tantrums; (b) tensions and dissatisfactions, as shown by frequent arguments but no outright crisis or fights; (c) the ability to give and receive love but with some difficulties, that is, there may be confusion between presence (Being) and power (Doing and Having); (d) the inability to reach consensus in negotiation or inefficiency in problem-solving strategies; (e) having received a primary prevention program but failing to complete it or benefit from it; or (f) having been in crisis, that is, having received tertiary prevention but now perhaps needing further booster shots (so to speak), in the form of further family enrichment and parenting training programs. Although functional families benefit from primary prevention programs, semifunctional ones may benefit from the combination of both primary and secondary prevention approaches.

The main issue here is distinguishing between functional and semifunctional families. Are functional families just at risk, but the risk for semifunctional families is so high that it reaches the level of need? More conceptual and empirical work is needed to answer this question. However, I will present and support the following position: Families at risk will profit from primary prevention programs or their equivalents, to be reviewed below. Families in need will profit from primary prevention *plus* administration of additional programmed materials (to be reviewed in the next chapter) exemplary of secondary prevention.

We can distinguish secondary prevention programs from primary prevention programs because they (a) deal with families through a different medium of communication, writing rather than speaking; (b) are much more specific and more clinically oriented than primary prevention programs, such as in dealing with clinical or troublesome behavior patterns in members of the family; and (c) are self-administered at home rather than administered by trainers, as in the case of primary prevention. However, as noted in the first chapter, there is a great deal of interchangeability between these two methods, to the extent that each can be transformed from the spoken to the written word or vice versa. Certain primary prevention programs, because of their structures, can be administered in

writing as extra homework assignments, just as written programmed materials can be administered to families orally.

Historical Background

For primary prevention, we have seen in the last two decades a
mushrooming of psychoeducational, assumedly preventive, programs for individuals, couples, and families (L'Abate, 1986a, 1987).
The purpose of this section is to review them briefly, from the
viewpoint of what they can offer to the field of primary prevention
with families at risk and select families in need.

The idea of making things better for already functioning families, which has been called *enrichment*, has historical roots in a variety of antecedents and influences. First, and most important, we
need to acknowledge the human potentials movement in stressing
the importance of loving and supporting, which, in practice,
became translated into the idea of programmed human relationships (L'Abate & Brown, 1969). This idea essentially assumed that
human relationships can be taught and, therefore, can be learned.
The forerunner of this position, of course, was Dale Carnegie, with
"how to make friends and influence people," and the franchising of
his methods to improve human relations in training institutes
throughout the United States.

A second influence, which was more oblique and indirect, was
the importance of play and games as pleasurable learning experiences, which, in practice, became translated into role-playing as the
best form of experiential as opposed to academic learning for interpersonal relationships (Kipper, 1986). Play is also important in family relations and personality development (L'Abate & Bryson, in
press). It represents surplus energy that can be used to make life
enjoyable. Healthy families like to play and enjoy themselves as
part of living, as shown by the ability to laugh and to poke fun at
oneself, at each other, and with intimate others. In fact, Ralph
Waldo Emerson (1803–1882) captured these qualities in ways that
would also define a functional family:

> To laugh often and love much; to win the respect of intelligent persons and
> the affection of children; to learn the approbation of honest critics and to
> endure the betrayal of false friends; to appreciate beauty; to find the best in

others; to give of one's self; to leave the world a bit better, whether by a healthy child, a garden patch or a redeemed social condition; to have played and laughed with enthusiasm and sung with exultation; to know that even one life has breathed easier because we have lived—this is to have succeeded.

The third influence in the enrichment movement was family life education (L'Abate, 1987; Leigh, Loewen, & Lester, 1986), which developed rapidly in many colleges and universities before World War II but began to slow down afterward. It emphasized too much information passively learned out of context, that is, it required people to learn family relations like any other kind of academic subject, without practical applications, real-life involvement, and possible improvement. Furthermore, it taught family relations to single individuals who could not transfer and apply the information to their families outside of the classroom. Consequently, family life education diminished in its influence because it did not meet the actual needs of its audience. It lacked any serious evaluation of its already questionable results and, outside of the classroom, had no delivery system. Nonetheless, it brought attention to the need to train and help people learn about family relations. Eventually, this approach metamorphosed into one of active and interactively experiential involvement, as required by the enrichment and social skills training movements (L'Abate & Milan, 1985). More recently, the National Council for Family Relations started to certify family life educators, an approach that hopefully will increase the level of professionalism as well as the standards of practice for this profession, whose members, by birthright and expertise, would certainly qualify well as primary preventers.

Marriage and family enrichment could be also viewed as being part of a much larger movement that stressed the importance of social skills training (SST; Hollin & Trower, 1986; L'Abate & Milan, 1985; McFall, 1988). Under this all-encompassing label, there are a variety of programs and emphases. Programs relevant to families are related to skill preparation for marriage, training for couples as partners, and training couples for more competent parenthood (L'Abate, 1986a). In fact, the most visible area of social skills training has been parenting, as shown by this list of partial references (Abidin, 1980; Alvy, 1988; Anthony & Benedek, 1970; Atkin &

Rubin, 1976; Belsky & Vondra, 1985; Biller & Meredith, 1974; Brock & Coufal, 1985; Budd, 1985; Carkhuff, 1985; Cohen, Cohler, & Weissman, 1984; Entwisle, 1985; Forehand & McMahon, 1981; Frank, 1982; Ginott, 1965, 1969; Group for the Advancement of Psychiatry, 1973; Lamb, 1976; Levant, 1986; Lynn, 1974; Moss, Abramowitz, & Racusin, 1985; Neville & Halaby, 1984; Phillips, 1978; Pollack & Grossman, 1985; Pruett, 1987; Rohner, 1986; Roosa, Fitzgerald, & Crawford, 1985).

The theoretical bases of the social skills movement can be found in L. Phillips's (1968) pioneer work. He expanded on White's (1960) early stress on the construct of competence. In fact, Phillips and his coworkers found significant relationships between social and occupational competence and psychopathology, that is, competence was positively related to psychological health and incompetence was related to psychopathology. Unfortunately, neither he nor those who followed him (Marlowe & Weinberg, 1985; Rathjen & Foreyt, 1980; Wine & Smye, 1981) stressed the importance of the family in the etiology and development of functionality and dysfunctionality. Nonetheless, all of the foregoing movements coalesced into producing a variety of parenting and marital skills training programs worthy of some, all too brief, consideration.

Marital Programs

In addition to the previous history the last two decades have seen the mushrooming of a variety of marital programs, such as, among too many others to review here, the Marriage Encounter movement (Calvo, 1975; L'Abate & McHenry, 1983), the Association for Couples in Marital Enrichment (ACME; Mace, 1986; Mace & Mace, 1976), and mostly church affiliated enrichment programs (Guerney, Guerney, & Cooney, 1985; Hopkins, Hopkins, Mace, & Mace, 1978; Joanning, 1985). Reviews of many marital programs are available (Bloom, Hodges, Kern, & McFaddin, 1985; Curran, Wallander, & Farrell, 1985; D'Augelli & D'Augelli, 1985; L'Abate & McHenry, 1983; Levant, 1986). Relationship Enhancement (RE) by Guerney (1988; Guerney & Guerney, 1985) and Couples Communication (CC) by Nunnally, Miller, and Wackman (1976; Wackman & Wampler, 1985) are the two best and most validated marriage growth programs.

McFall (1988), in his review of Hollin and Trower's handbook (1986), indicated some of problems that are still plaguing the SST movement and, by extension, the enrichment approach: (a) the conceptual inability to find consensus in the definition of social skills; (b) SST's assumption that behavioral deviance is determined by social skills deficits, which may not be valid; (c) methodological deficiencies demonstrated by the application of the same label to a very heterogeneous group of approaches; (d) empirical inabilities concerning the fact that different individuals (and families) and groups of individuals "have been treated indiscriminately with the same SST method" (McFall, 1988, p. 325); that empirical evidence for the efficacy of SST is still "equivocal," (because, as I—L'Abate, 1986a—also noted, there is no long-range follow-up to support the effectiveness of this approach, especially with families); and there are questions of generalization to other behaviors (that is, can we demonstrate that learning social skills transfers to other areas, such as the skills needed in intimate relationships?).

Parenting Programs

Parenting programs can be classified according to their origin and nature: One of the oldest parenting programs was developed by Dreikurs and Soltz (1964) following Adlerian thinking. This approach subsequently developed into the widely used STEP program, by Dinkmeyer and McKay (1976), which, together with the pioneer Parent Effectiveness Training (PET; Gordon, 1970), became one of the most applied parenting programs in North America. The Adlerian approach is also credited with the creation of a more recent and well-engineered parenting program by Popkin (1983).

Most other parenting programs have become an eclectic amalgam with various origins, mostly humanistic in orientation (Hoopes, Fisher, & Barlow, 1984; Levant, 1986). The remainder of parenting programs have their roots in behavioral approaches (Dumas, 1984; Forehand & McMahon, 1981; Forehand, Walley, & Furery, 1984; Patterson, 1985). The latter approaches also happen to have produced some of the most validated programs in the field of parenting.

In addition to skills training programs, a more recent movement, with less emphasis on skills training and more on caring, is on the rise: (a) family support groups (Kagan, Powell, Weissbourd, &

Zigler, 1987); (b) programs to strengthen families (Levine, 1988); and (c) the annual Nebraska Conference devoted to Family Strengths (Rowe et al., 1984; Stinnett, Chesser, & DeFrain, 1979; Stinnett, Chesser, DeFrain, & Knaub, 1980; Stinnett, DeFrain, King, Knaub, & Rowe, 1981; Stinnett et al., 1982).

Another important contribution to the whole structured approach to skills training can be found in the programs developed by the Child Welfare Institute of Atlanta,[1] under the direction and leadership of Tom Norton (personal communication, November 27, 1989). These programs consist of structured modules for social workers to use in training foster or adoptive parents. The major methods of training parents consist of lectures, handouts, role playing, group discussion, and written homework assignments. Their programmed structure is matched by that of programs developed by Hoopes, Fisher, and Barlow (1984). However, the most structured programs for couples and families are those described below that I have developed with my students.

Structured Enrichment Programs (SEPs)

To deal with functional and semifunctional couples and families, my collaborators and I have created a variety of SEPs to help a wide range of couples and families (L'Abate, 1977a, 1983, 1985c, 1987; L'Abate & Rupp, 1981). A program is composed of a basic unit called an "exercise", made up of a variety of questions asked of the couple or family around a single issue, for instance, "taking vacations" A group of exercises around a common topic ("having fun") is called a "lesson". A series of lessons in sequence around a specific subject ("leisure time") is called a "program". Thus far, 50 structured programs have been published, covering as many subjects relevant to improving family living (L'Abate & Weinstein, 1987). Case studies illustrating how this process of enriching families takes place can be found in L'Abate (1977a), L'Abate and Rupp, (1981), and L'Abate and Young (1987).

The functions of these programs are multiple, ranging from (a) didactic-propaedeutic, to train beginning students to work with functional and semifunctional families; (b) diagnostic-evaluative, that is, by trying to change families we can understand how they work or fail to work; (c) preventive-pretherapeutic, that is, if we can help families learn better ways of getting along and acquire a more mature sense of mastery and greater competence, perhaps we may forestall future problems; (d) to research the fourth function, which has helped show the usefulness of a structured, that is, verbatim, format in the administration of questions or instructions to families. Two doctoral dissertations, by Robert Wildman II (L'Abate, 1977a) and by Gary Ganahl (L'Abate, 1985c), and one large research project with Dug Smith (Smith & L'Abate, 1977a), helped to show short-term gains for couples and families. A research project by Kochalka (n.d.) attempts to validate a Family Profile Form to allow the matching of specific areas of dissatisfaction in couples with specific exercises in the same areas of dissatisfaction (as discussed in Chapter 4).

SEPs were created with the following guidelines in mind: (a) ease of administration with immediate applications possible without too much training or preparation for trainers; (b) ease of testability and verifiability, as can be achieved through the use of verbatim instructions; (c) a wide range of usefulness in application to a great variety of situations relevant to families with differing needs; (d) practical relevance in dealing with actual family matters; (e) efficiency and cost-effectiveness (these programs are relatively inexpensive because they can be administered by lay personnel or volunteers who do not charge or who charge minimal fees for their services); (f) a basis in established ethical and professional principles; (g) possession of prescriptive specificity, flexibility, and versatility (in the sense that they would be applicable to a wide range of families—rich and poor, educated and uneducated—with an even greater variety of issues and problems, from helping a family make up a budget to how to negotiate and problem-solve together); and (h) an eclectic derivation from both theory and experience, including many different theories (from Adler to Transactional Analysis).

To illustrate which topics and subjects are covered by SEPs, they are classified according to (a) developmental criteria, that is, according to family life stages (meeting, matching, and mating, man-woman relationships, expecting a child, becoming a parent, dealing with teenagers, facing death and widowhood) and (b) structural criteria, that is, according to a family's socioeconomic and educational conditions, level of competence, and special needs.

The selection of a specific program for a specific family—that is, matching a program to the family's perceived and stated needs—is based on the expressed needs of the family, qualified, however, by the enricher's (trainer's, facilitator's, trainee's) impressions and by a test battery (L'Abate & Young, 1987). On the basis of these three sources of information—the family, the trainer, and the test battery—three programs that seem to match the family's needs (as well as the conclusions derived from the trainer and from the test battery) are briefly described and offered to the family. Ultimately, each family chooses the program that seems closer to their needs and expectations. As indicated in Chapter 4, once we had identified nine different areas of family interaction (description, playing, touching, negotiating, and so on), my collaborators and I created an instrument, the Family Profile Form, to allow a closer match between a family's deficit areas and specific exercises designed to alleviate and improve these deficits (Kochalka, n.d.).

Evidence to Support the Usefulness of SEPs

Through a variety of studies performed over the years, we assessed the usefulness of SEPs with couples or families at risk. The first study was conducted in collaboration with Douglas K. Smith (Smith & L'Abate, 1977). It consisted of 55 clinical and nonclinical families with a total N of 217 subjects. *Clinical* families were defined as having one member identified as a patient and asking for help from me or my students. *Nonclinical* families were defined as not having an identified patient and not being in need of professional help at the time when they were asked to volunteer for this project. Each group was split into two groups—those who received enrichment and those who did not—for a total of four groups. Those families who did not receive SEPs were evaluated twice in two months (which is the average length of structured enrichment) just like the experimental families. All of these families were from a middle-class background and almost all included a father. A more detailed analysis of 37 families can be found in Golden (1974), who collected the data for the control families—those who did not receive SEPs.

The test battery, administered before and after enrichment consisted of four visual tests developed to assess families but not requiring the ability to read. The various studies validating this visual battery have been reviewed by L'Abate and Wagner (1985). The battery consisted of the following tests.

The Bell-Fagan Symbol Test is made up of 52 nonsensical symbols that correlate significantly with six emotional states: anxiety, anger, sadness, quietness, loving, and happiness. These cards were administered to each family member, who was instructed to separate them into piles representing self and each family member. Each card was then scored according to weights on the six emotional states obtained from correlational results from previous studies (Golden, 1974). Each family member received a composite score that represented the accumulated total weights from all family members and self. A total family score was obtained by summating individual scores. This test was administered first because we thought it was a good, nonthreatening icebreaker.

The Description of Feelings in the Family test consists of 72 pictures representing three degrees of intensity for four feelings— states—mad, sad, smug, and distracting—for six individuals, one male and one female adult, supposedly representing the parents, and one male and one female adolescent as well as a boy and a girl, representing the children. Scoring on this test was done for individual family members, although individual scores could have been summated to obtain a total family score.

The Situations in the Family test consists of 264 cards developed from Satir's typology of four dysfunctional stances: blaming, placating, distracting, and computing (L'Abate, 1976). These four stances were represented with six figures, two male and female adults, two male and female adolescents, and a boy and a girl. We scored individually but composite family scores could have been obtained.

The Animal Concept Picture Series was conceived to be more "projective" than the previous two, more like the Bell-Fagan Symbol Test but somewhat more threatening. It was administered last in the battery. It consisted of 90 animal pictures from which family members selected one card for self and one for other members. This administration was repeated four times, twice to measure the *actual* and twice the *ideal* perception of the family. Scoring, based on average semantic differential ratings of each card, included individual and family profiles.

Experimental families received six lessons of SEPs that best suited their needs. All of these programs were administered by graduate students in psychology or education under my supervision. Scores for each test were analyzed through ANOVA for main effects and interactions (for pre-post and enrichment/no-enrichment) for families as well as individuals (by sex and fathers, mothers, and children). Results showed that in the Bell-Fagan test only the sadness score was significantly influenced by enrichment ($F = 5.03$, $p < .05$) in the direction of greater intensity of feelings. In the description of feelings test, the number of cards selected was significant ($F = 12.97$, $p < .01$) from pretest to posttest, interacting significantly with the clinical-nonclinical classification ($F = 4.11$, $p < .05$). This result replicated Golden's (1974) results. This greater number of cards for clinical families significantly affected scores on the four feelings, differentiating clinical from nonclinical families at a high level of statistical significance. The same results were obtained for the Situations in the Family test. Clinical families chose significantly more cards than nonclinical families. Only the computing dimension interacted significantly with enrichment/no-enrichment. In the Animal Concept Pictures Series, enrichment produced significant main effects on dimensions of small-big, helpless-helpful, aggressive-passive, good-bad, strong-weak in the "actual" administration. In the "ideal" administration, enrichment produced a significant main effect and interaction with test-retest on the strong-weak dimension, and significant main effects or interactions were obtained for the aggressive-passive, dangerous-harmless, powerful-powerless, quiet-noisy, good-bad dimensions.

The ANOVA of individuals, divided by fathers, mothers, and children, yielded a variety of significant results above what we would expect by chance. In the Bell-Fagan test, enrichment produced main effects on the fathers' sorting of anxiety of their children and on mother's sorting of fathers on loving. The children's sortings showed a variety of main effects and interactions with clinical-nonclinical and before-after scores but were not influenced by enrichment. In the Description of Feelings in the Family test, only the children showed significant changes in their scores as a result of enrichment. In addition, identified patients chose significantly more cards than their well siblings. Both of these groups chose more cards than nonclinical controls. The same results were obtained on the Family Situations Picture Series, with no enrichment effects for parents and some effects for children. In the Animal Concept Picture Series, a significant interaction for the fathers for the "actual" dimension of good-bad, pre-post, and enrichment was found. Mothers failed to show any effect, and children showed significant pre-post changes on five of the ten dimensions. In the "ideal" administration, a variety of significant changes for fathers and mothers were found, but changes were not found for the children. This test appeared to be more sensitive to changes due to enrichment than any of the other tests in the battery. It is also the "cheapest" test because it gives a great deal of information about stereotyped male-female roles for the shortest length of administration—about five minutes.

The major shortcomings of this pilot study were in the relative newness of the measures used, the vast variability of scores, and the failure to use some old, tried-and-true, measures of family functioning that were nonexistent when this study was conducted (1972–1976). At the time, statistical measures that would be sensitive to families and individuals were still in their infancy. Consequently, it seemed necessary to conduct a second, more controlled study that would still compare effectiveness of structured enrichment with that of psychotherapy with clinical and nonclinical couples, defined according to the same criteria used in the previous study.

Wildman's study (1977) used four different groups of couples: Group I comprised 8 clinical couples (7 Caucasian couples and 1 Black) who received SEPs. They had been referred for enrichment by a community mental health center and private therapists. Enrichment was administered by graduate students. Group 2 comprised 11 clinical couples (10 caucasian couples and 1 Black) who received therapy in the Georgia State University Family Study Center from graduate students as well as in the community from private therapists. Group 3 comprised 25 nonclinical couples (21 Caucasian couples and 4 with race not listed) who received enrichment. Group 4 comprised 14 nonclinical control couples (13 Caucasian couples and 1 Black) who did not receive any kind of intervention. All of these couples were evaluated by a battery of tests consisting of an Identifying Information Sheet, a revision of the Marital Happiness Scale, a Marital Progress Sheet, and a Communication Reaction Form, all self-report, paper-and-pencil tests administered twice with a seven-week interval. Assignment to either Group 2 or Group 4 was random, but there was no random assignment for the other two groups.

Wildman measured change using a variety of measures derived from the test battery: A change score was obtained by subtracting pretest scores from posttest scores; then a total battery score was obtained by summing the scores on the three change measures, which, in turn, produced a total change score after subtracting the pretest score from the posttest score. Correlations among these measures were extremely high and statistically significant for both husbands and wives. This was the basis for combining the individual test scores into one overall score. Results indicated that the control group (Group 4) did not change its scores, while enrichment applied to nonclinical couples (Group 3) produced statistically significant changes denoting improvement in the enriched couples. The same kind of significant results were found for the positive effects of therapy (Group 2) as well as for the effects of enrichment on clinical couples (Group 1). As Wildman (1977, p. 177) concluded:

> All three intervention groups in this study showed significant increases on the Total Battery from pre- to post-test, and these increases were significantly greater than those found for a no-treatment control group . . . a dramatic finding of the present research was that enrichment applied to clinical couples was as effective as therapy.

As interpreted, Wildman's results support the usefulness of SEPs for clinically troubled marriages. Although I would not go that far, it would be feasible to include SEPs in an overall treatment plan of successive sieves for troubled couples and families (as suggested in chapter 3). There were shortcomings in this study as well, such as (a) not reporting the validity of the assessment instruments, which were all experimental and of questionable validity, and (b) using combined, averaged scores for husbands and wives that obscured individual variability. There were questionable statistical methods used that did not include ANOVA or other more sophisticated statistical techniques. Consequently, L'Abate and Rupp (1981) analyzed each test item separately in a treatment × time, 4 × 2 ANCOVA. Results from this analysis indicated that 94% of the items yielded a significant main effect for treatments; 65% of the items yielded a main effect for time; and 63% of the items showed a significant interaction effect between treatments and time.

Fry, Holly, and L'Abate (1979) evaluated three different methods of dealing with anger in relationships: (a) calm, rational discussion, à la Ellis (1976); (b) "fair fighting," à la Bach and Goldberg (1974); and (c) sharing of hurts and fears of being hurt, à la L'Abate (1977).

Two studies were performed. In the first one, videotaped role-playing procedures representing the three different methods were presented to 36 undergraduates. Their preferences indicated no support for the hypothesis of sex differences in dealing with conflict and some support for differential preferences for each of the three methods. In the second study, three structured enrichment lessons directly derived from the three theoretical and practical positions were administered through tape-recorded instruction to 11 couples in a random order, using each couple as its own control. Their reactions to the three methods demonstrated some support for the suggestion that intimacy may be found in the sharing of hurts, but the other two methods were demonstrated to be more suited for the negotiation of conflictual issues than for intimacy.

Wagner, Weeks, and L'Abate (1980) evaluated the use of paradoxically worded messages, one of the most common practices at the outset of family therapy at the time (L'Abate, Ganahl, & Hansen, 1986; Selvini-Palazzoli, Boscolo, Cecchin, & Prata, 1978), by combining them with SEPs. We evaluated 56 couples drawn from the student population with a test battery before and after a course of six sessions of marital enrichment. One group received no SEPs; a second group received SEPs only. A third group received linearly worded written messages at the end of the fourth lesson of SEPs; and a fourth group received paradoxically worded (i.e., circular) messages, also at the end of the fourth lesson of SEPs. Results failed to show any difference between linear or circular messages but supported the use of SEPs with some kind of written feedback, either linear or circular.

Ganahl (1981) set out to correct some of the weaknesses of previous studies by investigating the effects of SEP type, sex and number of trainers, and clients' level of adjustment. His Ss were 126 married couples and one cohabiting couple who participated as clients in the Family Study Center at GSU or undergraduates who volunteered for research credit as part of introductory psychology courses. Most Ss were in their late twenties, educated, and of diverse economic and occupational background, and had been married for an average of five years with an average of one child per couple. Most couples were Caucasian; the majority were either Protestant or with no religious preference. All trainers or therapists were graduate students in the family psychology program at GSU supervised by me or other faculty members.

The pre-post test battery scores of the nonclinical enrichment group (N = 51 couples) were compared with those of a no-treatment control group (N = 24), a nonclinical group receiving written homework assignments dealing with communication (n = 8), another enrichment group that had received additional homework assignments (n = 8), a clinical enrichment group composed of couples with marital difficulties (N = 18), and a clinical sample of couples receiving marital therapy (N = 18). No significant between-group differences were found for age, race, educational and occupational levels, length of marriage, and number of children.

The test battery scores were analyzed using one-factor ANOVA, with ANCOVA applied to positive results of groups that were significantly different from each other on pretest scores. Improvement was assessed by the Locke-Wallace Adjustment Test (MAT), the Primary Communication Inventory (PCI), the Marital Happiness Scale (MHS), and a composite test battery composed of questions concerning marital satisfaction with a variety of areas of functioning. All test were administered on a pre-post basis with a six- to seven-week interval in between.

Overall, the results from the foregoing analyses indicated that SEPs were effective in producing greater marital satisfaction and adjustment, at least as shown by the self-report, paper-and-pencil tests used with these couples. The clinical enrichment group achieved significant improvement on the MHS only, and the clinical therapy group showed significant improvement on the battery scores and on the MHS.

Sloan (1983) compared the effectiveness of two six-hour SEPs workshops administered in a group format in facilitating intimacy in marital adjustment. The major difference between the two workshops consisted of one group of couples being coached in sharing anger and hurt prior to negotiating while the other group was not coached. Sharing of hurt was hypothesized as the essential feature of intimacy in marriage as the deepest level of self-disclosure (as explained in Chapter 2). She assigned 24 Jewish couples at random to the two treatment conditions (i.e., SEPs with or without sharing of hurts). Analysis of scores on self-report measures of intimacy and marital adjustment administered one week before the workshop and six weeks after the workshop failed to show any differences between the two treatments. Although a relationship between pretreatment levels of intimacy and marital adjustment was found, changes in marital intimacy as a result of the workshop were not accompanied by concurrent changes in marital adjustment. Significant pre-post differences were found within the experimental group for intimacy and perceived ability to deal with relationship problems but not for marital adjustment. Only the pre-post difference in perceived ability to deal with relationship problems reached significance in the nonintimacy condition control group. Sloane interpreted these results as suggesting a trend toward more egalitarian emotional sharing among middle-class, college-educated couples who had been married 10 or more years. She suggested a series of developmental stages in intimacy facilitation built upon the intimacy model originally proposed.

The most critical issue in the results of these studies concerns long-term effects. All of the results dealt with short, posttreatment changes. We do not have information, as yet, on the long-range outcome of SEPs, except for a consumer satisfaction survey of all the couples and families who received SEPs during the 10 years since the survey's creation. Results indicated an 80% satisfaction rate (L'Abate & Rupp, 1981). There is a need for a more substantial follow-up of families who have been enriched with families who were evaluated without enrichment. A follow-up of this kind, to evaluate long term effects of SEPs, is now in progress (L'Abate & Cusinato, n.d.).

Discussion

What is the relationship, if any, between SEPs and other primary prevention programs developed by other authors? To illustrate this relationship, some of the best, better known, and more validated programs referred to above, such as Relationship Enhancement (RE), Couples Communication (CC), STEP, TIME (another program for marital growth developed by Dinkmeyer and Carlson, 1984), and ACME, will be compared according to the degree of structure and focus or content of the program. *Degree of structure* is defined by at least two emphases: at one extreme, emphasis on the program, such as in the verbatim instructions of SEP, or, at the other extreme, emphasis on the influence and leadership of the program facilitator(s). With a high degree of structure, the program itself is primarily responsible for producing any changes in the family, and the leader-facilitator is secondary to the program. With a medium degree of structure, both program and leader are approximately equal in their contribution to the process of growth and enrichment. With a low degree of structure, the leader is primarily responsible for the process, and the program is secondary to the leader.

In addition to degree of structure, a second independent variable needs to be considered in comparing various and different enrichment approaches, which is *degree of specificity*. For instance, SEPs have the highest degree of structure, and they also have the highest potential to make the family enrichment approach match or fit in a much more specific way than enrichment approaches like RE, CC, and ACME or parental approaches like PET or STEP. These approaches are general, all-purpose programs, that is, they are designed to fit the general needs of couples and families and not their specific needs. The same program fits all families. These "funnel" approaches assume that the same set of interpersonal skills, such as active listening and emotion-focused answers are basic to effective functioning in families. However, SEPs, with hundreds of lessons and more than 1,000 exercises, can be made much more specific, as indicated above, to each family's needs than these other approaches. SEPs, even though they contain lessons and exercises covering the exact types of skills stressed by other approaches, also contain a plethora of theory-derived, theory-independent, and, even theory-irrelevant lessons and exercises.

The degrees of structure and specificity of a program are important because they determine the level of training needed for the facilitator. For instance, training in SEPs is fast, almost instantaneous, but some of the other programs require up to 80 or 100 hours of training. However, SEP trainers usually work under supervision, at least in the beginning of training, but trainers for the other programs can then work independently. It may take the same length of time for SEP trainees to learn to work independently and to achieve a satisfactory level of proficiency. The major shortcoming of SEPs, in comparison with the other representative programs, is in their administration to one family at a time rather than to groups of families, as is the case with all other approaches.

Structure and specificity of approach are directly related to one another. If one wants a general, all-purpose program with low structure and specificity, one may choose ACME, which is an excellent model. On the other hand, if one wants a great deal of specificity, one may want to select SEPs, in which specificity for the individual needs of couples and families can be achieved easily. SEPs are highly structured and can be as specific as one wants to make them, as discussed above. RE, CC, TIME, and other well-validated enrichment programs gravitate toward the middle of this relationship, that is, they are in the middle of the distribution in degree of structure as well as specificity.

Most enrichment programs are administered to groups of couples, but SEPs are usually administered to one family at one time by one or two enrichers. This may be a disadvantage from an economic viewpoint. However, SEPs can and have been administered in a group format to four and five couples and up to two or three families at one time, with slight variations in the instructions.

From the viewpoint of theory, none of these programs is derived from any specific theory, except perhaps RE, which has its roots in the humanistic school. Although SEPs have specific, theory-derived programs focusing on the ability to love and the ability to negotiate, as well as theory-independent programs, RE, TIME, and CC are indirectly related to theory, to the extent that both of these topics are covered without a link to a specific theory. ACME, on the other hand, is rather unclear on its theoretical background, focusing instead, pragmatically, on effective communication for conflict resolution and learning to deal with anger creatively, in a group discussion format reminiscent of therapy. A summary comparison of these approaches according to degree of structure and specificity is contained in Table 5.1. Although most of these programs are either for couples as partners or for couples as parents, most of them, with the exception of RE, by definition exclude children. SEPs, on the other hand, do contain programs for families with children of all ages.

This comparison of different enrichment approaches is not done inviduously, to claim that one approach is "better" than another. There is absolutely no value judgment or conclusion made here about the comparative usefulness of one program over another. On the contrary, this comparison is made to show how these approaches differ from one another in their *functions*. For instance, for research purposes, and to make sure one needs to control what is said to couples or families, SEPs may be the approach of choice. On the other hand, if one wants to encourage and propagandize

TABLE 5.1: A Tentative Classification for Enrichment Programs

Exemplary Programs	Degree of Structure	Degree of Specificity	Content Focus		
			Negotiation	Love	Children
SE	High	High	Yes	Yes	Yes
RE, CC, PET, STEP, TIME	Medium	Medium	Yes	Yes	No
ACME	Low	Low	Not really specified	Not specified	No

*Except for RE, which includes programs for families with children and adolescents.

the cause of family and marriage enrichment, one would want to use the warm, personal contact found in ACME. This program is closer to a group therapy format than any of the other programs reviewed here, because it is low in both structure and specificity. Each approach has its advantages and disadvantages according to what criteria one wants to use. If research is a primary goal, establishing warm, personal contacts between enricher and family may be a secondary goal, even though both goals are not mutually exclusive and *both* could and should be fulfilled simultaneously, if at all possible.

Didactic Considerations

How do we teach trainees to work with families when they have never done so before? In the family therapy field trainees without experience begin by watching videotapes or live "gurus" at work with families through one-way mirrors. Primary prevention and secondary prevention can be taught through role-playing involvement with mock families first and with real families afterward. Most functional families (screened and selected) are eager to learn and lend themselves easily to the role of "guinea pig" for beginning students, provided they are aware there are controls, that is, that the trainee is being supervised. Thus the watchword for training in primary and secondary prevention is *gradualness*, through experiential rather than through book learning methods (Ganahl, Ferguson, & L'Abate, 1985; L'Abate & Jessee, 1981; L'Abate & Kochalka, 1983).

Gradualness in training means going from highly structured to less and less structured approaches. For instance, full-fledged professionals may know not only the most important primary and secondary prevention approaches, but also methods of evaluation. Middle-level professionals, specializing in prevention approaches, may start training with SEPs and then branch out and learn other more complex and leader-dependent approaches, such as RE, CC, STEP, TIME, and ACME. Volunteers and part-time trainees may learn just one approach and be supervised by middle-level professionals, according to the hierarchy introduced in Chapter 3 and expanded in Chapter 7.

Conclusion

A vast technology for primary prevention to intervene with functional and semifunctional families, hopefully to improve their levels of functioning and competence, is available. This technology can be used and administered by paraprofessional personnel (baccalaurate degree or equivalent) with a relative minimum of credentials and training and a maximum of interpersonal skills (warmth, genuine concern, unconditional regard, interpersonal maturity) to work with families. These paraprofessionals (volunteers, lay personnel, part- or full-time employees), specifically trained in one approach, would work under the direction, supervision, and support of middle- to upper-level professionals.

NOTE

1. The address of the Child Welfare Institute is 1365 Peachtree Street NE, Suite 700, Atlanta, GA 30309.

6

Programmed Materials as Secondary Prevention Tools

The purpose of this chapter is to introduce the concept of programmed materials and workbooks as tools in secondary prevention (L'Abate, 1987; L'Abate & Cox, in press). Although the main purpose of primary prevention is to increase the level of competence, and thus, hopefully, decrease chances of *possible* breakdown, the main purpose of secondary prevention is to decrease stress, dysfunctionality, and thus, hopefully, decrease chances of *probable* breakdown and crisis. The latter is clearly more oriented toward pathology and dysfunctionality than primary prevention, but not as much as tertiary prevention, in which the breakdown and crisis are *actual*—they have already taken place. In the first chapter, *secondary prevention* was defined as para-active, paratherapeutic, and oriented toward helping families *in need* rather than those families *at risk*. Both types of families were discussed previously; however, families in need will be described further here.

What Is a Family in "Need"?

We need to define *family in need*. Indeed, the task of future secondary prevention will be to find out which family will profit from this approach and which family will not. Secondary prevention hinges on our being able to discriminate between families *in need* and those *at risk*, and distinguish both types of families from those *in crisis*. These criteria will need to be much more objective than the fairly loose, admittedly qualitative criteria suggested here. It may be relatively easy to identify families at risk, as those, to begin with, who do not have an index, or identified, patient and who are or do not feel in need of professional help. On the other hand, a family in crisis is defined by at least those two characteristics that families at risk do not have, which are (a) an identified patient and (b) a need for professional help. Even though such a need is often denied by a family, a responsible professional has made the determination that the family is in crisis and is in need of professional help—whether or not the family agrees. Between these two extremes—risk and crisis—are those families that may not be dysfunctional enough to be in crisis but that could use some help nevertheless, even though the help may not be crisis oriented. They need some help *before* their condition, or the condition of one individual in the family, becomes critical enough to require tertiary intervention or, worse, medication, hospitalization, or incarceration.

Among the 14 criteria used in Table 1.1 in Chapter 1, a family in need is one at *very high risk* for probable breakdown, with a 66% or less chance that the referring condition will be irreversible without professional intervention. These families may already have individuals who are showing incipiently problematic, and possibly diagnosable, conditions, for instance, (a) families with anxious individuals (fear and compulsive worry) at risk for unhappiness and in need of some type of help, even though there may not be a crisis; (b) families with lonely or depressed individuals (sadness and feelings of inadequacy and hopelessness) who are at high risk for suicide or hospitalization and in need of help before things get worse, such as in families with senior citizens (Simson, Wilson, Hermelin, & Hess, 1983); (c) families with impulsive, self-defeating, or driven individuals, such as in adolescent pregnancy (McKenry, Walters, & Johnson, 1979), compulsive gambling (Peck, 1986), loneliness (Peplau & Goldston, 1984), runaways (Young, Godfrey, Matthews, & Adams, 1983), and individuals at high risk for incarceration and in need of help to learn how to reflect before acting out; (d) families composed by parents who were children of abusive (physically, sexually, substantively) parents; or (e) conflictful or polarized couples at risk for divorce and in need of learning better ways of interacting as partners rather than as individuals.

The foregoing list is not complete or definite. The last group mentioned, for instance, conflictful or troubled couples, may not display any of the conditions outlined above. However, many of these couples may not have enough of the skills to love and to negotiate to last for the long term, if that is what they want. Thus, from the viewpoint of the theory presented in Chapter 2, families at risk, as already noted in the previous chapter, know how to love and how to negotiate reasonably or fairly well. Their sense of self-importance is relatively free of conditionality for performance, perfection, production, or problem solving. Their sense of self-other importance is achieved through being together as equals, reciprocating freely and spontaneously feelings as well as actions and sharing victories as well as defeats. They are conductive and creative in how they interact with each other and with the outside world.

Families in need lack either one or both of these two abilities, to love and to negotiate. They are characterized by *reactivity* and *repetitiveness* in personal and interpersonal patterns. Their sense of self-importance is incomplete and, therefore, defective. Requirements and conditions are set for performance and production, with little or minimal presence and expression or sharing of positive or negative feelings. Doing and Having are stressed at the expense of Being. Consequently, there is an overreliance on external expressions and manifestations of importance, either through blind and uncritical conformity to rules and regulations or through rebellious rejection of social and interpersonal standards and conventional codes and laws. Reality is perceived in extreme, black and white dichotomies (right-wrong, true-false, and so on) with very little room for distinction or discrimination between extremes. Intimacy may be shared sporadically and occasionally but not on an ongoing basis as one would find in conductive families.

Families in crisis are usually but not always lacking in both areas of love and negotiation. They are characterized by both reactivity and repetitiveness *as well as* abuse and apathy in their family members. Their sense of self-importance is either extremely low or actually negative. There is no room for the equality, reciprocity, and intimacy found in families at risk. There may be chaotically symbiotic or contradictorily extreme feelings and actions, with no room for moderation, balance, or stability. Fighting and violence, that is, abuse, on one hand, may be counteracted by avoidance and withdrawal from them, that is, apathy, on the other hand.

Thus families in need of some kind of preventive approach may have some disturbing condition that may be either labeled (child of an alcoholic) or even diagnosable. An example is a member of the family showing an incipiently defeating and potentially destructive pattern that is troublesome to someone although not necessarily to that family member. The person could be a teacher, minister, physician, lawyer, or neighbor. Naturally, if secondary prevention approaches do not exist, it would be impossible to refer families to them. However, these approaches do exist and will be increasingly used in the future so families can avoid becoming critical and clinical.

Furthermore, we want to introduce the possibility that programmed materials and workbooks could be used alongside or in combination with primary *as well as* with tertiary prevention approaches. Reduced to written administration, they could become substitute, alternative, or additional forms of intervention for either primary or tertiary prevention approaches. Hence we need to introduce the use of the written word, basic to programmed materials, as one way of intervening preventively and therapeutically.

Historical Background

The historical roots of the use of programmed materials and workbooks in secondary prevention are in the practice of programmed writing. This practice started with undergraduates writing autobiographies in the 1950s and, more recently, senior citizens (Birren & Hedlund, 1987). There were a few clinical cases at the Menninger Clinic in the early 1960s. However, the most extensive use of writing for therapeutic purposes was the diary-journal approach started by Progoff (1980) in the middle 1960s. An APA symposium on what was then called "therapeutic writing" was published in the middle 1960s (Pearson, 1965). In the same year, Phillips and Wiener (1965) were the first ones to use programmed writing *at a distance*, that is, through the mail without contact between therapist and the undergraduates asking for help from a university counseling service. Another antecedent for programmed writing can be found in the programmed instruction (PI) move-

ment, now computer assisted instruction (CAI), leading to programmed interpersonal relations, then applied to intimate relations
(L'Abate & Brown, 1969).

Another, perhaps indirect, antecedent of programmed writing is
in the field of brief or short therapy (Barten, 1971; Barten & Barten,
1973; Budman, 1981; deShazer, 1982, 1985; Malan, 1976; Mann,
1973; Sifneos, 1987; Wolberg, 1980). This movement has attempted
to condense and shorten what at times appears to be an intermina-
bly expensive process into manageable time or sessions limits,
varying anywhere from 10 to 18 sessions. Even though many of the
authors cited above have attempted to create criteria for the selection of individuals and families, this field is still ill-defined. Especially when we deal with families, we do not know as yet which
family would benefit from which type of therapeutic approach:
short, long, or in between. However, we can safely assume that
purely reactive patterns, without apathy or abuse of any kind,
might have a better possible outcome in brief therapy than family
patterns characterized by abuse and apathy.

Relevant to the use of writing as an additional medium of therapeutic exchange, however, only Small (1971, p. 159), among the
proponents of brief therapy cited above, referred to writing and to
the work of Phillips and Wiener (1965) as a potentially therapeutic
source. The third modality of writing (after the verbal and the nonverbal modalities) has been essentially untapped by the therapeutic
community in its potential clinical and nonclinical preventive
applications.

I started working with written, systematic homework assignments (i.e., workbooks) for depression, negotiation, and intimacy
with individuals, couples, and families in crisis years ago (L'Abate,
1986b). This practice, which can be conceived as combining both
tertiary and secondary prevention approaches, led to the development of programmed writing as one type of secondary prevention
(L'Abate, 1987e; L'Abate & Cox, in press), in which programmed
materials and workbooks become an additional form of exchange
between the therapist and the family in addition to face-to-face
therapy sessions.

My students and I performed two pilot studies years ago to
study the extension of therapeutic interventions to homework
assignments. Wagner and L'Abate (1977) investigated the effects of
written homework assignments for 32 couples. They were all non-

clinical volunteers from undergraduate classes who needed experimental class credit. There were 8 couples for each of the following groups—Group 1: administration of SEPs plus written homework assignments and instructions on effective means of communication; Group 2: written homework assignments and instructions without SEPs; Group 3: SEPs without homework assignments; and Group 4: evaluation with the same test battery as the other three groups but with no intervention of any kind, or the control group. The test battery included the Locke-Wallace Marital Adjustment Test (MAT), the Primary Communication Inventory (PCI), the Marital Happiness Scale (MHS), the Communication Behaviors Rating Scale, and the Family Information Rating Scale for demographic background information.

Homework assignments consisted of six weekly lessons: (a) use of the *I* pronoun, (b) expression of and owning up to one's feelings, (c) suggestions on how to express feelings helpfully to one's partner, (d) adding the pronoun *We* to the *I* pronoun, (e) communicating effectively, and (f) practicing "I" messages more. Couples in the homework-assignments-only group only met formally with the trainer during the pre-post test sessions. Otherwise, during the six weeks of homework assignments, contact was kept at a minimum and only involved collecting the previous completed assignment and giving each couple the next assignment in a sealed envelope. Scores from the pre-post test were analyzed with correlations, percentages for change scores, Tukey's Multiple *t*-test, and Wilks's stepwise discriminant analysis. Correlations between husbands and wives were all significantly high, increasing in the postintervention testing. Change scores (posttest minus pretest) were classified as improved if they went over the median scores of the total distribution and as not improved if they went below the median. As a result, the following mean improvement scores (MIS) were found for the four groups—Group 1: MIS = +56.63 (S.D. = 118.39), with a percentage of improvement of 75; Group 2: MIS = +69.75 (S.D. 77.05), with a percentage of improvement of 62; Group 3: MIS = +3.75 (S.D. = 78.22), with a percentage of improvement of 37; Group 4: MIS = −23.64 (S.D. = 66.40), with a percentage of improvement of 25. Tukey's multiple t-tests compared the sum of the pre-post change scores across groups. Groups 1 and 2 were significantly different from the control group ($t = 3.33$; $p < .05$) and ($t = 3.38$; $p < .05$), respectively. In the discriminant analysis of 100 items in the four tests, approximately one-third of the items were found to contribute significantly to the scores of the most improved couples.

This study, therefore, was the first to suggest that synergistically positive effects can be obtained by combining two different methods of intervention, SEPs plus homework assignments. Alone, homework assignments were superior to SEPs and took much less time to administer, suggesting that this modality of treatment could be exploited more than it has been before.

Clark and L'Abate (1977) elaborated on the previous study using the same couples who received enrichment and who were used as controls, adding another similar group of 10 volunteer, nonclinical undergraduate couples. Each individual was asked to speak alone into a tape recorder for 10 minutes about one of five topics handed out in random order: the future, fears, sex, fantasies, feelings, and finishing up (the 6 Fs). Each assignment consisted of one brief written paragraph of instructions and introductory comments about the topic. After speaking individually into the tape-recorder, they were to get together to listen to their recordings and discuss their reactions to listening to them with each other. Contacts with the experimenter were kept to a minimum. Couples would hand in a tape and receive the next assignment. The same test battery administered in the previous study was used in this one, with the same kind of analysis of total change scores. Because of a different distribution of scores and subjects (26 instead of 32), the results were somewhat different for control and SEP groups. Scores yielded the following mean change percentages, respectively: control = 25%, SEPs = 50%, and tapes = 70%. Impressionistically, the couples receiving the tapes indicated that they enjoyed the process of confrontation and found it worthwhile for their relationship. Thus we found another cost-effective way of improving relationships, even though we remained mindful that these were young, enthusiastic, and somewhat selected couples.

The latest study summarized here is presented in detail elsewhere (L'Abate & Cox, in press). The purpose of this study was to evaluate the effectiveness of two workbooks for couples. One workbook attempted to teach couples to negotiate. The second workbook attempted to teach couples to become more intimate (L'Abate, 1986b). These two workbooks, consisting of six lessons each, were administered to volunteer undergraduate couples under two different experimental conditions. One group did weekly lessons *on their own*, with a minimum of therapist's time (up to but no more than 15 minutes), and another group answered the same lessons *in front of* a therapist (for 45 minutes). These two conditions plus the type of workbook (negotiation versus intimacy) were the two independent variables as well as the major influence on the outcome measures, made up of a battery of self-report, paper-and-pencil tests. The crucial issue in the administration of these workbooks, however, was the influence of the therapists, who in this study were advanced undergraduates. How much of the outcome was due to therapist influence and how much of the outcome was due to the workbooks' influence? The results for the two groups (maximum versus minimal "therapist" involvement) indicated that the influence of the therapist was indeed minimal. Neither group of couples showed any significant differences from the two treatment conditions. In other words, the outcome for couples with minimal therapist involvement was the same as for the couples with maximum therapist involvement. When two forms of treatment show the same result, we want to pick the treatment that costs less, in this case the one where expensive professional time is saved. The two workbooks, as expected, produced some differential effects, perhaps supporting the contention that negotiation should precede intimacy. It takes a certain degree of mastery and strength to show and share perceived weaknesses and negative aspects of oneself (L'Abate, 1986b).

All these studies were performed with an admittedly functional (i.e., nonclinical) population that had to fulfill class requirements. What would happen if we were to administer the same procedures to clinical couples or families? In my clinical practice, I have found it useful and time-saving to have selected clients write about whatever was upsetting them in an open, unstructured fashion ("Write about your depression whenever you feel like it"). From this relatively unstructured format, instructions then were administered in an increasingly structured, written (i.e., programmed) format. Instead of having clients write about depression whenever they felt like it, they were asked to follow a sequence of questions at preset times of the day on alternate days. The rationale for this structure was found in the notion of control elaborated elsewhere: "If you want to stop it, start it." Many written homework assignments were derived from theoretical models or from clinical experience that was at that time unrelated to theory. Few lessons mushroomed into workbooks and eventually programs (L'Abate, 1986b).

The technology of programmed materials has been applied over the years to depression (L'Abate, 1986b). For instance, instead of a single positive interpretation or reframing of depression, depression was reframed in ten different positive explanations. The client was asked to read and rank order these explanations in terms of how they apply to her or his experience. If the client did not like any of the explanations, he or she could come up with one of his or her own. After this lesson, where hopefully a more positive set about depression was induced, the symptom was then prescribed according to specific and detailed guidelines. This supposedly circular approach has been used in the design of various programmed materials, to be presented below. First, however, we need to introduce a typology of writing suggested, in part, by the studies cited above, because writing is the basis for programmed materials.

The practice of programmed writing is also supported by the study of Cox, Tisdelle, and Culbert (1988). They compared the effects of verbal versus written prescriptions on recall of self-reported adherence to therapeutic homework assignments (i.e., listening to relaxation tapes). Thirty adults were randomly assigned to the verbal and to the written conditions in a counterbalanced, within-Ss, crossover design. Their results showed that written prescriptions led to significantly better recall and adherence to homework assignments than verbal prescriptions.

Toward a Typology of Writing

It is arguable that the spoken word may be relevant to establish and maintain a therapeutic relationship. So-called relationships skills, discussed in Chapter 1, are nonrepeatable, unique features of the individual therapist's style. Words cannot be programmed because, in programming them, we lose the necessarily spontaneous quality needed to establish and maintain a therapeutic relationship. In the same way, the written word is necessary to deal with symptoms whose major feature is their repetitiveness. Why repeat the same instructions orally so many times? Why risk distortions and deletions on the client's part? Why not put these repetitive instructions in writing? Thus the relationship may depend on the spoken word. Dealing with the symptom, however, is more dependent on the written word. The differences between these two modalities are summarized in Table 6.1. In comparing the two modalities, it is obvious that the oral word cannot be controlled, predicted, programmed, or prescribed, while the written word can be controlled, predicted, and programmed. The spoken word is subject to more distortions or deletions than the written word. Furthermore, we can shift from the verbal to the written modality interchangeably in an easier fashion than going from the verbal to the nonverbal modality or vice versa. Hence we could conclude that, while the spoken word is necessary to deal with the relationship with clients, the written word can be used to deal with symptoms. The written word is specific, exacting, explicit, and programmable.

Dealing with symptoms during intervention can be described as "structuring skills" (as discussed in Chapter 1). Structuring interventions is easier (more comfortable, less time-consuming, less expensive) when it takes place through the written rather than through the oral modality. Instead of having to repeat instructions verbally and endlessly from one client to another and from one distressing condition to another, it is more economical, in terms of the therapist's time and energy, to assign the same instructions for the same situation or symptom in writing.

There are at least three types or degrees of structure for writing (L'Abate, 1987f), going from a relatively *open-ended*, unstructured format, such as autobiographies, diaries, and journals, to relatively more structured, *focused* instructions, such as suggesting that the respondent: "Write about . . . [depression, fears, deceptions, your breakup]," as in the two studies cited above (Clark & L'Abate, 1977; Wagner & L'Abate, 1977). From these two degrees of structure— open and focused—we can now move to an even more structured format, or *programmed* writing, as in the materials and workbooks described below.

Programmed Materials

Programmed materials and workbooks were written with the following criteria in mind: (a) *explicitness* of instructions and format, asking questions that are simple to understand and answer in a very concrete fashion; (b) *specificity* in content, focusing on objec-

TABLE 6.1: Summary of Relationships Between Spoken and Written Words as Modalities of Intervention in Preventive and Therapeutic Relationships

Spoken	Written
Necessary for Relationships[a]	Necessary for Structuring of Symptoms
Insufficient for Symptoms[b]	Insufficient for Relationships
Adaptive	Standardized
Uncontrollable	Controllable
Unpredictable	Predictable
Unprogrammable	Programmable
Nonprescribable or difficult to prescribe	Prescribable or easier to prescribe than the spoken word
Subject to distortions and/or deletions	Not as subject to distortions and deletions as the spoken word

a. Qualified in the text: There are some relationships, with impulsive and/or acting-out character disorders, for instance, in which the spoken word may be used for manipulative and distracting purposes. Under these conditions, the spoken word may become more of a hindrance than a help.
b. Questionable and open to empirical confirmation or disqualification.

tively definable conditions, such as depression or impulsivity; (c) *cost-effectiveness,* requiring little professional time and a great deal of involvement—time and energy—on the part of respondents rather than on the part of therapists or trainers; (d) *mass production and delivery,* relying on the written word, these materials can be mass-produced and delivered, provided, of course, that (e) professionals administering these materials follow ethically and professionally responsive and responsible practices. These materials, of course, cannot be administered without stressing the crucial importance of corrective feedback for each written lesson. This feedback can be given verbally or in writing, even through the mail, under certain conditions, as with incarcerated individuals or with families at risk rather than in need or in crisis.

Programmed materials include questionnaires and tests for evaluation. They may consist of loose, one-time lessons, three-lesson programs, or workbooks made up of a series of eight to twenty lessons related to a specific topic (depression, impulsivity, negotiation, intimacy). Each lesson is made up of questions (the Socratic method) that respondents need to answer *in writing.* Typically, there would be one lesson a week, for as many weeks as there are lessons—from two or three to as many as twenty—depending on the condition. Individuals would receive feedback from therapists while couples and families would compare and contrast their answers with each other as well as with the therapist, thus producing three "feedback loops" (to use a systems' cliché): (a) individual, or *monologic*; (b) dyadically interactional, or *dialogic*; and (c) between the family and the therapist, *corrective* or assumedly therapeutic.

For instance, in answering questions asked in each lesson, each respondent is now increasing the monologic function, hopefully increasing internal introspection and reflection, moving according to Schwartz and Garamoni (1989) from a negative internal monologue to a more functional and constructive internal dialogue. This change means going from considering just one side of an issue to including another side previously ignored. Once this task is accomplished, each respondent needs to discuss his or her answers with the partner or with other family members *on a regular basis*, through preset, prearranged appointments, comparing and contrasting their answers and, therefore, increasing the intimate dialogic function. When their lessons and discussions are then presented to a professional, he or she would add a third feedback loop, the corrective interpretation, explanation, or connection that the family may have missed either individually or dyadically.

The Functions of Programmed Materials

Programmed materials and workbooks fulfill a variety of functions. First, they may serve as preliminary preparation for either therapy or prevention. Considering the needs of many families in crisis and in need who drop out after a few sessions of therapy, we need to ask ourselves whether it would be less expensive to request that they work among themselves on workbooks designed to elicit reactions from each other. Considering the number of individuals, couples, and families on the waiting lists of many mental health clinics and hospitals, would it not be more cost-effective to have them start working on a workbook rather than just waiting? By decreasing or minimizing the probability of failure and attrition, which is so common in psychotherapy, the professional would not have spent as much time and energy in a loss.

Second, programmed materials and workbooks are useful in assessing motivation and competence to enter and stay in a personal, possibly prolonged, and, very likely close, professional relationship, requiring self-disclosure, confrontation, and support (L'Abate, 1986b). Evaluating and possibly increasing respondents' involvement in the process of change through programmed materials and workbooks is a process that reflects a paraphrase of Bronfenbrenner's (1979) dictum: "If we want to know how a family works, try to change it!" If a family is really motivated to change, the family will work for change. Consequently, family members can learn to work with each other through workbooks frequently (at least once a week) and faster (for at least one hour) among themselves and with a minimum of professional time and effort. Of course, the more dysfunctional, clinical, or critical the family, the more difficult it will be for them to start working together, at least at the beginning of the therapeutic relationship. As therapy normalizes the family, after the referring symptom or crisis has been taken care of, its members will increasingly become more able to work with each other, using the structure demanded by programmed materials. A lesson, a program, or a workbook presents a definite, concrete, and positive plan. They present a score to follow that oftentimes cannot be found in the spoken word.

Third, we can use programmed materials and workbooks in addition to traditional psychotherapy by employing a modality (i.e., the written one) different from the verbal or even the nonverbal. Traditional psychotherapy still suffers from the myth of uniformity (Kiesler, 1966). It is supposed to treat every conceivable psychological dysfunction known to humanity and, if people do not profit from it, it is because of their extreme dysfunctionality. But we can no longer subscribe to this view. How about considering, instead, the possibility that the verbal modality may not be the most appropriate modality for certain, yet to be identified, families? Workbooks, at least, offer an alternative route through which many families can relate *in addition* or *as an alternative* to the verbal and the nonverbal modalities. Of course, another task for the future will be to identify which family profits from this type of approach rather than another. After all, the idea that any form of psychological treatment based on the spoken word would be applicable to any deviant condition, as was assumed by psychoanalysis in its early days, is no longer tenable. Given a variety of treatment modalities, with differentiations within each modality, which family will benefit from which modality, at what cost, and with what kind of therapist, trainer, or facilitator?

Fourth, programmed materials and workbooks have the potential to increase generalization from the office to the home. Respondents are required to spend as much time working on weekly lessons as they would spend in face-to-face contact with a therapist. With families in need, we should be able to minimize oral interchange and maximize the individuals working together as a family through workbooks. In this way, respondents become more responsible for the process of change, relying more on their internal resources and less on the resources of the professional.

To sum up, these materials can be administered (a) before any face-to-face therapy takes place; (b) at the beginning of therapy; (c) in parallel with ongoing therapy, either with dual diagnoses, such as alcoholism and depression, or when the therapist is on vacation; and (d) after termination of traditional crisis therapy to deal with loose ends and incomplete, unfinished business. Workbooks can also be administered as an alternative to existing psychotherapeutic practices (a) with respondents (individuals, couples, or families) who may not be as proficient with the verbal modality as required by most types of psychotherapy; (b) with individuals who are resistant to or unable to deal with face-to-face interpersonal confrontation (acting-out individuals, addicts); and (c) with populations that cannot be reached through any other means, such as incarcerated individuals, missionary or military families, and others.

Furthermore, one of the main functions of workbooks is research. First, programmed materials and workbooks have the potential to help us deal with issues that cannot be dealt with, or are very expensive to deal with, using traditional psychotherapeutic approaches. For instance, programmed materials can help us control treatment and therapist variables that are too complex and too difficult to control in research. Second, they can help us verify theoretical and therapeutic approaches in a cost-effective fashion fulfilling criteria of *explicitness* and *specificity*. These characteristics are usually not found, or are difficult to find, in traditional therapeutic approaches, for instance, in (a) studying the differential effects of workbooks versus role-playing versus lecturing; (b) studying the effects of face-to-face relationship skills versus the effects of specific "therapeutic" feedback (i.e., structuring skills); (c) dealing with the matching hypothesis in psychotherapy (that is, which problem or symptom needs which form or type of treatment at what cost?), which can now be verified directly through the use of specific versus general workbooks rather than generally vague and hard to specify verbal psychotherapeutic practices; (d) comparing the outcome of specific workbooks produced by one author with the outcome of other workbooks produced by other authors; (e) comparing group versus individual administration of workbooks with high-risk populations, such as adjudicated criminals or juvenile populations; and (f) specifying and identifying polarized dimensions in couples, using two self-report tests derived from the selfhood model described in Chapters 2 and 4.

In addition to dealing with (if not solving) the whole problem of treatment-client match—which will remain insolvable as long as two humans come together through speech—programmed materials help us deal with another crucial therapeutic issue, which is: *generalization* from the therapist's office to the home or wherever clients reside (hospitals, halfway houses). How can we make sure that our directives, suggestions, and prescriptions in primary or tertiary prevention are going to make a difference to the family? How is a family to transfer skills and knowledge from outside the home to within it? Workbooks furnish the link between the office and the home that, hopefully, will increase the process of generalization, that is, transfer of learning from one setting to another.

Finally, programmed materials can help to deal with the common, dual diagnosis problem. Face-to-face therapy can be directed, for instance, toward the whole family, while selected individuals in the same family can work on specifically assigned workbooks, either dyadically or individually. This advantage will become clearer as different types of workbooks are described.

Types of Programmed Materials

The first three workbooks on depression, negotiation, and intimacy, plus a questionnaire for follow-up interviews, have already been published (L'Abate, 1986b). Other programmed materials, including evaluation forms, written homework assignments, and workbooks, are contained in a manual (L'Abate & Cox, in press). The purpose of this manual is to make available materials necessary for the practice of programmed writing to serve as secondary prevention tools. They can be conceived as being *paratherapeutic* methods of intervention, that is, they are to be used alongside of or parallel to tertiary prevention, that is, traditional psychotherapeutic techniques, or with primary prevention, that is, psychoeducational skills training approaches.

Materials for evaluation consist of original forms for instruments reviewed in Chapter 4, including instructions and weights to score them, like the Social Information Form with codes to score it, the Adjustment Inventory, the Self-Profile Chart, and the 240 items of the Problems in Relationships Test, with codes to score it.

Materials for individuals range from those for more severe to those for less severe conditions, starting with Alcoholics Anonymous (AA) 12 Steps, a program for addictive conditions, to the Social Training workbook for impulsive and acting-out individuals. This workbook is followed by 15 programs for the 15 revised Minnesota Multiphasic Personality Inventory (MMPI-2) Content Scales. Each of these scales represents 15 factor-pure dimensions. It is possible to derive lessons from the characteristics of each dimension, as in the case of the Social Training workbook already cited, designed to help change impulsivity. This workbook, however, was written independently of an MMPI-2 definition of impulsivity. Consequently, it will be possible to compare and contrast different workbooks, one related to and one independent from the MMPI-2. Their usefulness, for instance, could be compared in the case of three depression programs, one that I developed (L'Abate, 1986b), one that a collaborator developed (Levis, 1987), and a third from the MMPI-2 (Boyce & L'Abate, n.d.). If lessons on the same topic are found useful, it will be possible to use them together to deal with extreme conditions, as in the case of serious depression or other entrenched conditions. The same comparative evaluation can be made with anger. The three lessons about anger consist of one from the Social Training workbook, a second from the MMPI-2, and a third from the Social Growth workbook. There are two lessons on self-esteem—one from the MMPI-2 and the other from the Social Growth workbook (which is the final workbook for this section; it could be considered as a general, all-purpose program for anxious individuals or individuals without a specific behavior pattern).

Materials for couples consist of a program for *arguing or fighting* that includes the same paradoxical approach described above, that is, the first lesson requires a description of this pattern, the second lesson consists of ranking 10 positive "explanations" for the arguing, and the third lesson prescribes an argument or fight according to six suicidal patterns to be followed by the couple to have a really "dirty" argument: (a) using the *you* pronoun, (b) mind reading, (c) bringing up the past, (d) blackmailing and bribing, (e) giving ultimatums, (f) making excuses, and (g) using any other pattern that is peculiar to the couple. They are to tape-record their argument. After they return the tape to the therapist, it will be given back with instructions for a fourth lesson. The couple is to listen to the tape individually and score how often they use each of the patterns mentioned above. Once they come back with their frequency count (or content analysis) of the tape, they are assigned individual lessons that deal with the pattern that is primary in each of their arguments. When another pattern is secondary, it is assigned during the next session. Usually, arguments are dealt in five to six sessions and lessons.

Other couple programs consist of *codependency* and *sexuality*, with a workbook for *problems in relationships*, already described in relation to the selfhood model (Chapters 2 and 4). This model is part of the theory of interpersonal competence with a test designed to assign each lesson and a series of lessons according to the degree of polarization in the couple (as described in Chapter 4). A second workbook, *Building Relationships*, could be used independently or as a booster program for problems in relationships, because the overlap in lessons and orientation is pronounced.

Materials for families consist of programs in the same format as above: The first lesson is a description of the pattern; the second lesson contains positive explanations of the pattern that need to be ranked; and the third lesson consists of detailed guidelines to prescribe the disturbing behavior pattern. Programs start with general topics but progress and end with very specific topics. The nine family patterns, with three lessons each, are (a) negativity, (b) verbal abuse, (c) temper tantrums, (d) shyness, (e) stealing, (f) sibling rivalry, (g) domestic violence, (h) lying, and (i) binge eating.

Of course, there can be as many programmed materials and workbooks as the need and ingenuity of clinicians warrant. At this time, these materials and workbooks can be classified in at least three different ways according to their origins: (a) from clinically derived and devised hypotheses that test general as well as impressionistic clinical approaches, (b) from theory-derived models, and (c) from the phenomenally large self-help book literature.

Eclectic, clinically derived materials. These programs and workbooks are not derived from any particular theory. They were or are being written eclectically according to what is available in the literature on the subject, without any particular model in mind. Thus far, for instance, the following eclectic workbooks have been produced (a) *Social Training,* for impulsive, acting-out individuals; (b) *Social Growth,* for anxious individuals, individuals who cannot afford psychotherapy, or individuals whose motivation for psychotherapy is questionable; (c) *Building Relationships for Couples,* an eclectic workbook with no particular theoretical viewpoint but with emphasis on negotiation and intimacy—these workbooks, plus the evaluation instruments presented in Chapter 4, furnish the bulk of a first manual for programmed therapy (L'Abate & Cox, in press)— and (d) workbooks derived from literature on treating *addictions,* with one workbook for each specific addiction (L'Abate, Farrar, & Serritella, in press)—which are likely to furnish the major portion of a second manual.

Theory-derived workbooks. These are workbooks primarily designed to be theory-testing instruments. They are based on theoretical models derived from a developmental theory of interpersonal competence or to test any other theory (Chapter 2). (1) *Depression* for instance, as mentioned above, can be treated according to three workbooks—one, which I devised, uses a paradoxical interpersonal approach (L'Abate, 1986b); the other was derived from Beck's (Beck & Young, 1985) well-known cognitive approach reduced to workbook format (Levis, 1987); and the third was derived from the MMPI-2. With these three workbooks, we can compare and contrast one theoretical approach with the other (Boyce & L'Abate, n.d.). (2) There is a workbook on *negotiation* based on a model of negotiation derived from the original theory (L'Abate, 1986b). (3) The workbook on *intimacy* is derived from the same theory as for negotiation (L'Abate, 1986b). (4) As already described in Chapter 4, the *Problems in Relationships* workbook tests and verifies the major dimensions of reactivity in intimate relationships based on the four-part model of importance attribution (Chapters 2 and 4).

Workbooks derived from self-help books. The field is open to all sorts of possibilities, for instance, designing and deriving workbooks from existing self-help books, whose help remains questionable at best. Self-help books do not seem to offer the active and interactive involvement as well as the monologic and multiple feedback functions offered by workbooks. There are as many workbooks possible as there are available self-help books, and more. In fact, instead of having undergraduates write notoriously boring term papers as part of a class's requirements, I have had undergraduates reduce existing self-help books to workbooks in a child development class and in a psychology of adjustment class. These workbooks will furnish the bulk of a fourth manual devoted to self-help books dealing with (a) personhood, (b) partnership, and (c) parenthood issues. Guidelines for the creation of paratherapeutic workbooks, from whatever source one may wish to use, are summarized in Table 6.2.

The use of programmed materials and workbooks is not an accepted practice in either individual, marriage, or family therapy (L'Abate, Ganahl, & Hansen, 1986). Most of the active practice of homework assignments in marriage and family therapy is based either on single, crisis-oriented, ad hoc assignments (Haley, 1976) or on single-shot behavioral prescriptions of a verbal or written nature. At best, when instructions are given in writing, most of them are based on an attempt to deal with specific symptoms or problems (Shelton & Levy, 1981) with a pragmatic rationale. I have recently advanced the idea that one important aspect of the positive therapeutic outcome may be obtained from systematically written homework assignments (L'Abate, 1986). Because these written homework assignments are derived from a developmental theory of family functioning, they become another, hopefully more dynamic, way of testing this theory. Therefore, in addition to traditional, static paper-and-pencil tests (L'Abate & Wagner, 1985, 1988; Stevens & L'Abate, 1989), SEPs and programmed materials fulfill a theory-testing function.

The major implication concerns whether workbooks can be used as a cost-effective, mass-producible alternative or addition to existing mental health practices, which are based mainly on the oral rather than on the written word. Workbooks can reach a much larger audience than psychotherapy, because workbooks can be administered *at a distance* through the mail. For instance, I am working with inmates and acting-out juveniles who refused to join their families in therapy but agreed to work on the Social Training workbook through the mail. In my private practice, I have also

TABLE 6.2: Suggestions for Writing a Workbook

1. At the outset, do not worry about length, format, or style. It is best to start with an outline of the topics one wants to cover, assigning a lesson for each topic and following principles of sequencing between and within lessons. For instance, a workbook could be broken up into two or three sections, each one devoted to the different stages of the treatment process. Within each stage, one needs to allocate various lessons, each for a specific topic *in sequence*. Each lesson, and the questions within each lesson, should follow from the previous ones. For instance, one may start with the most immediate concerns, moving on to short-term and then to long-term concerns (past, present, and future). To increase the respondent's temporal perspective, give some daily, weekly, monthly, yearly, and longer-range goals. One needs to determine what is needed now, what will be needed later on, and what will be needed in the long run.

2. In writing each lesson, avoid brainwashing and lengthy instructions. If you find yourself explaining too much, you need to break the paragraphs into smaller steps, with a minimum of guidance and a maximum of letting the respondent come to find his or her own answers, step by step, gradually.

3. Follow a sequence in planning each lesson. Why are you asking the respondent to do what you are asking him or her to do? Which step should follow previous steps? In addition to the purpose of the workbook in general, you need to work out an outline that gives you a sequence within each of the stages mentioned in step 1, above. Each lesson should have its specific purpose. For instance, if the first lesson should be diagnostic, put all the diagnostic questions into the first lesson. The second lesson may concentrate on goals; the third lesson may concentrate on fulfilling daily goals; the fourth lesson may be devoted to weekly goals; and so on. Separate diagnostic from problem-solving questions. Give a title to each of your lessons. Use the notion of *sequencing* within each lesson and among lessons, with some degree of continuity and coherence from one lesson to another.

---

worked with adults with MMPI peaks on either the Depression or the Impulsivity scales. The Beck's, the MMPI-2, or the workbook already published have been used with severely depressed individuals (L'Abate, 1986b). These workbooks are used in tandem with each other and *in addition to* face-to-face traditional psychotherapy. Some acting-out, or character disordered individuals, on the other hand, have to complete working on the Social Training workbook before being seen for psychotherapy.

The advantages of these paratherapeutic workbooks are primarily in decreased costs and increased therapeutic effectiveness. Their main disadvantage is that they are not applicable, as yet, to illiterates or to unmotivated individuals, even though a program for unmotivated individuals, derived from a corresponding MMPI-2 scale, is available. All of these materials and workbooks, on the

TABLE 6.2 (cont.)

4. Build into each lesson weekly tasks or chores for the respondent to follow in detail. For instance, suggestions for controlling undesirable behavior could become weekly assignments for follow-up. The respondent needs to specify whether or not she or he followed the assignment, and why. How did he or she feel after doing the assignment (or not doing it)? Make sure that each homework assignment has feedback lines for answers at the beginning of the next lesson. For instance, one could have another lesson on completing homework assignments. How many of the assignments were completed? What was the outcome? If they were followed, what happened? If they were not followed, what happened? Each lesson needs to be closed at the end by homework assignments. The respondent needs to follow concrete, specific, and timely guidelines for behavioral tasks to be performed each week between lessons.

5. If the respondent speaks well but does not do the homework assignments, you may need to have a lesson on duplicity and lying to oneself, loved ones, peers, colleagues, friends, and so on. Stress pride as the antidote for shame and guilt. Are you proud of your behavior? Why? Why not? For instance, there is no sense giving a list of feeling adjectives if you do not follow them with specific instructions on feeling and emotions.

6. Make a tentative draft first. Send it to a few very critical friend-colleagues and ask for specific reactions and suggestions. Remember that this is the kind of workbook that you could use with your clients.

7. After receiving constructive feedback, revise the manuscript and try it out yourself, or give it to family members and/or friends who are not professionals to get their reactions. Use their reactions to revise it again.

8. Administer it to clients selectively and appropriately and on the basis of their feedback, revise it again.

other hand, could be administered by audio- or videotape and answered through the same media.

Conclusion

Programmed materials and workbooks provide an additional method of intervention that could be coupled with existing primary and tertiary prevention methods. Workbooks could be administered to selected individuals in families that are receiving SEPs or an equivalent primary prevention program. I have routinely used workbooks in my clinical practice, combining them with ongoing crisis therapy. In primary prevention, programmed workbooks could be administered without individualized feedback, although in secondary prevention, programmed workbooks would require individualized feedback to be given routinely with each lesson. In primary prevention, workbooks could be administered in a group format, lead by a middle-level professional, with feedback arising from group discussion. In secondary prevention, the format may be individual, with feedback from a professional given face to face or through the mail, depending on the particular situation.

These materials could (and, I believe, should) become extremely important tools for secondary prevention, when they are derived from (a) clinical experience and existing therapeutic practices, (b) theoretical models, and (c) self-help books. They can be used by middle- and upper-level professionals (who have an M.A. as well as experience) with credentials (for accurate assessment, selection, and matching of workbooks) and a minimum of training in how to administer them. Eventually, these workbooks could be administered by paraprofessionals under the supervision of middle- or upper-level professionals.

When we combine methods of intervention in primary, secondary, and tertiary prevention with a lattice and ladder of personnel, we can deal with more human problems and more families than was possible before. Workbooks are to secondary prevention what face-to-face contact is to tertiary prevention. The main issue here: Is change the outcome of systematically planned scripts, as in SEPs or in workbooks, plus corrective feedback, or the outcome of face-to-face relationships plus verbal interpretations? Workbooks can be used to research these questions.

7

Training Professional Preventers

Prevention, thus far, just like the family, has not been the province of any single discipline or profession (Jason, Hess, Felner, & Moritsugu, 1987; Price, 1983; Zolik, 1983). This chapter will introduce the possibility of creating a special profession devoted to the specialized delivery of primary and secondary prevention programs. The more a profession, or any complex system for that matter, develops and grows, the more it needs to differentiate into more manageable parts. The greater the degree of differentiation, the greater the need for specialization.

The mental health field in general has shown this progression. From one profession, namely, psychiatry, the mental health field has subdivided itself further into a variety of professions, and specializations within each profession, with family therapy one of the newcomers. With increasing specialization in the applied, clinical field, it is now apparent that the formal creation of a profession of preventers is growing near. The issue is whether this new profession will repeat the errors of its predecessors or whether it will be able to create standards well above those set by its predecessors in the mental health field.

However, before one talks about a profession of preventers, we need to ask ourselves what a profession is—what does it consist of? For instance, how is a profession different from a scientific society?

Prevention as a Profession

At the abstract level, a profession consists of a body of conceptual information, based on theoretical, experiential, practical, or empirical foundations. At a more practical level, a profession is also a body of recognized and recognizable professionals identified by a common bond, given by a title, professional identity, functions, and a body of commonly accepted practices and procedures. Most professions are like a guild society, with an accepted body of ethical and professional memberships, journals, meetings, and bylaws, based on fulfilling agreed-upon standards and functions (Goldstein, 1988). These include (a) establishing criteria for competence through standard-setting activities, such as educational criteria, entry requirements for membership, and licensing laws; (b) establishing mechanisms to implement and enforce established standards; (c) advocating legislative and administrative actions to protect the "image," mystique, and practical influence of the profession; (d) marketing the profession and its members through media and other channels; and (e) offering ancillary services to members, such as job placement, continuing education programs, and publications. According to these standards, prevention has a long way to go. However, as we shall see, a good beginning has already been made.

How About a Profession of Preventers?

Primary and secondary prevention approaches are based on strong convictions about their usefulness as well as on a growing common body of knowledge. Most professionals and laypeople are convinced that prevention is necessary, vital, and enduring. The problem, however, is *how* prevention is going to develop and grow. Years ago, I made some suggestions on how we should certify preventers not only through paper credentials, as in the already established mental health professions, but also through actual (objective) demonstrations of effectiveness in their interventions (L'Abate, 1983). Others made suggestions for prevention specializations in clinical psychology as well as the creation of a Ph.D. program in preventive psychology (L'Abate, 1987). A training program in family psychology, with evaluative and preventive components, has been in place for years (L'Abate, 1985a). The need for a profession of preventers is based on the following arguments.

First, the field of prevention with families already comprises many recognized, creative, and competent leaders, most of whom were reviewed in Chapter 5. Among the many are (a) David and Vera Mace, founders of ACME; (b) Don Dinkmeyer, with his STEP and TIME programs for parenting and marriage, respectively; (c) Tom Gordon, with PET; (d) Bernard and Luise Guerney, with RE; (e) Sherod Miller, with CC; and (f) David Olson and his ENRICH prevention program—to name just a few. Thus the field of prevention with families does not lack recognized, competent, and well-known leaders.

Second, there are many programs that, since 1970, have been created to train families in a variety of social, personal, marital, and parental skills (L'Abate, 1986a, 1987). These programs promise to develop into intermediate, cost-effective, and mass-oriented sieves for families at risk and in need. They are available to introduce primary and secondary prevention approaches from *nothing*, at the base, through tertiary prevention, that is, psychotherapy, medication, or institutionalization in either hospitals or jails.

Third, there have been embryonic developments in the creation of professional associations, like the almost defunct Interpersonal Skills Training and Research Association (ISTARA), the Association for Couples in Marital Enrichment (ACME), and others. Now a new association, the National Association of Prevention Professionals and Advocates (NAPPA), may succeed where others in the past may have failed to unify the variety of individuals committed to prevention in all of its aspects.

There is no doubt that prevention has its enemies, in the form of resistance to innovation and change, both at the ideological and at the delivery levels. For instance, many psychotherapists neither care about nor are interested in preventive efforts outside of their own fields, as discussed briefly in Chapter 1. Some of them seem to see preventive efforts as a threat to their livelihood or a waste of time and effort. Furthermore, they believe they are the real preventers. These differences suggest that preventers and therapists may have different value systems and different models. Prevention follows a public health model, with a long-range temporal perspective. Therapy, unless performed in public institutions, follows a crisis and private practice model. The help is given immediately on the basis of need and ability to pay. The issue is not whether one field is better than the other—*we need both*. In fact, we need as many models as will be useful to families. *We do not need mutually exclusive practices.*

In addition to inevitable bureaucratic hurdles and potential turf disputes, there is a great deal of resistance and downright opposition to innovation from the established mental health professionals. Recently, DeLuca (1989) reviewed the professional and bureaucratic hurdles, opposition, and resistance of psychologists opposed to the use of paraprofessional technicians in diagnosis, let alone in prevention.

I encountered the same kind of resistance, opposition, and fear when I first started to advocate the use of pre-, para- and quasi-professionals in the delivery of psychological services (L'Abate, 1964). It took a quarter of a century for this issue to come up again as one approach in the delivery of mental health services. Without a hierarchy of personnel, we are destined to try to build skyscrapers with our bare hands, as argued in Chapter 3. As Duhl and Cummings (1987, p. 1) indicated concerning the crisis in mental health services: "The crisis is real. The potential for a dramatic shift to a new ball game of mental health has never been greater. We do not know who the power hitters will be, nor do we know where the new ballpark will be. We only know that the game will change." This book suggests that the game allow a variety of players at different levels of expertise and human kindness. The ballpark will be the field of prevention, with families anywhere they want to play—in clinics, hospitals, schools, churches, and new structures, as discussed in the next chapter.

If there were to be, ideally, a new mental health profession of preventers, what would its needs be?

Needs of a Specialization in Prevention

More than a decade ago, we (L'Abate & O'Callaghan, 1977) outlined an educational curriculum that would consist of (a) courses in the whole field of family relations or family life education, with some simple, structured applications, such as SEPs at the undergraduate level; (b) at the graduate level, below the master's degree, specialization in the various primary and secondary prevention programs cursorily reviewed in Chapter 5, with a master's thesis comparing the effectiveness of one or two prevention programs; (c) at the Ph.D. level, above and beyond the master's, all of the knowledge covered at the two other levels, plus knowledge of statistics, research designs, techniques of program evaluation, and experience with tertiary prevention approaches; an internship and a doctoral dissertation on primary or secondary prevention would be necessary requirements.

More recently, I have outlined a whole educational curriculum in social skills training and primary prevention (L'Abate, 1987). Of course, no curriculum will be feasible unless jobs are available. As things are now, there are few paying jobs in the mental health field for those who perform prevention services. There are few if any job descriptions in state merit systems and state bureaucracies. Hence how can we train personnel if they cannot be employed? Openings can only be made when they are created by legislative action on the political level, a key area to investigate and to become involved in for those interested in promoting and promulgating prevention approaches. Ultimately, prevention will need to be accorded status as an important profession in its own right, assessed by credentialing and licensing boards, state merit systems, and the federal government. There is no question that prevention has a long way to go to fulfill all of the requirements listed above.

Training for Different Levels of Prevention

In addition to the academic curriculum outlined above, training in the application of primary and secondary prevention could take place according to three existing levels: (a) below the baccalaureate level, it could consist of clerical, semitechnical tasks requiring suitable personal qualities for the delivery of face-to-face services, such as the administration and computer scoring of structured diagnostic instruments; (b) baccalaureate-, or the equivalent, level training would consist of technical skills, a major in family life education, and beginning administration of simple, structured applications, such as SEPs, as already suggested; (c) master's degree, or the equivalent, at the semiprofessional level, with experiential knowledge through direct provision of services of various and more complex preventive approaches with couples and families; (d) Ph.D. or the equivalent for the professional level, with an ability to implement and combine methods of intervention based on primary, secondary, and tertiary prevention, using a variety of personnel, including oneself.

Combination of Prevention Levels

In family centers of the future, families could receive a variety of combinations of methods, for instance, (a) a combination of therapy and structured enrichment (Kochalka, Buzas, L'Abate, McHenry, & Gibson, 1987; L'Abate et al., 1976); (b) a combination of family therapy and workbooks with individuals in the same family (L'Abate & Cox, in press); (c) a combination of a variety of primary, secondary, and tertiary prevention methods, following a model of intervention that combines crisis intervention with tertiary, secondary (i.e., workbooks) and primary prevention approaches (L'Abate, 1986b).

Prevention has not as yet achieved credibility in some academic, bureaucratic, and professional circles. It has not proven itself to the point of becoming institutionalized through degree-granting curricula at undergraduate and graduate levels. However, what degree of proof will be necessary? To wait for proven prevention programs could require years and a major research commitment many of us can not make. Furthermore, the criteria for a profession are not the same as those required for a learned society. Although the major focus of a learned society is justification, as in the criteria of accountability, validity, and verifiability, the criteria for a profession are usefulness and satisfaction of existing public needs (L'Abate, 1964).

Ultimately, the major needs of preventive approaches will be in the areas of recruitment and delivery systems, that is, how can families at risk and in need be reached and recruited? How can we develop latent needs and market services to fulfill those needs? Bond and Wagner (1988), in their list of characteristics of effective prevention and promotion programs, listed the importance of identifying and securing resources and establishing alternative sources of resources to implement and maximize the likelihood of program utilization. To market prevention and promotion programs, Bond and Wagner listed five additional characteristics: (a) assessing the needs of service deliverers and program recipients; (b) creating translatable, adaptable programming; (c) encouraging a sense of ownership of the programs among service deliverers and program recipients; (d) embedding programs within existing institutions and structures; and (e) making programs engaging for their participants.

To strengthen and sustain prevention and promotion efforts, Bond and Wagner suggested that we will need to (a) establish ties with existing power structures, (b) educate policymakers and the public, and (c) train preventers. Hopefully, some of Bond and Wagner's points are a repetition of our discussion.

Consequently, prevention needs to develop individuals, couples, and even families whose major identification is that of preventer, at various levels of experience and competence. Prevention needs to have a hierarchy and lattice of various types and levels of skills and competencies (as advocated in Chapter 3). These individuals need to exercise pressure on existing structures, academic and political, for the institutionalization of prevention in courses, curricula, degrees, and job descriptions, with parallel salaries and recognition for the preventive services rendered.

Most of all, preventers will need to pay attention to research and evaluation and not repeat the errors of previous mental health professions. Preventers need to learn from the mistakes of the established mental health ideologies, professions, and specializations concerning the consistent denigration, downgrading, and downplaying, in training and in actual practice, of pre- and post-follow-up evaluations on an SOP basis. In addition, prevention approaches need to implement the institutionalization of *successive sieves* in service delivery, from (a) voluntary, for families at risk, to (b) obligatory, for families in need, to (c) mandatory or mandated, for families in crisis, according to criteria of cost-effectiveness as well as immediacy and nature of the needs (L'Abate & Cox, in press).

Conclusion

Prevention is here to stay, the issue is, however, *how* is it going to stay? Prevention can and should become a first-class profession, provided it keeps standards higher than traditional mental health professions (i.e., through evaluation, evaluation, evaluation).

8

Marriage Preparation

This chapter provides an example of how primary prevention can be applied directly to populations that have not been able to receive needed services. One of the most underserved and overlooked areas of need in primary and secondary prevention is marriage. It is the most important and, for some people, the longest-lasting relationship after relationships with siblings. Yet it has not received the attention it deserves. It has been taken for granted, just like personhood and parenthood in terms of the myths and sub-myths reviewed in the Preface.

The last generation has seen the phenomenal increase of professional associations dedicated to marriage and family therapy. However, the field of marriage preparation and promotion, as well as prevention of marital problems, has not often been in the eyes of the public and professionals and it has been low in the list of national priorities. We have more urgent problems to tackle than marriage. Yet we could argue that marriage has been taken for granted for too long at too many levels—cultural, institutional, and personal. We need to take decisive steps to make marriage the center of attention it deserves in primary and secondary prevention.

We recognize that marriage is a complex legal, economic, emotional, practical, social, and cultural process that is multileveled and multidimensional. Therefore, it needs the combined and concentrated efforts of a variety of people. For a lawyer, marriage is a contract. For a psychologist, marriage is a relationship. For a priest, marriage is a sacrament. For a sociologist, marriage is an institution. These and other disciplines need an institution where each viewpoint can be given the attention it deserves and where the unique contribution of each discipline is acknowledged within a dialogue of equals.

As already argued in the Preface of this book, three of the most destructive myths about marriage and the family concern equating chronological age with emotional and social maturity, especially in intimate relationships. To wit, (a) if we are older than 18 (or 21 depending on the state where one lives), we automatically become adults; (b) once we get married, we become instantaneously fully functioning partners; and (c) once we conceive a child, we instantaneously become parents. Many of us marry prematurely, strictly on the basis of short-lived infatuations and sexual urges, which, oftentimes, lead to premature parenthood. Many of us are completely unprepared to assume adult responsibilities such as marriage and parenthood. Consequently, we see the disastrous outcome of these three myths in illegitimacy, divorce, abuse, and neglect. Yet there is no institution, outside of the church and the therapeutic community, where people can learn to become more responsible persons and better prepared partners and parents. Oftentimes the process of becoming a partner takes place before one has become a fully functioning person. Oftentimes the process of becoming a parent even takes place before one can achieve adult and partner status.

Where is one to learn to achieve these levels of functioning? Educational institutions are not equipped to help, with the exception of a few academic and usually nonexperiential, or impractical, strictly academic marriage and family courses. How are we going to raise the consciousness of our nation to become prepared for marriage the way people prepare themselves to get a driver's license or even an occupation? One spends more time learning how to drive a car than learning how to become a person and a partner.

The institution of marriage has seen many drastic changes take place from one generation to the next. Although marital roles may have been clearly defined in the past, this is not the case today. The old-time, traditional notions of masculine and feminine roles are no longer operational in today's society. Equality of importance in a close and prolonged relationship is basic to the establishment of reciprocity and, ultimately, intimacy. Flexibility and creativity in role structures, decision making, and problem solving can take place provided both partners acknowledge and affirm their inherent equality of importance in different functions. Who is to say that housework is any less important than office work? Who is to say that raising children is only the major function and prerogative of women?

We can no longer subscribe to rigid and traditional views of marriage based on stereotyped and stultifying role functions. Equality, reciprocity, and intimacy in a relationship, however, are not given to us. We have to work hard to achieve them. The most we know about marriage is what we learned from our parents' marriage. Even if theirs was a good one, we can no longer assume that repeating what we learned from them will succeed in our marriage. There is too much variability in human behavior to expect that outcome. Furthermore, very few of us in the future will have the chance to see a working marriage from its inception to the death of its partners. Many of us will grow up in single-parent families or in nontraditional households. Who is going to teach us and how are we going to learn?

Marital Preparation

The field of family preparation is practically in its infancy (Gleason & Prescott, 1977; Haller & Olsen, 1951; Kon, 1983; Parker, 1986; Thurman, 1946) and seems to be characterized by confusion and inadequacy of purpose. For instance, where does marriage preparation end and marriage counseling begin (Schumm & Denton, 1979)? There are those who question whether marriage preparation can really take place on a before-marriage basis (Bader, Microys, & Sinclair, 1980). After all, how can one think appropriately when one is "in love"? By the same token, there are advocates of marriage preparation for divorced individuals (Messinger, Walker, & Freeman, 1978; Rolfe, 1985).

As the reader has seen throughout this book, we do not lack the technology to present marital programs. Given an abundance of riches, the issue here becomes one of selectivity. Which, among many programs, is more effective than other programs and how is one to choose?

Single Versus Multiple-Purpose Programs

The purpose of this section is not to review existing premarital preparation programs but to present programs for marital preparation that can be used responsibly. To select among the many available programs, we can start with a simpleminded distinction between single- and multiple-purpose programs. The same distinction was made in Chapter 5. Marital preparation programs can be classified into those that are specifically designed for a single purpose—a special, specific, and predetermined topic—versus those all-purpose programs designed to teach general interpersonal skills relevant in most if not all intimate relationships.

Among single-purpose programs, that developed by the British Columbia Council for the Family (1988), is highly recommended. It is probably the most eclectic and complete program available to date. Unfortunately, this program is so new that it lacks validating evidence as to its effectiveness. It is recommended, however, on the grounds of completeness and thoroughness of coverage as well as sensitivity to basic and important issues of marital preparation.

An excellent and up-to-date review of programs for premarital and newlywed couples can be found in Fournier and Olson (1986). They (1986, pp. 206–207) classified premarital programs into three categories: (a) family life education, (b) instructional counseling, and (c) enrichment. Their conclusion tends to dampen quick and easy enthusiasm about marital preparation: "In general, couples interviewed after marriage remember very little about the premarital program or did not follow through with the procedures after the program was completed" (p. 213)." Note that their tripartite division of premarital programs fits into the three levels of prevention presented in Chapter 1. For instance, family life education, with its emphasis on information giving and passive reception of information, would fit into primary prevention approaches with all couples, regardless of risk. Many of these couples will need further training, as found in enrichment, with stress on a more active involvement on the couple's side. The use of specially designed premarital workbooks would fit into secondary prevention. This approach would be more useful for couples in need of definite skills. Premarital counseling, on the other hand, would apply to couples already in crisis before marriage, who could or would not use either primary or secondary prevention approaches in the time of crisis. Fournier and Olson recommended that: "Premarital preparation should be seen as a national priority to help marriages get off on a good start. The prevention of divorce begins with providing good premarital preparation" (p. 226).

The simpleminded distinction between single- and multiple-purpose programs, however, breaks down in dealing with the SEPs reviewed in Chapter 5. This approach differs from the others that will be considered below. SEP's were designed to be administered with little preparation by nonprofessionals or paraprofessionals, such as volunteer couples, rather than by middle-level personnel, as in the case of the programs to be reviewed here and as suggested by Most and Guerney (1983). In other words, SEPs are both multipurpose as well as single-purpose. For instance, there are two programs for problem solving in courtship and premarriage as well as two programs for sexual attitudes and sexuality. Where is one to draw a line between the two? In addition, there is one program for newlyweds and eight programs for man-woman relationships, ranging from cohabitation to assertiveness, equality, reciprocity, negotiation, conflict resolution, and "working through." Again, where is one to draw the line? All of these programs are relevant to relationships, both before and after marriage. An example of an SEP with a dating couple has been given by Lutz and Weinstein (1987).

Multipurpose Programs

Many all-purpose skills training programs, reviewed in Chapter 5, follow a funnel approach and can be used in a variety of ways at all stages of the life cycle, including prior to marriage. Among the many available (Levant, 1986), there are a few that stand out in terms of completeness and supporting evidence for their short-term effectiveness:

Premarital Couples Communication Program (CC). This program is as well known as the (Minnesota) Couples Communication Program (L'Abate & McHenry, 1983; Wackman & Wampler, 1985).

Premarital Relationship Enhancement (PRE). This is probably one of the best documented premarital preparation programs (Avery, Ridely, Leslie, & Mulholland, 1980; Guerney, 1988; Guerney & Guerney, 1985; Guerney, Guerney, & Cooney, 1985; Ridley, Avery,

Harrell, Hayes-Clements, & McCunney, 1981; Ridley, Jorgensen, Morgan, & Avery, 1982).

ENRICH. This program has been applied to large populations by Olson and his associates. It has also been applied and validated extensively by Cusinato and his associates (1985) in Italy.

Converting the Need and the Dream into Reality[1]

The more we think about marriage, the more we realize how little is done for it in the areas of preparation, promotion, and prevention of marital problems. The family therapy movement and the mental health, psychotherapeutic establishments have focused on *crisis intervention* and the alleviation of many marital and family problems *after* a crisis has taken place. The National Institutes of Mental Health have focused on marriage and family therapy *research*. However, there is no center dedicated exclusively to marriage. There is the Palo Alto Behavioral Sciences "think tank," among many other think tanks scattered around the country. However, as we searched, we could not find one single place or institution whose sole aim was the promotion of marriage through preparation and prevention. Consequently, John Lantz and I founded the National Marriage Center in Decatur, Georgia, in 1988.

Functions of the National Marriage Center

The purpose of this section is to present a proposal concerning the foundation, formation, and construction of a national marriage center (NMC) *dedicated to the study, promulgation, and promotion of marriage fitness through marriage preparation and prevention of marital problems.* This center, as we see it, would serve a variety of functions not included together anywhere else in the world. Some of these functions may have been fulfilled in the past by separate institutions. Yet we lack a center that will encompass all of the many functions within one roof.

Clearinghouse. We need to have a central depository, a clearinghouse, for unifying and gathering together most, if not all, that is known about marriage from as many points of view as possible. Once this information is gathered, it needs to be distributed, disseminated, and, more important, applied responsibly. In the last generation, there has been more research devoted to marriage and the family than in all the previous years of recorded history. How is this information to be gathered together and processed for the improvement of marriage?

Think tank. We need a center where experts on marriage, from as many viewpoints and disciplines as possible, can come together and debate to sharpen their, and others', thinking about marriage. What would happen if we put together in a seminar *as equals* an artist, lawyer, psychiatrist, sociologist, clergyman or clergywoman, psychologist, nutritionist, and economist whose major interest, within their relative fields, is marriage?

This center would have as its primary motivation conducting a disciplined search for issues central and fundamental to marriage. This would be a neutral place, where different viewpoints would be given equal status and each viewpoint and discipline would receive support and nurturance. No single discipline would be primary at the expense of other disciplines. This would be a place where the best representatives from each discipline with expertise on marriage can come together and compare and contrast theories, research, and applications. This process would take place through the nomination of various visiting and/or resident fellows, interns, practicum students, and researchers. Each seminar or training course for professionals would include members of different professions and disciplines who would further the frontiers of thinking in their respective disciplines.

Research. We need to encourage and generate research that will have direct and indirect applications to marriage promotion and preparation and the prevention of marital problems.

Training center. We need to educate and train the public and many professionals to deal more and better with marital preparation, the NMC, and the promotion of marriage through a variety of media, such as symposia, conferences, workshops, lectures, and a newsletter and/or other publications. Training will take place for various levels, ladder and lattice, of pre-, para- and full-fledged professional personnel including training volunteers.

Service: Promotion of marital fitness. We will need to step up the pace and influence of preventive efforts to slow down and possibly decrease marital problems and marital breakdown. These preventive efforts would be focused on primary prevention for couples *at risk* and on secondary prevention for couples *in need*.

Some concrete steps have already been undertaken to convert the dream into a reality. (1) After a great deal of talking and discussing, we (John Lantz and I) have finally incorporated our National Marriage Center as a legal entity, as a not-for-profit organization. (2) We have been spreading the word through personal contacts, letters, TV appearances, and newspaper articles. The latter has brought the support and interest of a few select individuals from various fields of endeavor. We need to do more. We need to start talking to clubs, fraternal organizations, corporations, business, schools, and so on. We need to attract creative community activists to share our dream and help us convert it into a reality. This step would lead us into the next step. (3) We must get people involved organizationally to assume responsibilities, develop programs, and set up committees in order to go to the next step. (4) We need to create an organizational structure with people from all walks of life who will help us in the creation of a speakers' bureau, training courses, regular meetings, and plans and programs for the center and even volunteer to stuff envelopes and the like. (5) We need to solicit funds to allow us to start moving on a variety of fronts. (6) We will then be able to start creating a variety of boards, for instance, (a) a board of directors and an executive committee, (b) a board of professional advisers, and a (c) a board of volunteers. (7) These will include various classes of membership: (a) charter, (b) contributing, (c) sustaining, (d) professional, and (e) associate.

Ultimately, we will need a physical structure to house all of the various activities that this center will fulfill, including offices, conference rooms, a marriage library with subscriptions to all of the major professional and scientific journals devoted to the study of marriage, a communications area with computers for data processing and fax machines for the efficient distribution of information, and a printing room.

Creating of a Lasting Entity

Like our country's foresighted founding fathers, we want to create an institution to survive all of us and continue into the future. Institutions last, people do not. In order to make this a lasting institution, we need public support and corporate commitments and contributions; we will need to offer services and training for a fee; we will need research grants; and we will need to sell the information gathered. Currently, we are planning to start offering marriage preparation workshops in the following format.

Marriage Fitness Program: How to Achieve a Successful Relationship

The purpose of this program is to teach and help couples develop new and more successful ways of relating with each other. This program consists of six steps.

Step 1. Before being admitted to the workshop, a couple will need to accept *evaluation* with a thorough test battery consisting of the tests already described in Chapter 4, that is, the Social Information Form (85 items), Problems in Relationships (240 items), Intimacy and Negotiation (32 items), Marital Adjustment Inventory, the Self-Profile Chart, and the MMPI-2. On the basis of this evaluation, couples either will be admitted to the workshop, if their scores on the various tests of this battery fall within average ranges, or will be encouraged to seek therapy from qualified professionals elsewhere, if their scores fall outside of normal ranges. The purposes of this screening evaluation are to (a) assess the quality of the existing relationship, (b) determine whether a couple is ready for admission to this program, (c) establish a baseline against which progress at the end of this program can be reevaluated, (d) pinpoint areas of concern for each particular couple, and (e) collect basic research data for long-range evaluation of success in marriage. It will take approximately two hours of each partner's time to complete all of the questionnaires. Couples who have been referred elsewhere for counseling and therapy will be reevaluated on termination of therapy at no cost if they want to enter our program again. (An interesting sideline would be to select every other couple referred elsewhere to see whether we could help them work with specially designed lessons long distance through the mail.)

Step 2. We will present a *workshop*, consisting of a one-day group session with couples and two trainers. The tentative format for this workshop is to begin with each couple answering a brief questionnaire, "Beliefs about Marriage," where the many myths and submyths reviewed in the Preface will be presented on a true-false basis. The "true" answers will be discussed, because everybody should have answered "false." After this discussion, which we hope would involve all the couples, we would next administer a compatibility form to see how similar or different each couple is, with a subsequent discussion. Then, the topics of equality, reciprocity, and intimacy, taken from the equivalent SEPs exercises (L'Abate & Weinstein, 1987) would be introduced and discussed. These topics would be followed by that of the necessary skills for mature love, which are (a) seeing the good, (b) caring, (c) forgiveness, and (d) back to intimacy, as the sharing of hurts (L'Abate, 1986).

In the afternoon, couples will be able to break up into small groups to choose among such topics as "How to Fight in Love and Marriage: Fighting Clean and Fighting Dirty," using the forms already written on this topic (Chapter 6) consisting of three introductory lessons to describe, explain, and prescribe fighting or arguing, with the identification of destructive individual patterns. After this workshop, couples would be required to work on the next step.

Step 3. We would then assign *homework* consisting of lessons specifically created for each couple. On the basis of the initial evaluation, as well as their behavior during the workshop, each couple would be assigned homework assignments for two months with weekly meetings between partners for a total of eight lessons. Each couple will be required to answer each lesson individually, comparing and discussing their answers with each other, and mailing each lesson to the trainers, who, in turn, will evaluate the answers, giving written feedback to each couple, and send subsequent lessons through the mail. Depending on their needs, a couple could be administered one of the following workbooks: (a) *Negotiation* (9 lessons, L'Abate, 1986b); (b) *Problems in Relationships*, according to the process described in Chapter 6; (c) *Building Relationships* (Chapter 6); or (d) any of the workbooks developed from self-help books, described in Chapter 6.

As noted above, one of the major shortcomings of marriage preparation is the need for follow-through, because a one-day workshop is not sufficient to impart lasting skills. Consequently, a couple signing up for this workshop would commit itself to pre-post evaluation, as well as follow-through in this step, which would take place through correspondence by mail.

Step 4. The next stage is *reevaluation,* consisting of readministering all the questionnaires and tests (except the Social Information Form) originally administered at the beginning of the program.

Step 5. We will provide *feedback* in writing through the mail about the outcome of the reevaluation with possible recommendations for the future and a rebate of a portion of the original fee paid at the outset of the program.

Step 6. Finally we will follow up the couples on a long-term basis, yearly or biannually, using a follow-up format that is already available (L'Abate, 1986b). Thus in this program we plan to use all of the technology developed and described in Chapters 5 and 6.

Conclusion

We feel that we have the technology and know-how to start such a needed institution. Because both John Lantz and I live in DeKalb County, Georgia, this is where such a center will be built. Our complementary combination of legal skills and knowledge of marital preparation make us a good team to start it. We are both committed to the need for research as the basis of any kind of preventive work with couples. We want to add other professionals with different skills as we grow. If we do not build such a center, who will?

NOTE

1. This section was written in collaboration with John Lantz, J.D., Cofounder and Director of the National Marriage Center.

Appendix:
Where Structured Enrichment Failed—
A Case Study

The original purpose of this case was to illustrate how both SEPs and programmed homework assignments can be combined in interventions with functional and semifunctional couples. As defined in Chapter 5, semifunctional couples are at greater risk and, therefore, *in greater need* than functional couples or families for primary or secondary prevention approaches. Functional families *at risk* may benefit from primary prevention. Semifunctional families *in need* may benefit from a combination of primary (i.e., SEPs, Chapter 5) and secondary (i.e., programmed materials, Chapter 6) prevention approaches. Dysfunctional families *in crisis* will need tertiary prevention *plus* supplementary secondary and primary prevention approaches, after the crisis has subsided. Both primary and secondary prevention approaches lend themselves to this complementary combination. Although SEPs are usually administered directly by a trainer face to face, programmed materials are designed to be self-administered in addition to either primary or tertiary intervention. However, as indicated in Chapter 1, some SEPs may be interchangeable with secondary prevention once they are reduced to a written, self-administered rather than an oral trainer-administered format.

This couple's responses to the initial interview and assessment indicated the possibility of more serious problems in at least one partner, with strong tensions and dissatisfactions in the marital relationship. These problems were suggested by the man, who indicated that he was already in individual therapy and that both husband and wife had participated in some sessions of marital therapy. Thus, with the permission of the man's therapist, an approach of SEPs and systematic homework assignments complementary to ongoing individual therapy was planned.

Joe and Lynn Smith were interested in participating in a structured enrichment program for couples. The enricher, a first-year graduate student (M.A.) in the clinical psychology program without clinical experience was interested in learning primary and secondary prevention strategies with couples. This couple's participation was initiated by Joe, who volunteered himself and his wife to receive course credit for an introductory psychology class. After two sessions, Joe dropped his class but wished to continue the program voluntarily and forgo the credits.

Initial Interview and Evaluation:
Family History and Background Information

Joe had previously been married for seven years. He divorced after meeting Lynn in the Orient while stationed there in the military. His first marriage was one "without any feelings of love" and he felt like he was just "following in his father's footsteps." Both his father and his grandfather had been through divorces. Joe was in the military for ten years before he resigned. He later studied for three years at a midwestern university but did not receive a degree. Following this, he worked for a corporation, where he was able to work his way up to the position of vice president and bring home "100, 000 dollars a year." He left this position in 1986 after he discovered his wife, Lynn, had gone to another man for "support" during the period when their daughter was diagnosed with cancer. Although he had had affairs himself, Joe felt very hurt that he could not provide emotional support to his wife. This time in his life was "extremely difficult." He felt he "could not take much more." He felt he had had too many bad outcomes and experiences in his life and that "he must have done something wrong to cause the problems." He had been in individual therapy for the past two and a half years. For the previous year, he had also been involved in a men's group. These experiences had been helpful for him because he had been able to experience, express, and work through much of his anger. Three years before, he had been involved in a men's group on violence which he said he did not "enjoy" or "get much out of." He had a somewhat recent history of violent behavior that began when he struck Lynn in a fit of rage, focused around his jealousy for her receiving a bachelor's degree from college. Joe was currently enrolled in a university with a major in psychology, working part-time in a fast-food restaurant.

Lynn Smith, age 42, is the oldest of three children and was born and raised on a farm in the Midwest. Her parents are deceased; her mother died when she was 9 and her father died when she was 21, although he had emotionally abandoned her when she was a child. She described her father as a "binge alcoholic," who often had mood swings. Lynn had always enjoyed working and considered herself a very strong person. She moved away from home when she joined the service. After spending some time in the military and meeting Joe, Lynn resigned, worked for a while, and went to school to get her nursing degree. She described herself as "responsible," "independent, " and "emotional" but "able to keep herself together in times of stress." She belonged to a fundamentalist church and religion was an important part of her life. Lynn was currently employed as a nurse and said she "enjoyed her work."

Joe and Lynn met when they were both 27, in the military, when Joe was still married. Joe said he fell in love with Lynn and that they had had a lot of fun together on their days off. He was divorced within the next year and he and Lynn married when they were 28 years old. They had been married for 15 years and had four children. Joe described his children as "extremely bright" and reported the IQs of each of them; he also mentioned Lynn's IQ of "150, " and said her intelligence was what attracted him to her.

When asked more about themselves, Joe mentioned that he was very traditional in his views of men and women and it bothered him that he and Lynn's roles were reversed within a traditional sex role model. He felt "antagonistic towards women at times" and believed this was because of his upbringing. He felt burdened by the happenings in his life, specifically the diagnosis of his daughter with cancer in 1984. He described himself as feeling "like I was already carrying a heavy load and then my back was broken". During this time, Lynn was in nursing school. She had dealt with the situation by using the motto "that in everyone's life we are given a cross to bear and this was my cross." Joe felt that Lynn was so together and he was falling apart. He felt immense anger and emotion during this time; he described himself as feeling "like a woman in a man's body." In 1986, he quit his high-paying job. He became involved in therapy and a men's support group, where there were three homosexual members. He stated he had really enjoyed the group because he was around other men who were sensitive, as he viewed himself. It felt good to be able to be himself without being rejected. Joe seemed to feel that, if he were himself, he would be rejected by society, so he felt he must fit in with society by being macho, tough, and strong ("like men are supposed to be"). His goal was to be accepted for who he was and respected by Lynn so she would understand him better and they would be able to communicate better. He was frustrated by Lynn's emotional unexpressiveness and felt her use of the word "we" in statements prevented him from "knowing what she felt." He wanted to make his marriage work and loved Lynn very much, but at the same time he felt a strong need to develop his individuality.

Lynn was less talkative during the initial interview and said she didn't like to focus on problems. She felt she and Joe had gone through some tough times and that they were headed in the right direction, but she realized there were areas that needed work. Both Joe and Lynn felt that there were often underlying meanings to their communications so they never knew where they themselves were or their partner was. They needed a safe arena to express themselves and learn to negotiate their differences and were hoping to find structured enrichment helpful for meeting these needs.

Joe Smith, age 42, is one of five siblings, born and raised in the South. His parents were alive, married to each other, and lived near him. However, he was no longer on speaking terms with them. Joe reported how he came from "a dysfunctional family." During his childhood, Joe's father was only at home on weekends and Joe described him as a "workaholic." Joe described his relationship with his mother as being "sexually inappropriate," without elaboration. He was often put in the position of taking care of the family while his father was away. His father was very demanding and controlling and concerned that Joe be "manly." As a child, he felt he could never live up to his father's expectations. He felt that he "was always walking an extremely fine line," which was impossible for him. His father wanted him to be "a man" and Joe felt his father perceived him as "a wimp" because of his artistic and creative qualities. He experienced a strict Catholic upbringing and felt he was always in a "no-win situation." He "tried to do good in the eyes of the church," but when he was good he "would still get beat up" by his father. Although Joe described his father with anger in his voice, he also said he was impressed with his father's abilities and wanted to be like him. Joe felt the enrichment program would be very helpful for him and for Lynn. They had tried marital therapy before, but it fell through. The therapist felt that Joe "should work through his anger in individual therapy and a men's group on violence before marital counseling would be helpful." Joe was interested in learning about the "process of marital therapy." The enricher reemphasized that structured enrichment was *not* therapy. The difference was explained to them in terms of a continuum: Therapy dealt with clinical and critical conditions with little or no structure; SEPs were designed to make things better for a limited time span of six weeks, with a focus on areas the couple wanted to improve.

When asked what area they wanted to work on in the program and what their expectations were, both had difficulty pinning anything down specifically. They were presented with some general topics including parenting issues, men-women relationships, and communication patterns. They agreed on communication styles as their first choice and parenting issues as their second. It was explained that the enricher would use three sources of information, under supervision, to come up with a program: (a) the initial interview and a subjective impression by the enricher, (b) their stated needs and desires, and (c) test results.

Couple Evaluation

The instruments administered were the Family Inventory of Life Events and Changes (FILE): Family Environment Scale (FES); the Beck Depression Inventory (BDI); the SCL-90-R; and the Dyadic Adjustment Scale (DAS).

Results

The FILE was completed by Joe and Lynn together and was scored to determine the level of stress in their family. The family life events scores reflect the frequency of a "yes" response to stresses and changes. The weighted scores reflect the impact of specific changes on the family's overall level of stress, as shown in Table A.1.

Compared with "normal" families with school-aged children, Joe and Lynn's scores fell within the moderate range of stress. However, Joe and Lynn had very different strategies and strengths for coping with stress. In describing their coping with their daughter's diagnosis of cancer, Lynn was described as "strong and able to hold herself together" whereas Joe felt "hysterical" and experienced this stress as one that "broke his back." Joe appeared more vulnerable to additional stressors than Lynn. He admitted; she denied.

TABLE A.1: Family Inventory of Life Events

Subscales	Score	Weighted Score
1. Intrafamily strains	4	171
2. Marital strains	0	0
3. Pregnancy and childbearing	0	0
4. Finance and business strains	0	0
5. Work/family transitions and strains	4	172
6. Illness/family "care" strains	0	0
7. Losses	0	0
8. Transitions "in and out"	1	38
9. Family legal violations	1	75
Total	10	456

TABLE A.2: Family Environment Scale

| | Scaled Scores | |
Subscales	Joe	Lynn
Cohesion	31	53
Expressiveness	47	54
Conflict	54	65
Independence	20	53
Achievement orientation	47	47
Intellectual/cultural orientation	41	64
Active/recreational orientation	48	37
Moral/religious emphasis	51	46
Organization	48	26
Control	54	43
Total	441	488
Incongruence Score: 65		

Scores on the FES (Table A.2) suggested that Joe and Lynn were more incongruent in their perception of their family climate than a sample of "normal" families with six members (a score of 65 compared with 52). Joe's scores reflected a perception of his family as less cohesive, committed, and supportive to one another than Lynn's. He felt the family members were encouraged to express feelings directly and that there was a normal amount of expressed conflict. He saw his family as lacking assertiveness and self-sufficiency at times. His scores indicated an emphasis comparable to normal families in the areas of achievement, intellectual and cultural activities, moral and religious values, and participation in social and recreational activities. Joe felt it was important to have clear organization and structure in the family and felt control was useful for running family life. His scores were comparable to "normal" six-member family climates.

Lynn's scores on the same test indicated a perception of the family as committed to and supportive of one another and open to expressing their feelings directly. She indicated a high degree of conflict in the family expressed by anger and aggression. Her scores implied a perception of members as independent with an emphasis on achievement in the work and school settings. She saw her family as interested in political, social, and intellectual activities but saw the family as less interested in recreational activities. Her scores reflected her feelings that the family lacked organization and structure when planning family activities and delegating responsibilities. Overall, her scores were consistent with those of non-distressed six-member families.

On the BDI, Joe's score totaled 28 which placed him in the severely depressed range. Lynn's score, 9, was in the normal range for depressive symptoms.

On the SCL-90 (Table A.3), Joe reported significant disturbances on every scale except "phobic anxiety." His GSI, the most sensitive indicator of psychological distress, reflected a very high level of disturbance. He reported distress arising from perceptions of body dysfunctions, which corresponded to his verbal report of back pains. His distress within the obsessive-compulsive subscale was congruent with his desire to be "perfect." Joe also reported significant feelings of personal inadequacy and inferiority, particularly when comparing himself with others. He reported feeling "uneasy" around others and felt his emotions were more "feminine" than "masculine." He felt he was not understood by males and females and was uncomfortable with his emotions, which he described as often "overwhelming." His score on the depression scale was congruent with the BDI and reflected his feelings of hopelessness at times and dissatisfaction with his current situation (i.e., the role reversal when he went back to school and Lynn financially provided for the family). He reported feeling anxious and very hostile at times. This dimension reflected Joe's feelings of anger, resentment, and rage. Additionally, his scores reflected significant amounts of paranoid ideation and may have been related to his feelings of being responsible when things went wrong (i.e., for his abuse as a child and his daughter's diagnosis of cancer). He also reported a withdrawn life-style experience; although he actively participated as father and husband in a family of six, he often felt very emotionally unconnected and alone.

Lynn's scores were in the normal range and suggested she was not experiencing (or letting herself experience) significant amounts of psychological distress at the time of evaluation.

TABLE A.3: Results for the SCL-90

Symptoms	Standard Scores	
	Joe	Lynn
Somatization	*65	42
Obsessive-compulsive	*70	58
Interpersonal sensitivity	*70	53
Depression	*81	57
Anxiety	*71	44
Hostility	*63	49
Phobic anxiety	56	44
Paranoid ideation	*71	57
Psychoticism	*79	44
GSI	*81	51
PSDI	*65	44
PST	*69	53

*Indicates the most significant scores.

TABLE A.4: Dyadic Adjustment Scale

Subscales	Joe	Lynn
Dyadic consensus (DC)	23/65	44/65
Affectional expression (AE)	4/12	8/12
Dyadic satisfaction (DS)	30/50	37/50
Dyadic cohesion (DCoH)	13/24	15/24
Total	70	104

The DAS scores for this couple are presented in Table A.4. Each score was given in a ratio over the maximum score for each scale. These scores indicate that Joe and Lynn experienced a high degree of disagreement with each other. Although they reported feeling connected to one another, they had conflict in their affective expression. They reported feeling only fairly satisfied with their relationship. Overall, Joe's scores were more comparable to a sample of divorced couples. Lynn's scores were more congruent with married respondents.

Interpretation

Joe and Lynn appeared to be at different places in their individual levels of distress, with Joe experiencing significant amounts of distress in most areas of his personal life. His scores may have been indicative of the work he was doing in individual therapy. He focused on understanding his emotional development and depression and expressing himself in an appropriate manner. He reported he was in a "hostile" mood when completing the assessments. By all of the criteria given in Chapter 2, Joe fits into various categories and dimensions described by the theory. He fits the category of showing an apathetic-abusive pattern in his style with Lynn. At best, this pattern had become repetitive reactivity. This style would derive from a contradictorily confused identification on the likeness continuum, apparently symbiotic with his mother and apparently alienated from his father. On the level of self-definition, he could be categorized as "no-self," where no one wins with him and he seems to lose most of the time. When he wins, at least occupationally, he cannot handle success. In addition, his boundaries indicate a very loose, confused orientation to life, without direction except losses. He seems determined to lose in most areas of his life. His overemotionality is expressed at the expense of the other components of his resources—rationality and activity. He seems very close to a breakdown, barely holding on to reality and to tenuous controls. He is in a critical place in his life. His adjustment has reached the level of needing urgent clinical interventions, including medication or possible hospitalization.

Lynn's scores did not reflect any areas of distress. However, this denial may have indicated her style of "not focusing on the bad" and accepting whatever situation came her way in a relentlessly positive fashion that may have polarized the relationship even further. It may be that she was denying the conflicts in the relationship with Joe as a way of maintaining her strong role in the relationship. In spite of this overt level of "strength," and "goodness," it should be stressed that her level of adjustment was not any higher than her husband's. Her unrelenting stress on the positive and on strength is the same kind of reactive identification found in many adult children of alcoholics: "If I am good, grit my teeth, and show an outward facade of strength, I will be good and socially acceptable." This identification may be found in many invulnerable children who are relentlessly positive *in reaction* to very negative family backgrounds. What would happen to her if her husband were to abandon his relentlessly negative position?

This couple represents a level of dysfunctionality that falls within the boundaries of the AA and RR styles described in Chapter 2. They seem unable to break the many polarizations existing in their relationship. Where Joe needs to see himself as "sick," "incompetent, " and "weak," Lynn needs to see herself as "healthy," "competent," "good," and "strong." They are polarized in (a) the overemotionality (for Joe) versus overrationality (for Lynn) dimension; (b) the admission or approach (for Joe) versus denial or avoidance (for Lynn); and (c) goodness, strength, and positivity (for Lynn) and "badness," weakness, and negativity (for Joe). The predicted outcome of these polarizations, of course, is lack of intimacy, to the point that, while Joe tried to bootleg it through sexual affairs, Lynn had to use an extramarital affair to achieve a modicum of it.

Retrospectively, we can see that this couple is dysfunctional individually and dyadically. Therefore, they should not have been admitted to either structured enrichment or to any other course of primary or secondary prevention. According to the definitions given in previous chapters they are *in crisis* and, consequently, would need tertiary rather than any other prevention approach. However, to have dropped and rejected them from something they wanted might have added to their stress level even further. Consequently, they were accepted for a preventive course of action with many misgivings about their ability to complete it.

Recommendations

Following the initial interview, the assessment battery results, and a supervisory meeting to discuss the most appropriate and beneficial program for this couple, the following recommendations were made. Because of Joe's current involvement in therapy, a primary and secondary combined prevention program was deemed most appropriate. A structured enrichment program was the most feasible intervention at the marital level. First, this couple would need involvement in an enrichment program to negotiate the areas of their relationship in which they differed. Due to their diverging styles of emotional expressiveness, it was recommended that the negotiation program be used to focus on their communication styles and to develop a better understanding of their partners and of themselves. Due to Joe's involvement in individual and group therapy, to work on his anger and depression, it was recommended, second, that this couple receive the intimacy series (L'Abate, 1986b) on a trial basis, as homework assignments to complement the weekly negotiation sessions. The homework assignments would hopefully allow them to express themselves individually as well as to learn about their partner's position when they discussed the assignments together. Following the initial interview, the couple was to see the enricher for six weeks to complete the negotiation program. There would then be a closing assessment battery to determine any change and a closing interview. The couple would be seen in a three-month follow-up to determine continued levels of adjustment.

A release of information was obtained to monitor the clinical level of Joe in his concurrent individual and group therapies. Although this couple seemed to need tertiary intervention, it was agreed that structured enrichment might be helpful for them at the marital level as a supplement to therapy. At the closing of this program, their additional need to be actively involved in therapy would be addressed.

Session 1

As the session began, the couple was asked how it felt to fill out forms and Joe said he had been in a "hostile" mood when he did his. They felt they covered a wide range of areas and they liked that. Joe and Lynn were offered the following programs: reciprocity, assertiveness, and negotiation. Negotiation was recommended because it covered the areas they felt they needed help with in the communication domain. The goals of the negotiation program were defined as follows: (a) for couples to become aware of implicit rules that govern their interlocking marital system, (b) to increase awareness in the ways each partner communicates, and (c) to bargain effectively (i.e., "something for something").

Joe and Lynn decided they wanted to participate in the negotiation program. They were then asked if they would be interested in committing one hour of time on their own to do a homework assignment each week that focused on intimacy. They really seemed to like this idea and were eager to begin the program.

Lesson 11.1 Marriage Myths

Exercise 11.1.1: Reality and Fiction

What is a myth? Both Joe and Lynn felt that a *myth* was something that was presented as being true but in reality was not true. They both had thought that marriage would be the "answer." Because Joe had grown up in a dysfunctional family, he thought that certain marriages could be "perfect, with everyone happy," however, he had never had this experience. Having been married before, Joe claimed he had a little more understanding of what marriage was like, but because he had not felt "emotionally married," he didn't feel he had any more insight than Lynn. Joe imagined that Lynn would stay home and be "domestic," taking care of the home and children. He thought he would work and support the family. To Joe, marriage was a "logical choice rather than an emotional one." He perceived Lynn as domestic and strong and, because she had grown up on a farm, he thought she would want to be at home when they married.

To Lynn, marriage meant "togetherness and working toward common goals." When Lynn talked about this topic, she started to cry (she said she felt emotional after a difficult day at work). She wanted her family to be active in church and felt that children who grow up with a faith have a certain strength. Initially, she saw Joe as strong and responsible and these qualities attracted her to him.

Exercise 11.1.2 Apparent Discrepancies

Joe and Lynn were asked to describe what being in love was like during their courtship. They described their courtship as enjoyable. They spent a great deal of time together while they were stationed in the Orient. Joe remembered how it had been difficult too because they worked together. There were only 12 women in their duty station and other men were envious because Joe, who was an "ineligible" man, was dating Lynn. Joe also remembered feeling he had sacrificed many areas of himself (values, dignity as an officer) for Lynn to make her feel that he cared for her. He realized his biggest fear had been that she would leave him if he set limits between work and their relationship. Lynn had been "stronger" in this respect and had asked to be switched to another duty station because she felt the tension in their dual relationship. Joe talked about feeling angry about his sacrifices and his "weakness." He felt frustrated because he was so fearful of rejection. He had always resented Lynn for maintaining her responsibilities and keeping clear boundaries. Joe and Lynn also mentioned the good times they had getting pizza and enjoying their time together, but they described it as a "desperate situation."

Exercise 11.1.3: Real or Imagined Differences

The couple was asked to write down characteristics of men and women. After completing this exercise, Joe noticed that both he and Lynn had described women more negatively (weak, emotional, less athletic) and had glorified men (strong, independent). Joe felt he fit better with the female characteristics (more sensitive, creative, expressive, and verbal). Lynn said she was not as introspective, expressive, or sensitive as most females and felt she fit with the male characteristics. Joe expressed feelings of wanting to be valued and appreciated for the "risk" he was taking in moving toward more feminine characteristics. Lynn replied that she liked those qualities in Joe, and Joe said he needed to hear that more often.

In closing, the enricher gave Joe and Lynn the first lesson of the intimacy series (caring) and told them to fill it out individually, talk about their ideas together, and bring any questions about the homework to the next session.

Supervision

We reviewed primary and secondary prevention approaches. Enrichment was primary because the focus was on areas in which the couple wanted to do better. The homework assignments were secondary; they added something to the primary approach. Tertiary prevention approaches would include clinical work where issues were more toxic in how they affected the relationship and the functioning of the system. We discussed how a combined approach might strengthen a prevention model. This approach was different from the traditional orientation of separating prevention and therapy and allowed for a continuum rather than separate activities.

We discussed how the traditional sequence of homework assignments should include depression, negotiation, and then intimacy. We were aware of Joe's depression and how this might affect the success of the homework assignment. The intimacy series might have been premature and inappropriate at the time. We decided we would ask them how it went and, if they found it helpful, we would continue with the intimacy homework. Joe's depression was being dealt with in his individual therapy and we felt it was important to focus on bringing this couple closer together in their communication and behavior styles.

Session 2

Homework Assignment 1: Love and Caring

This session reviewed some of the issues and concerns that were brought up in the intimacy homework. They had completed the assignment separately; however, they did not have the extra time together. They found time to do it alone and felt it was helpful. They felt coming to the sessions allowed them a "safe environment to express themselves"; otherwise they would keep many of their feelings and perspectives hidden.

The couple was asked to define *love*. For Lynn, love was similar to caring, but more. She said she cares about a lot of people, but truly loves very few. She saw love as unconditional giving. Joe, on the other hand, had a difficult time with this question and said he became angry when he tried to come up with a definition. He came to the conclusion that there "is no such thing as love." *Love* is just a word to describe an intense feeling one has at a particular moment. He also said the word *love* is used to satisfy the expectations of the one who wants to hear it.

When asked, "What is caring?" Joe had a much easier time. He felt caring was genuine and believed there was a difference between "caring" and "loving". He could not understand how one could "say they loved you" and then "beat you up or walk all over you". He got angry just thinking about it and felt "love" was very fake and superficial. Lynn believed she could show she cared physically and mentally but had difficulty showing her care emotionally.

The homework assignment served as a perfect lead in to the negotiation program.

Lesson 11.2: Focus on the Relationship

Exercise 11.2.1—Who Am I?

Joe and Lynn faced each other and asked each other the following questions while the enricher wrote down the answers. "Who are you?" Joe responded that he was "trustworthy, honest, a father, a person who cares about Lynn, and insecure." Lynn responded that she was "emotional, dependable, conscientious, sad, and a person who is interested in growth".

"What can I give you?" To this question, Joe answered "insightfulness, trustworthiness, yourself, a home, and a chance to prove myself." Lynn responded that she could give "understanding of where I come from, respect, emotional support, time, and forgiveness."

"What can you give me?" To this final question, Lynn began by answering "The chance you asked for, caring, appreciation, dependability, and respect." Joe answered, "Your freedom (you said you wanted to be free, independent, not to be needed, and not to be there for me), equality, what you wanted (which had to do with all of the things you asked for a long time ago), and whatever you want."

This exercise created a great deal of emotion. Both Joe and Lynn cried and looked at each other for long periods of time. They started to talk about divorce and even discussed child custody. At this point, the enricher interjected to try and get back to the program. It seemed important that they recommit to each other to keep working and try to strengthen their relationship. Joe said his biggest fear was putting out an either/or statement (i.e., "I leave or we work it out."). Lynn responded that she would just deal with whatever happened. Lynn reminded Joe that she had lived with him for 15 years and he recognized and appreciated her statement; he did see it as a sign of her love and commitment to him and their marriage.

The enricher asked if they wanted to continue the intimacy homework and they said they really wanted to do that. They were given the next homework assignment at the end of the session.

Supervision

When getting back the intimacy homework, it was important to look at each partner's individual answers and push for them to discuss them together. Joe and Lynn needed to be responsible for discussing them together and making the time for each other.

We discussed the difference between *reactivity* and *spontaneity*. *Spontaneity*, or a positive agreement to do something on impulse, is what a couple strives for; one can only be spontaneous when one has intimacy. Anger is often manipulative and reactive. When Joe was angry, he didn't have to look at himself. This assumption was congruent with his feelings of resentment toward Lynn when she had finished her degree a few years before. He felt that his world was falling apart and she was keeping herself together and getting the degree he wanted so badly for himself. This envy created enormous anger and he reacted against Lynn through his emotions and physical abuse. When Joe was mad at Lynn, he projected what is going on with him onto her.

This pattern may indicate "no-self" in both members: Nobody wins. It seems that Joe had set the situation so he was "bad" and Lynn was "good"; but neither one of them could win because Lynn was frustrated by his insecurity and resentment toward her. There is no equality in a reactive type of relationship. Only in a reciprocal relationship can there be two winners. Joe and Lynn's current style of interaction was self-defeating. Joe reported feeling abusive, "out of control," when he projected onto Lynn.

Because of his intense reactivity, Lynn appeared apathetic and lacking emotional responsiveness, which further frustrated Joe.

It was important to ask Joe if he was aware of how self-sabotaging he was. Did he need a scapegoat to be himself? Also, it was recommended that the enricher look through the data to see if Lynn was denying the problems in the relationship. Did they disagree in the way they described each other's individual style and interaction pattern? Did Lynn need to be strong because Joe was so weak? It seemed the good-bad polarization occurred because Joe took the "one-down" position forcing Lynn into the "one-up" and strong position. Therefore, she was strong by default. This pattern followed the description Joe gave of their courtship. Lynn was strong enough to say "no" when it came to crossing the line into a dual relationship and she actively made arrangements to be away from Joe to avoid further difficulties. Joe, on the other hand, was insecure about the relationship and sacrificed many of his values and job ethics for the relationship. He spoke of feeling frustrated by his lack of control and weakness.

Although it seemed enrichment was not enough for this couple, they were committed to the contract and stated they were getting a great deal from the program. Perhaps this couple would benefit from clinical intervention when they finished with the structured, initial type of format.

Session 3

Homework Assignment 2: Seeing the Good

Joe and Lynn arrived 20 minutes late, which limited the session to 35 minutes. They were interested in discussing the homework assignment on "seeing the good." Joe was interested in what Lynn had to say and the enricher realized they had not made time to discuss their answers together before arriving at the session. When asked what "seeing the good" meant, Joe said "appreciating value in others". For Joe, it was often difficult for him to focus on the good because he had been let down so many times. It was even more difficult to see the good in himself, although he realized he was more fortunate than some other people (i.e., he was "physically attractive, not mutilated"). Although he described himself as having a "poor self-image," he was able to characterize himself as "intelligent, personable, witty, humorous, artistic, talented, patient, kind, and understanding." When asked about his negative characteristics, Joe replied he felt "angry, sometimes insensitive, unstable, adventurous to a fault," and that he "strove to be perfect." He found it equally difficult to see the good and the bad because he "externalizes so much." He felt it was easier to see the faults of others because of his strong judgmental background. For Joe, it was most difficult to see the good in Lynn. He was curious as to why that was, and Lynn suggested it was because his expectations had been so great of her and she had failed to live up to them. Joe agreed.

For Lynn, "seeing the good" meant looking for positive qualities in people; she felt she could always find something good to focus on in people. She described herself as caring, willing to help, willing to try, and optimistic but admitted it was difficult to talk about the "good qualities." She did not give these qualities much value because seeing the good in oneself was "not valued in her family"; "negative aspects were dwelled on more." In describing her negative points, she said she was "resentful, selfish, stubborn, had difficulty accepting criticism, and difficulty admitting when she was wrong." She said it was most difficult to see the bad because she did not like to think of those qualities and make herself "feel awful." Lynn wrote that it was moderately difficult to see the good in Joe because "she lives with him every day" and moderately difficult to see the good in her father because "he was dead and had abandoned [her] as a child."

After Joe and Lynn discussed their differences, time had run out and the enricher decided to continue with the third lesson of the negotiation program the following week.

Supervision

Joe and Lynn needed to discuss the homework assignment between themselves before coming to the session. If they were unable to comply, the homework assignments should not have been included. We also talked about writing a contract before departing for the three-week vacation break that was coming up. This contract was to be typed and state that they would complete the homework assignments that were left (at that time, it was assignments 5 and 6). They would sign the contract and keep a copy. The advantage of homework assignments is that they maintain continuity with the enrichment and regulate the couple's level of reactivity while breaks or vacations do not permit contact sessions. The enricher was to give Joe and Lynn this contract the week after the following one, before the break period.

Session 4

Homework Assignment 3: Love and Forgiveness

As the session began, the enricher decided to hold off on any discussion of the homework until the enrichment lesson was completed.

Lesson 11.3 Communication in Marriage

Exercise 11.3.1: Definition

Joe and Lynn were asked, "What does the word communication mean?" For Joe, it meant knowing what the other person was thinking without fear of rejection. For Lynn, it meant expressing feelings and listening to others. When asked how they had communicated in the past, they laughed and said "We haven't!" Joe mentioned his use of abuse and violent behavior to communicate his feelings and needs. He was aware of Lynn's nonverbal style of communicating and said she was often silent; he interpreted her silence as a rejection of himself and a lack of interest in his person. He said her gestures were often defensive and he felt this was her way of controlling him. He felt very hurt when Lynn responded (or didn't respond) to him in this way and it made him angry that she controlled him in her "subtle" way. Joe was also cognizant of Lynn's nonverbal communication when she opened her arms up for hugs. Joe said he appreciated the emotional communication from Lynn but was eager for her to communicate to him directly and verbally so he would know what she was feeling and "who she was." Lynn stated that Joe's nonverbal behavior was easy to read. He would give her a glare and she knew to stay out of his way. It is interesting that this situation usually continued with Lynn keeping silent and Joe becoming frustrated and angry.

Exercise 11.3.2: Communicating Feelings

In this exercise, Lynn was told to communicate a feeling to Joe without the use of any words. She communicated the feeling "I love you" by touching him playfully with her feet and smiling. Both giggled and it was nice for the enricher to see them open and sweet with each other. Joe reported receiving the feeling that was sent. Both partners said they didn't have trouble reading the emotional messages being sent but felt they didn't get many of their needs met through their current communication styles.

Exercise 11.3.3: Incongruent Stances

It was very easy for Joe and Lynn to slip into the roles of placator, blamer, avoider, and preacher. Lynn said she was much like the "placator" and "avoider" in real life and that Joe was a "blamer." To get the most out of the exercise, they acted out the comfortable role of their partner to get a feel for their partner's style. They delved into some toxic issues during the role-play and it was obvious that "acting" made it easier for them to discuss some very intense difficulties. After 10 minutes of role-play, the exercise was processed. They felt it was difficult to play the roles and Lynn specifically did not like "feeling like a bully"; she would much rather smooth over the differences.

Exercise 11.3.4: Speaking for Self; *I* Statements

This last exercise, with the enricher guiding them to switch and begin new sentences, consisted of emotionally laden conversation. They actively engaged in conversation using sentences beginning with "it," "you," "we," and then finally "I." They said they felt much more comfortable with the *I* statements except that Joe had noticed that Lynn no longer made statements of her own but only responded to his statements. He felt her conversation lacked substance. He noticed that, when they were using the *you* statements, Lynn had anger in her voice and was forceful in her statements, which had a blaming content. He said it felt good to him to hear her talk out some real feelings and was disappointed when it stopped with the *I* statements. This, he said, had been an issue in the beginning of the sessions (i.e., when Joe had said he was frustrated not knowing where Lynn stood on issues and what was going on with her).

With these accusations, Lynn became upset with Joe and said, "The whole conversation was only a game." At this point, Joe started to push Lynn to talk about a personal issue of hers. She responded by saying he had better stop or she was going to leave. She was upset that he had started to bring up the past. He continued to push her and Lynn asserted herself by stating he was "not being fair" and she was leaving; and she did.

Joe and the enricher talked for a while. He said he found himself pushing Lynn's buttons when he wanted a response from her. He loved her very much and needed some feedback and felt this was the only way to get it. He also opened up and spoke about an extramarital affair that Lynn had had (the topic of the past *not* to be discussed) and added he had had them too. He was hurt by the affair because he felt Lynn had gone to another man to make her feel feminine, cared for, and supported. He said he "would have given anything to make her feel that way." He was also upset that Lynn had not shared any of her past in the sessions and really hoped she would next time.

At the end of this session, Lynn had•already turned in her homework assignment and Joe had not completed his. He said he would finish it and bring it back with assignment 4 the next week.

Supervision

During supervision, the enricher spoke of her uneasy feelings about the situation during the session. It had not been appropriate to sit and talk with Joe while Lynn was not involved. The enricher would bring this up at the beginning of the next session and process the situation, apologizing to Lynn for having a "session" without her present. The next session would be the last one before the break and would be the time to go over the homework contract.

Session 5

The morning before this session, Joe called to say that he and Lynn were canceling their involvement in the enrichment program. He felt the sessions had "turned into a bitching time" and did not feel it was helpful for their relationship. He felt he had controlled the sessions in this way and believed that the goals of enrichment were not being met. He also said that he felt "therapied out" and said that it was just too much for him. The enricher spoke to Lynn, who also felt the sessions were not helping to bring them closer together but were instead creating more problems. Neither of them felt the need for a closing session to further process their feelings about the program.

Summary

This case is an example of a program of structured enrichment that failed. As a couple, Joe and Lynn had critical needs that could not be addressed in the structured setting of enrichment. We thought they might have been able to benefit from a combined primary and secondary prevention approach; however, it appears they were beyond this stage and were more appropriate for tertiary intervention. This case is also exemplary of moving too fast in selecting a complementary homework assignment. This failure supports the flow that should have been followed (as suggested by L'Abate, 1986): the depression homework, followed by negotiation, and then intimacy. The couple was unable to develop intimacy (i.e., they never made the time to discuss their assignments together) and, therefore, the overall program was not successful. The trainer may have failed in keeping control of sessions, especially the last one, allowing Joe to take control to berate Lynn. She should have stopped whenever the couple went out of the boundaries of structured enrichment. Both structured enrichment and homework assignments were too much too soon for this couple. They were not ready for either primary or secondary prevention because too many issues from the past, both individual and dyadic, were still intruding on the present.

This failure also demonstrates the need for careful evaluation and acting on the basis of the data rather than on the basis of altruistic, missionary goodwill. However, this failure also shows the function of structured enrichment as a diagnostic approach ("If you want to know how a family works, try to change it"). Most of the defeating patterns found during enrichment had become too evident during the first interview and the evaluation. Another function of structured enrichment, the dydactic, was fulfilled by having the student become painfully aware of how clinical and critical couples may not only defeat each other but possibly other help-givers.

NOTE

1. This case was conducted by Linda A. Owens under my supervision.

References

Abidin, R. R. (Ed.). (1980). *Parent education and intervention handbook*. Springfield, IL: Charles C Thomas.

Albee, G. W. (1984). A competency model must replace the defect model. In J. M. Joffe, G. W. Albee, & L. D. Kelly (Eds.), *Readings in primary prevention of psychopathology: Basic concepts* (pp. 228–245). Hanover, VT: University Press of New England.

Albee, G. W. (1986). Toward a just society: Lessons from observations on the primary prevention of psychopathology. *American Psychologist, 41*, 891–898.

Alvy, K. T. (1988). Parenting programs for Black parents. In L. A. Bond & B. M. Wagner (Eds.), *Families in transition: Primary prevention programs that work* (pp. 135–169). Newbury Park, CA: Sage.

American Psychological Association. (1986). *Marketing psychological services: A practitioner's guide*. Washington, DC: Author.

Anderson, C. M., Reiss, D. J., & Hogarty, G. E. (1986). *Schizophrenia and the family: A practitioner's guide to psychoeducation and management*. New York: Guilford.

Anthony, E. J., & Benedek, T. (Eds.). (1970). *Parenthood: Its psychology and psychopathology*. London: Little, Brown.

Arnhoff, F. N., Rubinstein, E. A., & Speisman, J. C. (Eds.). (1969). *Manpower for mental health*. Chicago: Aldine.

Atkin, E., & Rubin, E. (1976). *Part-time father: A guide for the divorced father*. New York: Vanguard.

Avery, A. W., Ridley, C. A., Leslie, L. A., & Mulholland, T. (1980). Relationship enhancement with premarital couples: A six-month follow-up. *American Journal of Family Therapy, 8*, 23–30.

Bach, G., & Goldberg, H. (1974). *Creative aggression*. New York: Doubleday.

Bader, E., Microys, G., & Sinclair, C. (1980). Do marriage preparation programs really work? A Canadian experiment. *Journal of Marital and Family Therapy, 6,* 171–179.

Barker, R. C. (1968). *Ecological psychology: Concepts and method for studying the environment of human behavior.* Stanford, CA: Stanford University Press.

Barnett, R. C., Biener, L., & Baruch, G. K. (Eds.). (1987). *Gender and stress.* New York: Free Press.

Barten, H. H. (Ed.). (1971). *Brief therapies.* New York: Behavioral Publications.

Barten, H. H., & Barten, S. S. (Eds.). (1973). *Children and their parents in brief therapy.* New York: Behavioral Publications.

Beck, A. T., & Young, J. E. (1985). Depression. In D. H. Barlow (Ed.), *Clinical handbook of psychological disorders* (pp. 206–244). New York: Guilford.

Bell, R. Q., & Harper, L. V. (1977). *Child effects on adults.* Lincoln: University of Nebraska Press.

Belle, D. (1987). Gender differences in the social moderators of stress. In R. C. Barnett, L. Biener, & G. K. Baruch (Eds.), *Gender and stress* (pp. 257–277). New York: Free Press.

Belsky, J., & Vondra, J. (1985). Characteristics, consequences, and determinants of parenting. In L. L'Abate (Ed.), *Handbook of family psychology and therapy* (pp. 523–555). Homewood, IL: Dorsey.

Bem, D. J., & Allen, A. (1974). On predicting some of the people some of the time: The search for cross-situational consistencies in behavior. *Psychological Review, 81,* 506–520.

Bem, D. J., & Funder, D. C. (1978). Predicting more of the people more of the time: Assessing the personality of situations. *Psychological Review, 85,* 485–501.

Biller, H., & Meredith, D. (1974). *Father power.* New York: David McKay.

Birren, J. E., & Hedlund, B. (1987). Contributions of autobiography to developmental psychology. In N. Eisenberg (Ed.), *Contemporary topics in developmental psychology* (pp. 384–415). New York: John Wiley.

Bloom, B. L., Hodges, W. F., Kern, M. B., & McFaddin, S. C. (1985). A preventive intervention program for the newly separated: Final evaluations. *American Journal of Orthopsychiatry, 55,* 9–26.

Bond, L. A., & Wagner, B. M. (1988). What makes primary prevention programs work? In L. A. Bond & B. M. Wagner (Eds.), *Families in transition: Primary prevention programs that work* (pp. 343–354). Newbury Park, CA: Sage.

Boyce, J., & L'Abate, L. (n.d.). The comparative effectiveness of three depression workbooks [Research in progress]. Georgia State University, Department of Psychology, Atlanta.

British Columbia Council for the Family. (1988). *Every marriage needs responsible decisions: Marriage preparation, a resource book for instruction.* Vancouver, BC: Author.

Brock, G., & Coufal, J. D. (1985). Parent education as skill training. In L. L'Abate & M. Milan (Eds.), *Handbook of social skills training and research* (pp. 263–282). New York: John Wiley.

Brody, N. (1980). Social motivation. *Annual Review of Psychology, 31,* 143–168.

Bronfenbrenner, U. (1979). *The ecology of human development.* Cambridge, MA: Harvard University Press.

Buckner, J. C., Trickett, E. J., & Corse, S. J. (1985). *Primary prevention in mental health: An annotated bibliography* (Publication No. 85–1405). Rockville, MD: U.S. Department of Health and Human Services.

Budd, K. S. (1985). Parents as mediators in the social skills training of children. In L'Abate & M. Milan (Eds.), *Handbook of social skills training and research* (pp. 245–261). New York: John Wiley.

Budman, S. H. (Ed.). (1981). *Forms of brief therapy.* New York: Guilford.

Burgess, E. W. (1926). The family as a unity of interacting personalities. *Family, 7,* 3–9.

Burgess, E. W. (1927). The family and the person. *Publications of the American Sociological Society, 20,* 133–143.

Calvo, G. (1975). *Marriage encounter.* St. Paul, MN: Marriage Encounter.

Carkhuff, R. C. (1985). *Productive parenting skills.* Amherst, MA: Resource Development Press.

Ciotta, D. (1984). *L'educazione permanente nell' esperienza dei gruppi famiglia.* Torino, Italy: Borla.

Clark, D., & L'Abate, L. (1977). Enrichment and tape recordings with couples. In L. L'Abate, *Enrichment: Structured interventions with couples, families, and groups* (pp. 203–213). Washington, DC: University Press of America.

Cohen, R. S., Cohler, B. J., & Weissman, S. H. (Eds.). (1984). *Parenthood: A psychodynamic perspective.* New York: Guilford.

Congressional Record. (1973). American families: Trends and pressures, 1973. Washington, DC: Government Printing Office.

Cowen, E. L. (1983). Primary prevention in mental health: Past, present, and future. In R. D. Felner, L. A. Jason, J. N. Moritsugu, & S. S. Farber (Eds.), *Preventive psychology: Theory, research, and practice* (pp. 11–30). New York: Pergamon.

Cowen, E. L. (1984). Demystifying primary prevention. In J. M. Joffe, G. W. Albee, & L. D. Kelly (Eds.), *Readings in primary prevention of psychopathology: Basic concepts* (pp. 37–51). Hanover, VT: University Press of New England.

Cox, D. J., Tisdelle, D. A., & Culbert, J. P. (1988). Increasing adherence to behavioral homework assignments. *Journal of Behavioral Medicine, 11,* 519–522.

Crandall, R. (1984). Work and leisure in the life span. In M. D. Lee & R. N. Kanungo (Eds.), *Management of work and personal life: Problems and opportunities.* New York: Praeger.

Curran, J. P., Wallander, J. L., & Farrell, A. D. (1985). Heterosexual skills training. In L. L'Abate & M. Milan (Eds.), *Handbook of social skills training and research* (pp. 136–169). New York: John Wiley.

Cusinato, M. (1985). *Formazione permanente coniugale: Manuale per il consulente.* Treviso, Italy: Centro della Famiglia.

D'Augelli, A., & D'Augelli, J. F. (1985). The enhancement of sexual skills and competence: Promoting lifelong sexual unfolding. In L. L'Abate & M. Milan (Eds.), *Handbook of social skills training and research* (pp. 170–218). New York: John Wiley.

DeLuca, J. W. (1989). Neuropsychology technicians in clinical practice: Precedents, rationale, and current deployment. *Clinical Neuropsychologist, 3*, 3–21.

deSantis, F. (1979). *L'educazione permanente.* Firenze, Italy: La Nuova Italia.

deShazer, S. (1982). *Patterns of brief family therapy: An ecosystemic approach.* New York: Guilford.

deShazer, S. (1985). *Keys to solution in brief therapy.* New York: Norton.

Dinkmeyer, D., & Carlson, J. (1984). *Training in marriage enrichment.* Circle Pines, MN: American Guidance Service.

Dinkmeyer, D., & McKay, G. (1976). *Systematic training for effective parenting (STEP).* Circle Pines, MN: American Guidance Service.

Dreikurs, R., & Soltz, V. (1964). *Children: The challenge.* New York: Hawthorn.

Duhl, L. J., & Cummings, N. A. (Eds.). (1987). *The future of mental health services: Coping with crisis.* New York: Springer.

Dumas, J. E. (1984). Interactional correlates of treatment outcome in behavioral parent training. *Journal of Consulting and Clinical Psychology, 52,* 946–954.

Dunst, C., Trivette, C., & Deal, A. (1988). *Enabling and empowering families: Principles and guidelines for practice.* Cambridge, MA: Brookline.

Edelstein, B., & Michelson, L. (Eds.). (1986). *Handbook of prevention.* New York: Plenum.

Edwards, J. H. (1988). *Attrition in family and marital therapy.* Unpublished manuscript. Georgia State University, Department of Psychology, Atlanta.

Efron, D., & Rowe, B. (1987). *The strategic parenting manual.* Ontario, Canada: JSST Press.

Ekehammer, B. (1974). Interactionism in personality from a historical perspective. *Psychological Bulletin, 81,* 1026–1048.

Ellis, A. (1976). Techniques for handling anger in marriage. *Journal of Marriage and Family Counseling, 2,* 305–315.

Ellsworth, R. B. (1968). *Nonprofessionals in psychiatric rehabilitation: The psychiatric aide and the schizophrenic patient.* New York: Appleton-Century-Crofts.

Emmons, R. A. (1989). Exploring the relations between motives and traits: The case of narcissism. In D. M. Buss & N. Cantor (Eds.), *Personality psychology: Recent trends and emerging directions* (pp. 32–44). New York: Springer-Verlag.

Endler, N. S., & Magnusson, D. (1976). Toward an interactional psychology of personality. *Psychological Bulletin, 83,* 956–974.

Entwisle, D. R. (1985). Becoming a parent. In L. L'Abate (Ed.), *Handbook of family psychology and therapy* (pp. 557–585). Homewood, IL: Dorsey.

Falloon, I. R. H., & Liberman, R. P. (1983). Behavioral family interventions in the management of chronic schizophrenia. In W. R. McFarlane (Ed.), *Family therapy in schizophrenia* (pp. 117–137). New York: Guilford.

Felner, R. D., Jason, L. A., Moritsugu, J. N., & Farber, S. S. (Eds.). (1983). *Preventive psychology: Theory, research, and practice*. New York: Pergamon.

Foá, U. G., & Foá, E. B. (1974). *Societal structures of the mind*. Springfield, IL: Charles C Thomas.

Ford, M. E. (1985). The concept of competence: Themes and variations. In H. A. Marlowe, Jr., & R. B. Weinberg (Eds.), *Competence development: Theory and practice in special populations* (pp. 3–49). Springfield, IL: Charles C Thomas.

Forehand, R. L., & McMahon, R. J. (1981). *Helping the noncompliant child: Children's guide to parent training*. New York: Guilford.

Forehand, R. L., Walley, P. B., & Furery, W. M. (1984). Prevention in the home: Parent and family. In M. C. Roberts & L. Peterson (Eds.), *Prevention of problems in childhood: Psychological research and applications* (pp. 342–368). New York: John Wiley.

Fournier, D. G., & Olson, D. H. (1986). Programs for premarital and newlywed couples. In R. F. Levant (Ed.), *Psychoeducational approaches to family therapy and counseling* (pp. 194–231). New York: Springer.

Frank, M. (Ed.). (1982). *Primary prevention for children and families*. New York: Haworth.

Franken, D. A., & van Raaij, W. F. (1982). Satisfaction with leisure time activities. *Journal of Leisure Research, 24*, 337–351.

Fry, J., Holly, J., & L'Abate, L. (1979). Intimacy is sharing hurt feelings: Comparison of three conflict resolution methods. *Journal of Marriage and Family Therapy, 5*, 35–41.

Galdston, I. (Ed.). (1961). *The family: A focal point in health education*. New York: International Universities Press.

Ganahl, G. F. (1981). *Effects of client treatment and therapist variables on the outcome of structured marital enrichment*. Unpublished doctoral dissertation, Georgia State University, Atlanta.

Ganahl, G. F., Ferguson, L. R., & L'Abate, L. (1985). Training in family psychology. In L. L'Abate (Ed.), *Handbook of family psychology and therapy* (pp. 1249–1279). Homewood, IL: Dorsey.

Garfield, S. L. (1986). Research on client variables on psychotherapy. In S. L. Garfield & A. E. Bergin (Eds.), *Handbook of psychotherapy and behavior change* (pp. 213–256). New York: John Wiley.

Gaylin, W., & Person, E. (Eds.). (1988). *Passionate attachments: Thinking about love*. New York: Free Press.

Gesten, E. L., & Jason, L. A. (1987). Social and community interventions. *Annual Review of Psychology, 38*, 427–460.

Ginott, H. G. (1965). *Between parent & child*. New York: Macmillan.

Ginott, H. G. (1969). *Between parent & teenager*. New York: Macmillan.

Gleason, J., & Prescott, M. P. (1977). Group techniques for premarital preparation. *Family Coordinator, 26*, 277–280.

Goglia, L. (1985). *Personality characteristics of adult children of alcoholics*. Unpublished doctoral dissertation, Georgia State University, Atlanta.

Golden, R. P. (1974). *A validation study of the Family Assessment Battery*. Unpublished doctoral dissertation, Georgia State University, Atlanta.

Goldstein, L. D. (1988, February). APA's evolution from learned society to professional organization model. *Psychology Monitor*, p. 3.

Goldston, S. E. (1986). Primary prevention: Historical perspectives and a blueprint for action. *American Psychologist, 41*, 453–460.

Gordon, T. (1970). *Parent effectiveness training*. New York: Macmillan.

Gore, W. R. (1979). Sex differences in the epidemiology of mental disorder: Evidence and explanation. In E. S. Gomberg & V. Franks (Eds.), *Gender and disordered behavior: Sex differences in psychopathology* (pp. 23–68). New York: Brunner/Mazel.

Gottlieb, H., Kavkewitz, M., & L'Abate, L. (1977). The laboratory evaluation and enrichment of sexuality: Method and some preliminary results. In L. L'Abate, *Enrichment: Structured interventions with couples, families, and groups* (pp. 106–121). Washington, DC: University Press of America.

Grosser, C., Henry, W. E., & Kelly, J. G. (Eds.). (1969). *Nonprofessionals in the human services*. San Francisco: Jossey-Bass.

Group for the Advancement of Psychiatry. (1973). *The joys and sorrows of parenthood*. New York: Scribner.

Guerney, B. G., Jr. (Ed.). (1969). *Psychotherapeutic agents: New roles for nonprofessionals, parents, and teachers*. New York: Holt, Rinehart & Winston.

Guerney, B. G., Jr. (1988). Family relationship enhancement: A skill training approach. In L. A. Bond & B. M. Wagner (Eds.), *Families in transition: Primary prevention programs that work* (pp. 99–134). Newbury Park, CA: Sage.

Guerney, L., & Guerney, B., Jr. (1985). The relationship enhancement family of family therapies. In L. L'Abate & M. Milan (Eds.), *Handbook of social skills training and research* (pp. 506–525). New York: John Wiley.

Guerney, B. G., Jr., Guerney, L., & Cooney, T. (1985). Marital and family problem prevention and enrichment programs. In L. L'Abate (Ed.), *Handbook of family psychology and therapy* (pp. 1179–1216). Homewood, IL: Dorsey.

Guidelin, E. (1981). *Educazione permanente*. Firenze, Italy: La Nuova Italia.

Gurman, A. S., Kniskern, D. P., & Pinsoff, W. (1986). Research on the process and outcome of marital and family therapy. In S. Garfield & A. Bergin (Eds.), *Handbook of psychotherapy and behavior change* (pp. 565–624). New York: John Wiley.

Haley, J. (1976). *Problem-solving therapy*. San Francisco: Jossey-Bass.

Hall, W. C. (1987). *The efficacy of a marital contracting approach to the treatment of remarried couples*. Unpublished master's thesis, Georgia State University, Atlanta.

Haller, A. O., & Olsen, W. (1951). Courses in preparation for marriage in 113 colleges and universities. *A. K. Deltan, 22*, 7–10.

Harriman, L. C. (1986) Teaching traditional vs. emerging concepts in family life education. *Family Relations, 35*, 581–586.

Hayes, S. C., Nelson, R. O., & Jarrett, R. B. (1987). The treatment utility of assessment: A functional approach to evaluating assessment quality. *American Psychologist, 42,* 963–974.

Hefferman, J. A., & Albee, G. W. (1985). Prevention prospectives: From Vermont to Washington. *American Psychologist, 40,* 202–204.

Hermalin, J., & Morell, J. A. (Eds.). (1981). *Evaluation and prevention in human services.* New York: Haworth.

Hermalin, J., & Morell, J. A. (Eds.). (1987). *Prevention planning in mental health.* Newbury Park, CA: Sage.

Hermalin, J. A., & Weirich, T. W. (1983). Prevention research in field settings: An interpersonal problem-solving approach. In R. Hess & J. Hermalin (Eds.), *Innovations in prevention* (pp. 31–48). New York: Haworth.

Hess, R., & Hermalin, J. (Eds.). (1983). *Innovations in prevention.* New York: Haworth.

Hirschman, E. C. (1984). Leisure motives and sex roles. *Journal of Leisure Research, 16,* 209–223.

Hobbs, N., Dokecki, P. R., Hoover-Dempsey, K. V., Moroney, R. M., Shaybe, M. W., & Weeks, K. H. (1984). *Strengthening families.* San Francisco: Jossey-Bass.

Hoffman, L. W., Gandelman, R., & Schiffman, H. R. (1982). *Parenting: Its causes and consequences.* Hillsdale, NJ: Lawrence Erlbaum.

Hollin, C. R., & Trower, P. (Eds.) (1986). *Handbook of social skills training* (Vols. 1–2). Oxford: Pergamon.

Hoopes, M. H., Fisher, B. L. & Barlow, S. H. (1984). *Structured family facilitation programs: Enrichment, education, and treatment.* Rockville, MD: Aspen Systems Publications.

Hopkins, L., Hopkins, P., Mace, D., & Mace, V. (1978). *Toward better marriages: The handbook of the Association of Couples for Marriage Enrichment.* Winston-Salem, NC: ACME.

Hunter, D. E. K., Hoffnung, R. J., & Ferholt, J. S. (1988). Family therapy in trouble: Psychoeducation as solution and problem. *Family Process, 27,* 327–338.

Jason, L. A., Hess, R. E., Felner, R. D., & Moritsugu, J. N. (Eds.). (1987). *Prevention: Toward a multidisciplinary approach.* New York: Haworth.

Jensen, L. C., & Kingston, M. (1986). *Parenting.* New York: Holt, Rinehart & Winston.

Joanning, H. (1985). Social skills training for divorced individuals. In L. L'Abate & M. Milan (Eds.), *Handbook of social skills training and research* (pp. 192–217). New York: John Wiley.

Joffe, J. M., Albee, G. W., & Kelly, L. D. (Eds.). (1984). *Readings in primary prevention of psychopathology.* Hanover, NH: University Press of New England.

Joint Commission on Mental Health of Children. (1969). *Crisis in child mental health: Challenge for the 1970's.* New York: Harper & Row.

Joint Commission on Mental Illness and Health. (1961). *Action for mental health.* New York: Science Editions.

Juster, F. T., & Stafford, F. P. (Eds.). (1985). *Time, goods, and well-being.* Ann Arbor: University of Michigan, Institute for Social Research.

Kagan, S. L., Powell, D. R., Weissbourd, B., & Zigler, E. F. (Eds.). (1987). *America's family support programs.* New Haven, CT: Yale University Press.

Kahn, A. H., & Kamerman, S. B. (1982). *Helping America's families.* Philadelphia: Temple University Press.

Kazdin, A. E. (1986). The evaluation of psychotherapy: Research design and methodology. In S. L. Garfield & A. E. Bergin (Eds.), *Handbook of psychotherapy and behavior change* (pp. 21–68). New York: John Wiley.

Kelly, J. G. (1970). The quest for valid preventive interventions. In C. D. Spielberger (Ed.), *Current trends in clinical and community psychology* (Vol. 2). New York: Academic Press.

Kelly, J. G., & Hess, R. E. (Eds.). (1986). *The ecology of prevention: Illustrating mental health consultation.* New York: Haworth.

Keniston, K., & Carnegie Council on Children. (1977). *All our children: The American family under pressure.* New York: Harcourt Brace Jovanovich.

Kessler, M., & Albee, G. W. (1975). Primary prevention. *Annual Review of Psychology, 26,* 557–591.

Kiesler, D. J. (1966). Some myths of psychotherapy research and the search for a paradigm. *Psychological Bulletin, 65,* 110–136.

Kipper, D. A. (1986). *Psychotherapy through clinical role playing.* New York: Brunner/Mazel.

Kiresuk, T. J., & Sherman, R. E. (1968). Goal attainment scaling: A general method for evaluating comprehensive community mental health programs. *Community Mental Health Journal, 4,* 443–453.

Klarman, H. E. (1969). Economic aspects of mental health manpower. In F. N. Arnhoff, E. A. Rubinstein, & J. C. Speisman (Eds.), *Manpower for mental health* (pp. 67–92). Chicago: Aldine.

Klein, D. C., & Goldston, S. E. (Eds.). (1977). *Primary prevention: An idea whose time has come.* Rockville, MD: National Institute of Mental Health.

Kochalka, J. (n.d.). Validity and reliability of family-related assessment instruments to prescribe structured enrichment programs. [Research in progress, title tentative]. Georgia State University, Atlanta.

Kochalka, J., Buzas, H., L'Abate, L., McHenry, S., & Gibson, E. (1987). Structured enrichment: Training and implementation with paraprofessionals. In L. L'Abate, *Family psychology: Vol. 2. Theory, therapy, enrichment, and training* (pp. 279–287). Lanham, MD: University Press of America.

Kochalka, J., & L'Abate, L. (1983). Structure and gradualness in the clinical training of family psychologists. In L. L'Abate, *Family psychology: Theory, therapy, and training* (pp. 287–299). Washington, DC: University Press of America.

Kon, I. S. (1983). Preparing youth for marriage and family life. *Sociological Research, 1,* 190–193.

L'Abate, L. (1964). *Principles of clinical psychology.* New York: Grune & Stratton.

L'Abate, L. (1965). *The laboratory method in clinical psychology.* Atlanta: Georgia State University, Pullen Library.

L'Abate, L. (1969). The continuum of rehabilitation and laboratory evaluation: Behavior modification and psychotherapy. In C. M. Franks (Ed.), *Behavior therapy: Appraisal and status* (pp. 476–494). New York: McGraw-Hill.

L'Abate, L. (1971). Receptive-expressive functions in kindergarten children and adolescents. *Psychology in the Schools, 8,* 253–259.

L'Abate, L. (1973). The laboratory method in clinical psychology: Three applications. *Journal of Clinical Child Psychology, 2,* 8–10.

L'Abate, L. (1976). *Understanding and helping the individual in the family.* New York: Grune & Stratton.

L'Abate, L. (1977a). *Enrichment: Structured interventions with couples, families, and groups.* Washington, DC: University Press of America.

L'Abate, L. (1977b). Intimacy is sharing hurt feelings: A reply to David Mace. *Journal of Marriage and Family Counseling, 3,* 13–16.

L'Abate, L. (1979). Aggression and construction in children's monitored play-therapy. *Journal of Counseling and Psychotherapy, 2,* 137–158.

L'Abate, L. (1983). Prevention as a profession: Toward a new conceptual frame of reference. In D. R. Mace (Ed.), *Prevention in family services: Approaches to family wellness* (pp. 49–62). Beverly Hills, CA: Sage.

L'Abate, L. (1985a). A training program in family psychology: Evaluation, prevention, and family therapy. *American Journal of Family Therapy, 13,* 7–16.

L'Abate, L. (Ed.). (1985b). *Handbook of family psychology and therapy.* Homewood, IL: Dorsey.

L'Abate, L. (1985c). Structured enrichment (SE) for couples and families. *Family Relations, 34,* 169–175.

L'Abate, L. (1985d). The status and future of family psychology and therapy. In L. L'Abate (Ed.), *Handbook of family psychology and therapy* (pp. 1417–1435). Homewood, IL: Dorsey.

L'Abate, L. (1986a). Prevention of marital and family problems. In B. Edelstein & L. Michelson (Eds.), *Handbook of prevention* (pp. 177–193). New York: Plenum.

L'Abate, L. (1986b). *Systematic family therapy.* New York: Brunner/Mazel.

L'Abate, L. (1987). *Family psychology: Vol. 2. Theory, therapy, enrichment, and training.* Lanham, MD: University Press of America.

L'Abate, L. (in press). Understanding addictive behaviors. In L. L'Abate, J. E. Farrar, & D. A. Serritella (Eds.), *Handbook of differential treatment for addictions.* Needham Heights, MA: Allyn & Bacon.

L'Abate, L., & Bagarozzi, D. A. (in press). *Sourcebook for marriage and family evaluation.* New York: Brunner/Mazel.

L'Abate, L., & Brown, E. C. (1969). An appraisal of teaching machines and programmed instruction. In C. M. Franks (Ed.), *Behavior therapy: Appraisal and status* (pp. 396–414). New York: McGraw-Hill.

L'Abate, L., & Bryson, C. (in press). *A theory of personality development*. New York: Brunner/Mazel.

L'Abate, L., & Colondier, G. (1987). The emperor has no clothes! Long live the emperor! A critique of family systems thinking and a reductionistic proposal. *American Journal of Family Therapy, 15*, 19–33.

L'Abate, L., & Cox, J. (in press). *Programmed writing: A self-administered approach with individuals, couples, and families*. Pacific Grove, CA: Brooks/Cole.

L'Abate, L., & Cusinato, M. (n.d.). A follow-up of the long term effects of structured enrichment programs [Research in progress]. Georgia State University, Department of Psychology, Atlanta.

L'Abate, L., & Dunne, E. E. (1977). The family taboo in psychology textbooks. *Teaching of Psychology, 5*, 115–117.

L'Abate, L., Farrar, J., & Serritella, D. (Eds.). (in press). *Handbook of differential treatments for addictions*. Needham Heights, MA: Allyn & Bacon.

L'Abate, L., & Fresh, E. (n.d.). Development and validation of a problem in relationships test [Research in progress]. Georgia State University, Department of Psychology, Atlanta.

L'Abate, L., Ganahl, G., & Hansen, J. C. (1986). *Methods of family therapy*. Englewood Cliffs, NJ: Prentice-Hall.

L'Abate, L., & Harel, T. (in press). Deriving a theory of developmental competence from resource exchange theory: Implications for preventive interventions. In U. Foá (Ed.), *Recent contributions and applications of resource exchange theory*. Hillsdale, NJ: Lawrence Erlbaum.

L'Abate, L., & Hewitt, D. (1988). Toward a classification of sex and sexual behavior. *Journal of Sex and Marital Therapy, 14*, 29–39.

L'Abate, L., & Hewitt, D. (1989). Power and presence: When complementarity becomes polarity. In J. Crosby (Ed.), *When one wants out and the other doesn't: Doing therapy with polarized couples* (pp. 136–152). New York: Brunner/Mazel.

L'Abate, L., & Jessee, E. (1981). Enrichment role-playing as a step in training of family therapists. *Journal of Marriage and Family Therapy, 7*, 507–514.

L'Abate, L., & Kochalka, J. (1983). Clinical training in family psychology. In B. F. Okun & S. T. Gladding (Eds.), *Issues in marriage training and family therapists* (pp. 63–71). Ann Arbor, MI: ERIC/CAPS.

L'Abate, L., & McHenry, S. (1983). *Handbook of marital interventions*. Orlando, FL: Grune & Stratton.

L'Abate, L., & Milan, M. (Eds.). (1985). *Handbook of social skills training and research*. New York: John Wiley.

L'Abate, L., & O'Callaghan, J. B. (1977). Implications of the enrichment model for research and training. *Family Coordinator, 26*, 61–64.

L'Abate, L., O'Callaghan, J. B., Piat, J. D., Dunne, E. E., Margolis, R., Prigge, B., & Soper, P. (1976). Enlarging the scope of intervention with couples and families: Combination of therapy and enrichment. In L. Wolberg & L. Aronson (Eds.), *Group therapy 1976: An overview* (pp. 62–73). New York: Stratton Intercontinental Medical Books.

218 BUILDING FAMILY COMPETENCE

L'Abate, L., & Rupp, G. (1981). *Enrichment: Structured interventions for family life.* Washington, DC: University Press of America.

L'Abate, L., & Thaxton, M. L. (1981). Differentiation of resources in mental health delivery: Implications for training. *Professional Psychology, 12,* 761–768.

L'Abate, L., & Wagner, V. (1985). Theory-derived, family-oriented test-batteries. In L. L'Abate (Ed.), *Handbook of family psychology and therapy* (pp. 1006–1031). Homewood, IL: Dorsey.

L'Abate, L., & Wagner, V. (1988). Testing a theory of developmental competence in the family. *American Journal of Family Therapy, 16,* 23–35.

L'Abate, L., & Weinstein, S. (1987). *Structured enrichment programs for couples and families.* New York: Brunner/Mazel.

L'Abate, L., Wildman, R. W., II, O'Callaghan, J. B., Simon, S. J., Allison, M., Kahn, G., & Rainwater, N. (1975). The laboratory evaluation and enrichment of couples: Applications and preliminary results. *Journal of Marriage and Family Counseling, 1,* 351–358.

L'Abate, L., & Young, L. (1987). *Casebook of structured enrichment programs for couples and families.* New York: Brunner/Mazel.

Lamb, M. E. (Ed.). (1976). *The role of the father in child development.* New York: Wiley-Interscience.

Langsley, D. G., & Kaplan, D. M. (1968). *The treatment of families in crisis.* New York: Grune & Stratton.

Lauffer, A., & Gorodezky, S. (1977). *Volunteers.* Beverly Hills, CA: Sage.

Lazarus, R. S., & Folkman, S. (1984). *Stress, appraisal, and coping.* New York: Springer.

Lee, M. D., & Kanungo, R. N. (1984). Work and personal-life coordination in a changing society. In M. D. Lee & R. N. Kanungo (Eds.), *Management of work and personal life: Problems and opportunities.* New York: Praeger.

Leigh, G. K., Loewen, I. R., & Lester, M. E. (1986). Caveat emptor: Values and ethics in family life education and enrichment. *Family Relations, 35,* 573–580.

LeMasters, E. E. (1970). *Parents in America: A sociological analysis.* Homewood, IL: Dorsey.

Lemkau, J. (1984). Reflections on selflessness in the lives of women. *Women & Therapy, 3,* 31–36.

Lengrad, P. (1973). *Introduzione all'educazione permanente.* Roma, Italy: A. Armando.

Lerner, R. M., & Spanier, G. B. (1978). *Child influences on marital and family interaction: A life-span perspective.* New York: Academic Press.

Levant, R. F. (1986). *Psychoeducational approaches to family therapy and counseling.* New York: Springer.

Levine, C. (Ed.). (1988). *Programs to strengthen families: A resource guide.* Chicago: Family Resource Coalition.

Levis, M. (1987). *Short-term treatment for depression using systematic homework assignments.* Unpublished doctoral dissertation, Georgia State University, Atlanta.

Lewis, J. M., Beavers, W. R., Gossett, J. T., & Phillips, V. A. (1976). *No single thread: Psychological health in family systems.* New York: Brunner/Mazel.

Lieberman, E. J. (1976). The prevention of marital problems. In H. Grunebaum & J. Christ (Eds.), *Contemporary marriage: Structure, dynamics, and therapy* (pp. 315–332). Boston: Little, Brown.

Littell, J. H. (1986). *Building strong foundations: Evaluation strategies for family resource programs.* Chicago: Family Resource Coalition.

Lorion, R. P. (1983). Evaluating preventive interventions: Guidelines for the serious change agent. In R. D. Felner, L. A. Jason, J. N. Moritsugu, & S. S. Farber (Eds.), *Preventive psychology: Theory, research, and practice* (pp. 251–268). New York: Pergamon.

Lorion, R. P., Tolan, P. H., & Wahler, R. G. (1987). Prevention. In H. C. Quay (Ed.), *Handbook of juvenile delinquency* (pp. 383–416). New York: John Wiley.

Lutz, J., & Weinstein, S. E. (1987). A dating couple. In L. L'Abate & L. Young. *Casebook of structured enrichment programs for couples and families* (pp. 5–16). New York: Brunner/Mazel.

Lynn, D. B. (1974). *The father: His role in child development.* Monterey, CA: Brooks/Cole.

Mace, D. R. (Ed.). (1983). *Prevention in family services: Approaches to family wellness.* Beverly Hills, CA: Sage.

Mace, D. R. (1986). Marriage and family enrichment. In F. P. Piercy, D. H. Sprenkle et al., *Family therapy sourcebook* (pp. 187–212). New York: Guilford.

Mace, D. R., & Mace, V. (1976). Marriage enrichment: A preventive group approach for couples. In D. H. L. Olson (Ed.), *Treating relationships* (pp. 321–336). Lake Mills, IA: Graphic Publishing.

Malan, D. H. (1976). *The frontier of brief psychotherapy: An example of the convergence of research and clinical practice.* New York: Plenum.

Mann, J. (1973). *Time-limited psychotherapy.* Cambridge, MA: Harvard University Press.

Marlatt, G. A. (1988). Matching clients to treatment: Treatment models and stages of change. In D. M. Donovan & G. A. Marlatt (Eds.), *Assessment of addictive behaviors* (pp. 474–483). New York: Guilford.

Marlowe, H. A., Jr., & Weinberg, R. B. (Eds.). (1985). *Competence development: Theory and practice in special populations.* Springfield, IL: Charles C Thomas.

McFall, R. M. (1988). Not just another handbook [Review of Hollin & Trower's *Handbook of social skills training*]. *Contemporary Psychology, 33*, 324–325.

McKenry, P. C., Walters, L. H., & Johnson, C. (1979). Adolescent pregnancy: A review of the literature. *Family Coordinator, 28*, 17–28.

Mencarelli, M. (1976). *Scuola di base e educazione permanente.* Brescia, Italy: La Scuola Editrice.

Messinger, L., Walker, K. N., & Freeman, S. J. J. (1978). Preparation for remarriage following divorce: The use of group techniques. *American Journal of Orthopsychiatry, 48*, 263–272.

Miller, S. M., & Kirsch, N. (1987). Sex differences in cognitive coping with stress. In R. C. Barnett, L. Biener, & G. K. Baruch (Eds.), *Gender and stress* (pp. 278–307). New York: Free Press.

Moos, R. H. (1976). *The human context: Environmental determinants of behavior.* New York: John Wiley.

Moss, H. A., Hess, R., & Swift, C. (Eds.). (1982). *Early intervention programs for infants.* New York: Haworth.

Moss, N. E., Abramowitz, S. L., & Racusin, G. R. (1985). Parental heritage: Progress and prospect. In L. L'Abate (Ed.), *Handbook of family psychology and therapy* (pp. 499–522). Homewood, IL: Dorsey.

Most, R., & Guerney, B., Jr. (1983). An empirical evaluation of the training of lay volunteer leaders for premarital relationship enhancement. *Family Relations, 32,* 239–251.

Murphy, L. B., & Frank, C. (1979). Prevention: The clinical psychologist. *Annual Review of Psychology, 30,* 173–207.

Murstein, B. I. (1988). A taxonomy of love. In R. J. Sternberg & M. L. Barnes (Eds.), *The psychology of love* (pp. 13–37). New Haven, CT: Yale University Press.

Nash, K. B., Jr., Lifton, N., & Smith, S. E. (Eds.). (1978). *The paraprofessional: Selected readings.* New Haven, CT: Advocate Press.

Neville, H., & Halaby, M. (1984). *No-fault parenting.* New York: Facts-on-File Publications.

Nickols, S. A., Fournier, D. G., & Nickols, S. Y. (1986). Evaluation of a preparation for marriage workshop. *Family Relations, 35,* 563–571.

Nunnally, E. W., Miller, S., & Wackman, D. B. (1976). The Minnesota couples communication program. In H. A. Otto (Ed.), *Marriage and family enrichment: New perspectives and programs* (pp. 180–192). Nashville, TN: Abington.

Olson, D. H. (1983). How effective *is* marriage preparation? In D. R. Mace (Ed.), *Prevention in family services: Approaches to family wellness* (pp. 65–75). Beverly Hills, CA: Sage.

Olson, D. H., Fournier, D. G., & Druckman, J. M. (n.d.). *Enrich II: leader's guide.* Circle Pines, MN: American Guidance Service.

Parker, M. (1986). Developing a marriage preparation course. *Marriage Guidance, 22,* 18–21.

Patterson, G. R. (1985). Beyond technology: The next stage in developing an empirical base for parent training. In L. L'Abate (Ed.), *Handbook of family psychology and therapy* (pp. 1344–1379). Homewood, IL: Dorsey.

Pearson, L. (Ed.). (1965). *The use of written communication in psychotherapy.* Springfield, IL: Charles C Thomas.

Peck, C. P. (1986). A public mental health issue: Risk-taking behavior and compulsive gambling. *American Psychologist, 41,* 461–465.

Peplau, L. A., & Goldston, S. E. (Eds.). (1984). *Preventing the harmful consequences of severe and persistent loneliness.* Rockville, MD: National Institutes of Mental Health.

Phillips, E. L. (1978). *The social skills basis of psychopathology: Alternatives to abnormal psychology.* New York: Grune & Stratton.

Phillips, E. L. (1985a). *Psychotherapy revisited: New frontiers in research and practice.* Hillsdale, NJ: Lawrence Erlbaum.

Phillips, E. L. (1985b). Social skills: History and prospect. In L. L'Abate & M. Milan (Eds.), *Handbook of social skills training and research* (pp. 3–21). New York: John Wiley.

Phillips, E. L. (1987). The ubiquitous decay curve: Service delivery similarities in psychotherapy, medicine, and addiction. *Professional Psychology: Research and Practice, 19,* 650–652.

Phillips, E. L., & Wiener, D. N. (1965). *Short-term psychotherapy and structured behavior change.* New York: McGraw-Hill.

Phillips, L. (1968). *Human adaptation and its failures.* New York: Academic Press.

Pollack, W. S., & Grossman, F. K. (1985). Parent-child interaction. In L. L'Abate (Ed.), *Handbook of family psychology and therapy* (pp. 586–622). Homewood, IL: Dorsey.

Popkin, M. H. (1983). *Active parenting.* Atlanta: Active Parenting.

Powell, D. R. (1987). Methodological and conceptual issues in research. In S. L. Kagan, D. R. Powell, B. Weissbourd, & E. F. Zigler (Eds.), *America's family support programs* (pp. 311–328). New Haven, CT: Yale University Press.

Price, R. H. (1983). The education of a prevention psychologist. In R. D. Felner, L. A. Jason, J. N. Moritsugu, & S. S. Farber (Eds.), *Preventive psychology: Theory, research and practice* (pp. 290–296). New York: Pergamon.

Price, R. H., Cowen, E. L., Lorion, R. P., & Ramos-McKay, J. (1989). The search for effective preventive programs: What we learned along the way. *American Journal of Orthopsychiatry, 59,* 49–58.

Price, R. H., Ketterer, R. F., Bader, B. C., & Monahan, J. (Eds.). (1980). *Prevention in mental health: Research, policy, and practice.* Beverly Hills, CA: Sage.

Price, R. H., & Smith, S. S. (1985). *A guide to evaluating prevention programs in mental health* (DHHS Publication No. 85–1365). Rockville, MD: National Institute of Mental Health.

Progoff, I. (1980). *The practice of process mediation: The intensive journal way to spiritual experience.* New York: Dialogue House.

Pruett, K. D. (1987). *The nurturing father.* New York: Warner.

Quay, H. C. (1987). Institutional treatment. In H. C. Quay (Ed.), *Handbook of juvenile delinquency* (pp. 244–265). New York: John Wiley.

Rappaport, J., Swift, C., & Hess, R. (Eds.). (1983). *Studies in empowerment: Steps toward understanding and action.* New York: Haworth.

Rathjen, D. P., & Foreyt, J. P. (Eds.). (1980). *Social competence: Interventions for children and adults.* New York: Pergamon.

Reilly, J. W., Rohrbaugh, M., & Lackner, J. M. (1988). A controlled evaluation of psychoeducational workshops for relatives of state hospital patients. *Journal of Marital and Family Psychology, 14,* 429–432.

Richmond, W. K. (1978). *Educazione permanente nella societa' aperta*. Roma, Italy: A. Armando.

Rickel, A. U., & Allen, L. (1987). *Preventing maladjustment from infancy through adolescence*. Newbury Park, CA: Sage.

Ridley, C. A., Avery, A. W., Harrell, J. E., Hayes-Clements, A. A., & McCunney, N. (1981). Mutual problem-solving skills training for premarital couples: A six month follow-up. *Journal of Applied Developmental Psychology, 4*, 179–185.

Ridley, C. A., Jorgensen, S. R., Morgan, A. C., & Avery, A. W. (1982). Relationship enhancement with premarital couples: An assessment of effects on relationship quality. *American Journal of Family Therapy, 10*, 41–48.

Roberts, M. C., & Peterson, L. (1984). Prevention models: Theoretical and practical implications. In M. C. Roberts & L. Peterson (Eds.), *Prevention of problems in childhood: Psychological research and applications* (pp. 1–39). New York: John Wiley.

Rohner, R. P. (1986). *The warmth dimension: Foundations of parental acceptance-rejection theory*. Beverly Hills, CA: Sage.

Rolfe, D. J. (1985). Preparing the previously married for second marriage. *Journal of Pastoral Care, 39*, 110–119.

Roosa, M. W., Fitzgerald, H. E., & Crawford, M. (1985). Teenage parenting, delayed parenting, and childlessness. In L. L'Abate (Ed.), *Handbook of family psychology and therapy* (pp. 623–629). Homewood, IL: Dorsey.

Rowe, G., DeFrain, J., Lingren, H., MacDonald, R., Stinnett, N., Van Zandt, S., & Williams, R. (1984). *Family strengths: Continuity and diversity*. Newton, MA: Education Development Center.

Sager, C. J. (1976). *Marriage contracts and couple therapy: Hidden forces in intimate relationships*. New York: Brunner/Mazel.

Sauber, S. R., & contributors. (1983). *The human services delivery system: Mental health, criminal justice, social welfare, education, and health services*. New York: Columbia University Press.

Schratz, P. (1988). *Ego development and marital adjustment: A structural-developmental approach*. Unpublished doctoral dissertation, Georgia State University, Atlanta.

Schumm, W. R., & Denton, W. (1979). Trends in premarital counseling. *Journal of Marital and Family Therapy, 22*, 23–32.

Schwartz, R. M. & Garamoni, G. L. (1989). Cognitive balance and psychopathology: Evaluation of an information processing model of positive and negative states of mind. *Clinical Psychology Review, 9*, 271–294.

Seitz, V. (1987). Outcome evaluation of family support programs: Research design alternatives to true experiments. In S. L. Kagan, D. R. Powell, B. Weissbourd, & E. F. Zigler (Eds.), *America's family support programs* (pp. 329–344). New Haven, CT: Yale University Press.

Selvini-Palazzoli, M., Boscolo, L., Cecchin, G., & Prata, G. (1978). *Paradox and counterparadox*. New York: Jason Aronson.

Shaver, P., Hazan, C., & Bradshaw, D. (1988). Love as attachment: The integration of three behavioral systems. In R. J. Sternberg & M. L. Barnes (Eds.), *The psychology of love* (pp. 68–99). New Haven, CT: Yale University Press.

Shelton, J. L., & Levy, R. L. (1981). *Behavioral assignments and treatment compliance.* Champaign, IL: Research Press.

Sifneos, P. E. (1987). *Short-term dynamic psychotherapy: Evaluation and technique.* New York: Plenum.

Simson, S., Wilson, R. B., Hermalin, J., & Hess, R. (Eds.). (1983). *Aging and prevention: New approaches for preventing health and mental health problems in older adults.* New York: Haworth.

Sloan, S. Z. (1983). *Assessing the differential effectiveness of two enrichment formats in facilitating marital intimacy and adjustment.* Unpublished doctoral dissertation, Georgia State University, Atlanta.

Sloan, S. Z., & L'Abate, L. (1985). Intimacy. In L. L'Abate (Ed.), *Handbook of family psychology and therapy* (pp. 305–329). Homewood, IL: Dorsey.

Small, L. (1971). *The briefer psychotherapies.* New York: Brunner/Mazel.

Smith, D. K., & L'Abate, L. (1977). The laboratory evaluation and enrichment of families. In L. L'Abate, *Enrichment: Structured interventions with couples, families, and groups* (pp. 89–105). Washington, DC: University Press of America.

Snyder, J., & Patterson, G. R. (1987). Family interaction and delinquent behavior. In H. C. Quay (Ed.), *Handbook of juvenile delinquency* (pp. 216–243). New York: John Wiley.

Sobey, F. (1970). *The nonprofessional revolution in mental health.* New York: Columbia University Press.

Sprafkin, J., Swift, C., & Hess, R. (Eds.). (1983). *Rx television: Enhancing the preventive impact of TV.* New York: Haworth.

Stamps, S. M., & Stamps, M. B. (1985). Race, class, and leisure activities of urban residents. *Journal of Leisure Activities, 17,* 40–55.

Sternberg, R. J., & Barnes, M. L. (Eds.). (1988). *The psychology of love.* New Haven, CT: Yale University Press.

Sternberg, R. J., & Grajek, S. (1984). The nature of love. *Journal of Personality and Social Psychology, 47,* 312–329.

Stevens, F. E., & L'Abate, L. (1989). Validity and reliability of a theory-derived measure of intimacy. *American Journal of Family Therapy, 17,* 359–368.

Stinnett, N., Chesser, B., & DeFrain, J. (1979). *Building family strengths: Blueprints for action.* Lincoln: University of Nebraska Press.

Stinnett, N., Chesser, B., DeFrain, J., & Knaub, P. (1980). *Family strengths: Positive models for family life.* Lincoln: University of Nebraska Press.

Stinnett, N., & DeFrain, J. (1985). *Secrets of strong families.* Boston: Little, Brown.

Stinnett, N., DeFrain, J., King, K., Knaub, P., & Rowe, G. (1981). *Family strengths: Roots of well-being.* Lincoln: University of Nebraska Press.

Stinnett, N., DeFrain, J., King, K., Lingren, H., Rowe, G., Van Zandt, S., & Williams, R. (1982). *Family strengths: Vol. 4. Positive support systems.* Lincoln: University of Nebraska Press.

Stolz, S. B. (1984). Preventive models: Implications for a technology of practice. In M. C. Roberts & L. Peterson (Eds.), *Prevention of problems in childhood: Psychological research and applications* (pp. 391–414). New York: John Wiley.

Swensen, C. H., Jr. (1985). Love in the family. In L. L'Abate (Ed.), *Handbook of family psychology and therapy* (pp. 357–377). Homewood, IL: Dorsey.

Thaxton, L. (1989). *Issues of control among children of alcoholics.* Unpublished doctoral dissertation, Georgia State University, Atlanta.

Thurman, F. C. (1946). College courses in preparation for marriage. *Social Forces, 24,* 332–335.

Wackman, D. B., & Wampler, K. S. (1985). The couples communication program. In L. L'Abate & M. Milan (Eds.), *Handbook of social skills training and research* (pp. 457–476). New York: John Wiley.

Wagner, V., & L'Abate, L. (1977). Enrichment and written home work assignments with couples. In L. L'Abate, *Enrichment: Structured interventions with couples, families, and groups* (pp. 184–202). Washington, DC: University Press of America.

Wagner, V., Weeks, G., & L'Abate, L. (1980). Enrichment and written messages with couples. *American Journal of Family Therapy, 8,* 36–44.

Wandersman, A., & Hess, R. (Eds.). (1985). *Beyond the individual: Environmental approaches and prevention.* New York: Haworth.

Weeks, G., & L'Abate, L. (1982). *Paradoxical psychotherapy: Theory and practice with individuals, couples, and families. New York: Brunner/Mazel.*

Weissman, M. M., & Klerman, G. L. (1979). Sex differences in the epidemiology of depression. In E. S. Gomberg & V. Franks (Eds.), *Gender and disordered behavior: Sex differences in psychopathology* (pp. 381–425). New York: Brunner/Mazel.

White, R. W. (1959). Motivation reconsidered: The concept of competence. *Psychological Review, 66,* 297–333.

White, R. W. (1960). Competence and the psychosexual stages of development. In M. R. Jones (Ed.), *Nebraska Symposium on Motivation* (pp. 97–141). Lincoln: University of Nebraska Press.

Wildman, R. W., II. (1977). Structured versus unstructured marital interventions. In L. L'Abate, *Enrichment: Structured interventions with couples, families, and groups* (pp. 154–183). Washington, DC: University Press of America.

Wine, J. D., & Smye, M. D. (Eds.). (1981). *Social competence.* New York: Guilford.

Winter, W. D., & Ferreira, A. J. (1969). Interaction process analysis of family decision-making. In W. D. Winter & A. J. Ferreira (Eds.), *Research in family interaction: Readings and commentary* (pp. 232–241). Palo Alto, CA: Science and Behavior Books.

Wolberg, L. W. (1980). *Handbook of short-term psychotherapy.* New York: Thieme-Stratton.

Wolchik, S. A., Sandler, I. N., & Braver, S. L. (1987). Social support: Its assessment and relation to children's adjustment. In N. Eisenberg (Ed.), *Contemporary topics in developmental psychology* (pp. 319–350). New York: John Wiley.

Wynne, L. C. (1988). *The state of the art in family therapy research: Controversies and recommendations.* New York: Family Process.

Young, R. L., Godfrey, W., Matthews, B., & Adams, G. R. (1983). Runaways: A review of negative consequences. *Family Relations, 32,* 275–281.

Zautra, A., Bachrach, K., & Hess, R. (Eds.). (1983). *Strategies for need assessment in prevention.* New York: Haworth.

Zigler, E. F., & Freeman, J. (1987). Evaluating family support programs. In S. L. Kagan, D. R. Powell, B. Weissbourd, & E. F. Zigler (Eds.), *America's family support programs* (pp. 352–361). New Haven, CT: Yale University Press.

Zolik, E. S. (1983). Training for preventive psychology in community and academic settings. In R. D. Felner, L. A. Jason, J. N. Moritsugu, & S. S. Farber (Eds.), *Preventive psychology: Theory, research and practice* (pp. 273–289). New York: Pergamon.

Author Index

Subject Index

About the Author

LUCIANO L'ABATE was born in Brindisi, and educated in Florence, Italy. He came to the United States as an exchange student under the auspices of the Mennonite Central Committee of Tabor College in Hillsboro, Kansas, from which he graduated with high honors in two years with majors in English and psychology. After receiving a UNESCO scholarship at Wichita University, where he received an M.A., he earned a Ph.D. from Duke University. After working for two years as a clinical psychologist at the Pitt County Health Department (Greenville, North Carolina), and teaching in the extension division of East Carolina College, he received a U.S.P.S. postdoctoral fellowship in child psychotherapy at Michael Reese Hospital, Chicago. After this training, he became Assistant Professor of Psychology in the Department of Psychiatry at Washington University School of Medicine, St. Louis, Missouri. He and his family moved to Atlanta, Georgia, when he became Associate Professor and Chief Psychologist in the Child Psychiatry division of the Department of Psychiatry at Emory University School of Medicine. Since 1965, he has been Professor of Psychology at Georgia State University, where since 1972 he has been Director of the Family Psychology Training Program.

He is a Diplomate and Examiner of the American Board of Examiners in Professional Psychology and is a Fellow and Approved Supervisor of the American Association of Marriage and

Family Therapy. He is a Fellow of the American Psychological Association, Life Member of American Orthopsychiatric Association and Charter Member of the American Family Therapy Association. He is also a member of other professional associations including the National Council for Family Relations. He is on the editorial board of eight journals and serves as a consultant to various publishing houses. He is the author or coauthor of more than 200 papers, chapters, and reviews in professional journals and 20 books; 4 additional books are in press. His work has been translated into Japanese, Finnish, Spanish, Italian, French, and German. Recently awarded the 1983 Alumni Distinguished Professorship in the School of Arts and Sciences, in 1984, he was named "Outstanding Citizen" by the House of Representatives in the State of Georgia. In 1986, he received the "Outstanding Achievement & Service" award from the Tabor College Alumni Association. In 1987, he received recognition by the Georgia Association for Marriage and Family Therapy for "outstanding contribution."

NOTES

NOTES